THE SUPERVISOR'S BIG BOOK OF LISTS

by George Fuller

Also by the Author

✤ ✤

The Supervisor's Portable Answer Book, 1990, Prentice Hall

The Negotiator's Handbook, 1991, Prentice Hall

The SUPERVISOR'S BIG BOOK OF LISTS

GEORGE T. FULLER

PRENTICE HALL
Englewood Cliffs, New Jersey 07632

Prentice-Hall International (UK) Limited, *London*
Prentice-Hall of Australia Pty. Limited, *Sydney*
Prentice-Hall Canada, Inc., *Toronto*
Prentice-Hall Hispanoamericana, S.A., *Mexico*
Prentice-Hall of India Private Limited, *New Delhi*
Prentice-Hall of Japan, Inc., *Tokyo*
Simon & Schuster Asia Pte. Ltd., *Singapore*
Editora Prentice-Hall do Brasil, Ltda., *Rio de Janeiro*

©1994 *by*
George T. Fuller

10   9   8   7   6   5   4   3   2   1

Library of Congress Cataloging-in Publication Data

Fuller, George.
    The supervisor's big book of lists / by George Fuller.
        p. cm.
    Includes index.
    ISBN 0-13-336850-5. — ISBN 0-13-122771-8 (pbk.)
    1. Supervision of employees—Handbooks, manuals, etc.
I. Title.
HF5549.12.F827   1994   93-48158
658.3'02—dc20   CIP

ISBN 0-13-336850-5
      0-13-122771-8 (pbk)

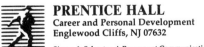

PRENTICE HALL
Career and Personal Development
Englewood Cliffs, NJ 07632
Simon & Schuster, A Paramount Communications Company

Printed in the United States of America

Introduction

❧ ❧

Whether your supervisory responsibilities consume the bulk of your time as a first-line supervisor, or are secondary to your other duties as a middle manager, you will probably agree that the problems associated with managing people produce most of your work-related difficulties. It's hard to deny that supervising people in a work environment is both a difficult and time-consuming task. After all, it takes patience, persistence, and a host of other virtues to successfully steer subordinates with individual personalities and skills toward the completion of their assigned duties.

What makes a supervisor's role even harder is that job demands don't always give you the luxury of carefully thinking through every action you take. As a result, you are forced to make hasty decisions, even when you would prefer more time to analyze the situation. This makes it inevitable that mistakes will be made, which is to be expected in the pressure cooker environment in which first-level supervisors and middle managers work.

Unfortunately, when something goes wrong, upper management doesn't want to hear that you're overworked and/or understaffed. "Get it done on time, and get it done right," is a rough version of the performance parameters you have to operate under. On the other end of the scale, subordinates place added demands on both your time and sanity. All of which leaves you constantly overworked and with insufficient time to do everything that should be done.

The goal of *The Supervisor's Big Book of Lists* is to assist you in overcoming this double-barreled whammy of too much work and too little time. In this book there are 115 detailed lists, containing well over a *thousand* time-tested tips, to assist you in solving the many complex problems you face in performing your daily tasks. These detailed lists can make your job easier in several ways.

First, they are a quick reference guide to follow before you attack a particular problem. This will help you avoid missing a critical step or action that can happen when you are under the gun trying to do ten things at once. And for those inevitable situations where you are called upon to act first and think later, the lists will provide insurance that nothing has been overlooked.

Another advantage of the subject-specific lists in *The Big Book of Lists* is their wide-ranging coverage. You will, of course, find lists with hundreds of tips covering such common supervisory problems as how to deal with troublemakers, delegate effectively, control absenteeism, and the many other daily dilemmas you have to deal with. However, the lists go beyond these aspects of supervision to cover subjects that occur less frequently, but can be a real can of worms when they arise. These include such quandaries as how to protect your department against cutbacks, and how to handle unreasonable workload demands.

Beyond operational issues, your own job satisfaction and career success can't be ignored. For this reason, you will find plenty of solid advice on personal issues, such as dealing with stress, protecting yourself against back-stabbers, and even managing your own boss, which is equally as important to your career success as managing subordinates.

There are several other aspects of this book that you should find useful. One is that *The Big Book of Lists* not only gives you the comprehensive coverage of supervision that you need, but its lists make it quick and easy to use. This format lets you readily find and read everything on a single topic in a matter of minutes, without wading through either abstract theory, or lengthy narrative.

Another positive feature of *The Big Book of Lists* is its value as a repetitive working tool, rather than simply being a one-time read. The many topic-specific lists make it a book you can refer to every time a new problem rears its ugly head.

Finally, it should be mentioned that this book should be of equal value to both relatively inexperienced supervisors, as well as seasoned veterans, although perhaps not for the same reasons. If your status as a boss is relatively recent, you may use this book in greater depth and frequency than your more experienced counterparts. On the other hand, if you are a seasoned supervisor, the book's primary benefits may be as a memory jogger, and a check to make sure you have covered all of the bases in dealing with individual issues. It will also serve you well in subject areas you only encounter on rare occasions.

Above all else, for everyone, either newcomer or seasoned boss, first-level supervisor or middle manager, this book should help you avoid one of the major hazards every overworked supervisor dreads. And that is, the embarrassing after-the-fact question often asked by a boss, another superior, or perhaps a career-competitive critic, which is "Why don't you do this or that?" This book should substantially reduce that risk for you in the future.

Contents

❧ ❦

Chapter Two
SHARPENING YOUR SUPERVISORY COMMUNICATION SKILLS 25

Chapter Three
STRATEGIES TO IMPROVE INDIVIDUAL EMPLOYEE PERFORMANCE 51

Chapter Four

TACTICS TO IMPROVE YOUR GROUP'S PRODUCTIVITY 77

Chapter Five

COPING WITH PROBLEM EMPLOYEES AND EMPLOYEE PROBLEMS 99

Chapter Six
WHEELING AND DEALING
WITH YOUR BOSS AND OTHERS 123

Chapter Seven
HANDLING HIRING, FIRING,
AND OTHER PERSONNEL MATTERS 151

· Chapter Eight

MANAGING AROUND CRISIS AND PANIC SITUATIONS 179

Chapter Nine

CONQUERING THE DAY-TO-DAY DETAILS OF YOUR JOB 207

Chapter Ten

SUPERVISORY SELF-IMPROVEMENT PRACTICES 241

INDEX 263

Chapter One

AVOIDING THE TIME TRAPS OF SUPERVISION

One of the major hassles facing anyone with supervisory responsibilities is the lack of time needed to fully deal with problems as they arise. That's easy enough to understand, since you not only have to handle the functional responsibilities of your job, but must also supervise others in the performance of their duties. How much time each involves is to a large degree dictated by the requirements of your position and the number of people you have to supervise. Whatever your particular situation is, the demands on your time can make it seem like you have two jobs for the pay of one.

Of course, everyone faced with the dilemma of too much work, and too little time, attempts to cope in one way or another. This may mean arriving at work early and/or leaving late. Other supervisors may take paperwork home, while a few determined individuals may try a time management program only to discover it doesn't have any more lasting value than the latest diet fad.

In the end, for most supervisors, coping with time pressures boils down to concentrating on the hottest problem of the moment and putting everything else on the back burner. The end result of this approach is generally frustration at being unable to accomplish things the way you want to. It can also mean mistakes are made, deadlines are missed, and your boss is breathing down your neck to speed things up. Meanwhile your in-basket is overflowing and your phone is ringing nonstop.

You may have long since decided that constant time pressures are a necessary evil you have to live with, as distasteful as that may be. However, it doesn't have to be that way, and you can conquer the time demands placed upon you if you first recognize one simple fact. You may well be doing two, or even three or four jobs, for the pay of one. Sound crazy? It isn't, and here's why.

Supervision lends itself to being a time trap brought about by doing the work of other people. To a large extent, the culprits are the very people you supervise. For example, they come to you with a problem and you solve it. Of course, sometimes that's both proper and practical. However, in many instances, employees will seek out a boss on matters they could resolve themselves, or in conjunction with co-workers. After all, getting the boss's approval is the path of least resistance, unless workers are encouraged to exercise more initiative in doing their jobs.

An even more time-consuming supervisory trap is for a supervisor to take the particular chore over, rather than simply telling the subordinate how to go about resolving the issue. This frequently happens when a worker approaches a busy boss who, after quickly hearing the problem, says something such as, "I'll look into that and get back to you." What has happened is that an already overburdened boss has just accepted another assignment—from a subordinate no less.

Apart from the need to avoid assuming work that is properly done by subordinates, there are several other common time-eaters that can—and should—be dealt with. These include all sorts of pests who interrupt you throughout the workday for one or another petty reason.

Of course, reducing the constant stream of paperwork that flows across your desk is another way to gain time to concentrate on more important objectives. And even with routine tasks, sometimes habit-forming procedures are used which may not be the most effective in terms of the time taken to accomplish them.

The topical lists in this chapter have but one purpose, which is to free up more of your time for productive pursuits. They cover how best to accomplish more in less time in terms of such duties as holding meetings, coping with deadlines, and controlling paperwork. Perhaps of even greater importance, they will help you to unload existing duties in ways that will both make your group more productive, and yourself less pressured.

1.1

♧

Ten Ways to Control Interruptions
by Two-Legged Pests

Needless interruptions not only waste your time, but they may also disturb your thought process when you're busily engaged in trying to resolve another matter. Although by themselves many interruptions are brief, the cumulative time lost to intruders during the work week can be significant. Using some of the following techniques will rapidly cure this problem.

1. *Beware of your behavior.* Your personality and temperament are more important than anything in discouraging interruptions. If you encourage schmoozing and small talk, you'll get plenty of it. So keep your distance in terms of socializing, and don't have lunch and/or coffee with subordinates, since it fosters a familiarity that promotes interruptions throughout the day.

2. *Encourage decision making.* Give employees the authority to act on their own. This will cut down on the number of times you're interrupted to get routine guidance. To make this approach work, be careful about criticizing workers when they make mistakes.

3. *Make sure assignments are understood.* When new and/or difficult projects are assigned, make sure workers understand what to do. This will avoid countless interruptions later on. It also helps if you specify when and if they are to report back to you.

4. *Visit others so they won't visit you.* Make a habit of stopping by subordinates' work stations or offices. This lessens the need for them to see you, and puts you in control of the time spent doing this. It also discourages goofing off when workers know the boss is likely to drop by.

5. *Promote alternatives.* Encourage your subordinates to get answers elsewhere, such as from co-workers, other departments, and written policies and procedures.

6. *Establish a procedure for appointments.* You might want to establish a set time of day for employees to see you with routine questions. Early in the morning works best for dealing with that day's issues, while late in the day works well for future assignments. If you adopt this approach, raise questions and expect answers. This will discourage workers from

besieging you with trivial matters and prevent them from dumping problems in your lap for resolution.

7. *Minimize the opportunity for interruptions.* Simple logistical practices can discourage potential intruders. These include:

   a. Remove any chairs for guests from your office. It's easier to keep people moving if they are already standing.

   b. Position your desk so the back of your chair faces the door. This discourages passers-by from dropping in.

   c. Close your office door. If you choose to practice an "open door" policy, then get in the habit of closing the door when you don't want to be disturbed.

   d. Have someone field your phone calls, since in some jobs the telephone will interrupt you more than individuals.

8. *Discourage persistent pests.* Usually, it will just be a few subordinates who commit most of the unwanted intrusions upon your time. Deal with these hard-core pests in a hard-nosed manner. Tell them you don't want to be interrupted about tasks they can handle themselves. If that doesn't work, give them assignments that will keep them out of your hair for a while, such as long written reports, or the dirtiest and/or least desirable job under your control.

9. *Make it unpleasant.* When subordinates insist on seeing you when you're busy, insist on seeing them when they want to go home. For instance, when someone interrupts you, say, "I'm busy right now, Bob; see me at five o'clock." (Quitting time) You know Bob will be there before five, since he wants to leave on time. Make sure to keep the discussion going for about fifteen minutes past quitting time.

10. *When all else fails—hide.* There will be times when you need a block of uninterrupted time to complete a task, and no matter how adept you are at controlling interruptions, the phone will ring, or someone will knock on a closed door. Rather than get frustrated, or work into the night when everyone else has left, find yourself an escape spot. Usually, a vacant conference room somewhere will do the trick. Just don't defeat the purpose by telling everyone where you're going.

NOTE: With the corporate tendency toward participative management and open-door policies, you might think controlling interruptions works against this trend. To the contrary. What you are doing is eliminating idle and wasted time. Furthermore, by encouraging workers to solve problems themselves, you are actually furthering employee involvement in the decision-making process.

1.2

Fifteen Ways to Tell People to Get Lost

After you have taken steps to prevent and control interruptions, you should notice a significant reduction in terms of unnecessary intrusions. However, an equally important time-eater are those people you meet with for legitimate purposes who just don't know when it's time to leave. This can be a hassle, since no one wants to be rude. The unfortunate result is that good manners tend to aid and abet malingerers who knowingly or unknowingly are killing time at your expense. Let's look at a few ways you can edge people along who have overstayed their welcome.

1. Once you have the essence of what someone is talking about, start to summarize and then make a statement designed to end the conversation, such as, "Let's do what you suggested and see what happens in the next few weeks."

2. When people don't take the hint when you make a concluding remark, stand up, pick up the phone as if to make a call, or make some other gesture to plainly signify the meeting is at an end.

3. When people won't budge, even with hints, get up, excuse yourself by saying, "I've got to go to a meeting," and leave the office yourself.

4. When the discussion no longer serves a valid purpose there's nothing wrong with telling it like it is and saying, "You'll have to excuse me now. I have work to do." Don't worry about being rude. You're getting paid for working, not socializing. After all, the same joker who wants to hang around your office may be the one who walks by on the way out at 5:00 P.M., while you're still working away at your desk.

5. Interrupt people who ramble on. Some people can never stop talking. When you encounter such an individual, be prepared to interrupt and abruptly bring the discussion to an end.

6. Keep your responses as brief as possible. The more you say, the greater the opportunity for the other party to continue the discussion.

7. Suggest taking a break. Going for coffee accomplishes your main purpose, which is to get people out of your office. to discourage their return say something similar to, "I've got some work to catch up on," and leave them in the company cafeteria.

8. Walk them back to where they came from. A quicker variation than going for coffee is to stand up and say, "I need a drink of water. Let's talk on the way back to your office." This gives the impression the discussion can continue—which it will—at least until you reach the other person's office.

9. Fix 'em up with someone else. Frequently, the subject will be such that you can palm the person off on someone else. At an appropriate point say something similar to, "Let's go talk to Mary about this." After spending a couple of minutes in a three-way conversation, just bow out gracefully and head back to your office.

10. Practice prevention by establishing a time limit at the start of an impromptu meeting. For example:

    a. "Fred, I can only give you five minutes." (This approach is good where you feel no obligation to explain the reasoning for a time limit.) or,

    b. "I can only talk for ten minutes, Arthur, since I have another meeting at eleven." (Where you feel an explanation for the time limit is necessary, either as a matter of courtesy, or because of the person's status.)

11. For formal preplanned meetings you may want to establish time limits in a memo that goes out beforehand. Once you have reached the time limit, quickly summarize, and announce the meeting is concluded. Otherwise, setting a time limit will be a useless exercise.

12. You may be hesitant about trying to nudge someone such as your boss along if he or she overstays their welcome, but it can be done. For instance, "Good morning, Dan, did you want to see me? I'm scheduled to meet with Quality Control in ten minutes to see about getting the testing speeded up on the McDermott order." Try saying something similar to this when you're working on a project you know the boss wants completed as soon as possible. Only an incompetent boss will waste your time when you appear to be busy. Be careful here about the

office politics angle, and if you do give an excuse, make sure it's either valid, or you don't get caught lying.

13. Prearrange with someone to get you off the hook. If possible, you can make arrangements with your secretary, or a trusted subordinate to interrupt you at a pre-arranged time, say fifteen minutes after a meeting has begun. This is an especially useful ploy to use with someone who habitually overstays their welcome, or has a habit of camping out in other people's offices. Of course, when the interruption takes place, you have the option of continuing the discussion if it's of value, or calling a halt based on the guise of more pressing business in the form of your preplanned interruption.

14. Stage a mini-crisis. Everyone relates to the real or imagined work panics that occur regularly. If you want to edge someone along, stage your own. It doesn't have to be anything elaborate. For instance, suddenly blurt out, "Heck, I forgot to turn in the time sheets this morning," and hastily excuse yourself.

15. Use the phone. Any incoming call can be an excuse to say, "Excuse me, I'll be on this call a while. I'll get back to you when I'm done." If your constantly ringing phone has chosen to remain silent just when you need it most, don't despair. Initiate a call yourself by saying something such as, "Can I interrupt a minute? I promised to call Mr. Jones at ten o'clock." Then, either call someone you need to contact, or if necessary, the pre-recorded weather message, and then state you will get back to your visitor.

1.3

Twelve Time-Saving Techniques
for Routine Tasks

Daily routines at work are usually overlooked as potential sources for saving time. For one thing, it's a natural habit to keep doing things the way they have been done in the past. In addition, individual matters of a routine nature don't always consume a big block of time. Yet, many perfunctory tasks can be simplified, combined, or eliminated, to give you additional time for higher priority projects. To some extent, your particular job will dictate where the most effective changes can be made. The following suggestions are common to most any supervisory position.

- Discipline yourself to stay on top of routine matters, since letting things drag makes them more difficult to deal with later.

- Relay general information in group meetings, rather than repeating something one-by-one several times over.

- Delegate routine tasks, such as ordering supplies, to subordinates.

- Don't fill in for absent subordinates. Instead cross-train workers to handle other jobs.

- Assign periodic responsibilities—such as training new employees—to subordinates.

- Avoid clutter so time isn't wasted searching for things.

- Don't write memos if you can call someone, unless there is an imperative reason to have a permanent record.

- Look for repetitive reports that can be eliminated.

- Shorten, eliminate, or combine meetings. (See Sec. 1.8 on how to do this.)

- Learn to recognize what never has to be done, and forget about it. A good example are standard memos and reports which receive widespread circulation, but are irrelevant to most recipients.

- Use personal downtime, such as waiting for meetings to start and coffee breaks, to do "minimal thought" chores such as going through routine reading matter.

- Have people from other departments come to see you rather than you going to see them.

1.4

Thirteen Guaranteed Practices That Will Control Your Paperwork

A common complaint for many supervisors is the amount of paperwork they have to handle. What often makes this burden even more irksome is that much of the paper flow is both unnecessary and unwanted. To make matters worse, new technology often adds to the problem. Computers churn out printouts, faxes flow freely, and even voice mail and E-mail can contribute indirectly by making it easier to reach you with yet another request for some form of written response. All of which probably leaves you chuckling when you read where some futurist has made another prediction about the paperless office of the future. Believe it only when you see it. Until then, your personal salvation rests with controlling the amount of paperwork you have to deal with. It's not easy, but it is doable, and adopting some of the following practices will help you succeed.

1. Write only when you have to. Written responses are time-consuming, so always consider other alternatives before either initiating or replying in writing. There are exceptions, but as a good general rule for when you should put something in writing, do so if:

    - Your boss or other superiors require and/or expect a written format.

    - The material is of such a nature that the recipient will better understand it if it's in written form.

    - A permanent record is required. (EX: a disciplinary action.)

2. Whenever possible, you can save time by replying to requests directly on the memo or letter rather than preparing a separate reply.

3. Use your subordinates to lighten your load. Look for certain types of paperwork that can be handled by a trusted employee rather than processing it yourself. When you do delegate paperwork to subordinates, be sure they understand exactly what you want and encourage them to be as brief as possible.

4. Avoid wasting time trying to understand the meaning of confusing correspondence. If practical, contact the writer for clarification. Otherwise, unless you must respond immediately, leave difficult reading matter until you have sufficient quiet time to struggle through it at a slow pace.

5. Eliminate distractions when you're handling the bulk of your paperwork, since they disturb your concentration. Fatigue can also slow the process down, so if possible try to tackle your paperwork early in the morning while your energy levels are high.

6. Be careful with the filing process. One of the biggest time-wasters associated with paperwork is having to look for something that was

filed—but no one knows where. This also applies to computers, since if something gets misfiled on a disk, you will have to scan the files to find it.

7. Purge your files periodically. This saves space, but even more important it saves time when you're looking for that illusive piece of paper.

8. Minimize the amount of time you spend reading material that isn't directly related to your job. It's a good habit to practice tearing pages from reports, newspapers, and magazines that you need, and then toss the rest without either reading or skimming it. Incidentally, computers and fax machines add to the flow of information, so be selective about what you want to read and retain.

9. See what paperwork you can eliminate that originates elsewhere. For example, get your name removed from distribution lists for material you have no use for. People tend to haphazardly put others on distribution lists without first checking whether or not they need and/or want to receive the information.

10. Avoid procrastination in replying to written material. Often, when letters, memos, and other correspondence is received there's a tendency to read it and then put it aside for later reply. The problem is that by the time you get around to it again, you have to read it all over again, since you've long since forgotten what it said. Answering correspondence right away avoids this. Of course, this isn't always possible, and some correspondence requires additional information before it can be replied to. But even here, you may want to jot your thoughts down in the margin of the correspondence the first time you read it, so as to save time when you go back to it later.

11. Avoid the in-basket trap. The most commonly recommended way to reduce paperwork is to handle it only once. This isn't always possible as noted above. But there is much to be said for the general value of this practice. In fact, if you want to try something extreme to cut down on the paperwork piling up in your in-basket, just remove the receptacle. This will force you to deal with paperwork right away to keep it from piling up on your desk.

12. Look for ways to eliminate some of the writing you do now. For example, memos confirming meetings and similar matter are fertile ground for elimination.

13. Last, but not least, always remember when you have to write, keep it short. It saves you writing time, and will hopefully encourage others to be equally brief.

1.5

⇓

Seven Proven Ways to Delegate Your Duties to Others

As a supervisor, one of the best ways to increase your personal efficiency, as well as your group's productivity, is to delegate duties more effectively. If done correctly, it can also reduce your personal job stress, since you won't be struggling to do everything yourself. This will also make you a better supervisor, since you will be able to spend more of your time on supervisory responsibilities rather than wasting it on detail work.

However, one of the major drawbacks to a greater use of delegation is the fear that the work won't be done right. Nevertheless, this is a hurdle that can be overcome by carefully planning how, what, and to whom you delegate tasks. Using the following procedures will help in this regard.

1. Establish specific goals to be accomplished. Decide exactly what you want done, the deadline for completion, and the priority of the task in relation to other work.

2. Select the right subordinate for the job. Although routine tasks can be pretty much farmed out at random, more difficult assignments should be delegated based upon the talents and workload of subordinates.

3. Discuss the details of what you want accomplished with the person selected for the task. Try to make assignments that will challenge workers without overwhelming them. Encourage workers to contribute their ideas as to how the job should be done. It's also critical to furnish suggested ways to complete the task, since some workers will be reluctant to ask questions and will flounder around trying to figure out where to start. Be sure any instructions are easy to understand, since there's a natural tendency to be casual about things we are familiar with, not realizing it is unfamiliar to someone else.

4. Be clear about priorities. Let the worker know how the assigned task fits in with other work assigned to the individual.

5. Establish controls in the form of periodic checkpoints where the worker should brief you on the progress of the work. This will allow you to monitor how well the employee is moving ahead toward the completion date for the task. There are two prime considerations when setting checkpoints. The first is, of course, the difficulty of the assignment. The other is the capability of the individual to operate independently. Some people will require more scrutiny than others, which is especially true for newer and less experienced workers.

6. Determine limits on what the employee can and can't do in completing the assignment. It's also important at the outset to make certain the employee has the necessary resources to do the job.

7. Support the results. Even if the delegated project doesn't work out well, refrain from criticizing the employee if the worker made a good faith effort to succeed. When workers aren't criticized for failure they will be far more willing to accept the challenge of new assignments. Not every assignment will work out as planned, but those that don't succeed can contribute to the learning process—for both you and your subordinates.

CAUTION: To prevent things from getting off track, a limited amount of follow-up is necessary. This is particularly true for assignments where periodic checkpoints aren't feasible. However, too much follow-up will discourage workers from moving ahead on their own to complete the task. On the other hand, if you don't follow up at all, there's a danger that the worker will make little or no progress toward completing the project.

Therefore, the level of follow-up is a balancing act between too much and not enough. How much is appropriate depends upon the ease or difficulty of the task, the capabilities of the worker selected for the job, and your own style of supervision. Careful selection of the individual assigned, and first-rate instructions before the work begins should make the amount of follow-up minimal in most cases.

1.6

✲

Commonsense Methods for Using Your Time Effectively

One of the hardest obstacles to overcome as a supervisor is trying to meet the seemingly impossible demands placed upon your time. Beyond being responsible for overseeing the operations you supervise, there's plenty of paperwork, an endless string of meetings, and countless conferences with subordinates or your boss. If that isn't enough work to wear you out, there's always the occasional special project or rush assignment which is supposed to supersede everything else. With all of these claims on your time, the only practical way to keep your head above water is to look for ways to make better use of the available hours. Using a combination of the following techniques should inject a little breathing room into your busy schedule.

1. *Concentrate on priorities.* Keep a list of what you have to do ranked by priorities. A lot of time can be wasted just thinking about what has to be done next, or bouncing from one assignment to another without wrapping anything up. Always do the highest priority tasks first. Sometimes there's a tendency to do lower priority items because they happen to be less difficult.

2. *Set realistic deadlines.* Leave some slack time when you estimate how long a project will take. Not allowing enough time initially can leave you scrambling to finish a task which can result in careless errors being made. It also doesn't allow for coping with the inevitable emergencies which occur from time to time.

3. *Change your habits.* Think about some of the ways you can change your routine to free up some time. Giving up reading the paper before work, or shortening your coffee breaks, doesn't seem like a great time saver. However, if you save even fifteen minutes a day, over the course of a year this adds up to well over a week's worth of time. That, in the long run, could be the extra week's vacation you take next year, which you may have skipped in the past because you were too busy.

   On a more general level, you may want to revamp your management style. For example, if you practice being a highly visible manager by spending most of the day conferring with subordinates, try setting aside an hour or two daily to work with your office door closed. This lower profile will give you the time you need to stay on top of your deskbound duties.

4. *Eliminate nonessential chores.* Look for minor chores that you handle that can be either eliminated or delegated to subordinates. No matter what management level people are at, they often perform repetitive tasks which can just as easily be done by someone else. For instance, a first-level supervisor may make out time sheets, while a more senior manag-

er may conduct a daily staff meeting. In both of these situations, the function can probably be assigned to a trusted subordinate.

5. *Learn to say "No."* It's impolite to be rude, and for this reason, as well as your inclination to be helpful, people may continually seek your counsel on both business and personal matters. This can become a real headache when you're trying to get some work done. As a result, you have to learn to say something such as, "I'm busy right now. I'll get back to you as soon as I can." Anyone who is reasonable can understand this. But if you're worried about being rude, remember that someone who is considerate wouldn't interrupt you in the first place when they see that you're busy.

6. *Use technology wisely.* Personal computers, voice mail, and all of the other modern equipment available can be either a productivity booster or productivity buster. Naturally, it's easy to assume that only good things can happen from using the most up-to-date technology. But if you're not careful, these productivity enhancers can turn into real time-eaters if they're not used wisely.

   To counter this tendency, it's important to not become a captive of a particular piece of equipment. For example, electronic mail messages can be just as useless as the hard-copy junk that clogs up your in-basket before you get around to tossing it in the wastebasket. So learn to simply ignore the nonessential messages that pop up on your computer monitor. The same sort of screening should also be applied to voice mail and telephone call-back requests. Unless there's a practical and/or political reason for responding (EX: a message left by a superior), learn to ignore these secondary demands upon your time.

   On the other hand, take advantage of technology when it will act as a time saver. What it all comes down to is using technology when it will boost your efficiency, and ignoring it when it won't. The extent to which this will save you time will vary with the nature of your job, and the equipment you have at your disposal.

7. *Use scheduling aids.* You can use your time more effectively if you keep track of present and future projects. What method you use to do this basically boils down to what you feel most comfortable with. What you want to avoid is the sort of detailed accounting that is in itself time-consuming. Any of the following basic types of memory joggers are useful.

   • Appointment calendars—To show name, telephone number, and purpose of appointments.

- Desk or wall calendar—To jot down notes on upcoming projects, deadlines, and so forth.

- Tickler file—This file, which is organized by dates, has sections to file correspondence and notes.

- To-do list—A list showing what has to be done based on the priority of the project.

Of course, if you have your own computer you can set up your own scheduling format, or use a commercially available software program. If you want to go beyond the basics with your scheduling, you may also consider buying one of the several organizers on the market.

And for even greater control, you may want to try a time management program. However, any of the simpler aids are adequate for most purposes.

8. *Find time to think.* There are certain tasks that can't be done properly unless you have sufficient time to consider the best way to proceed. These include fairly complex projects, new assignments, and written responses which require a great deal of thought. If you fail to allocate a block of time for these efforts, they will either be continually postponed, which may result in missed deadlines, or performed piecemeal, which will reflect on the quality of your work. Alternatively, you may find yourself burning the midnight oil at work or home in an effort to stay on top of your job. Therefore, when you're trying to cope with time pressures at work, don't neglect "thinking time." It's very easy to overlook this factor by unconsciously reasoning that you're too busy to have any quiet time. On the contrary, the busier you are, the more you need a little bit of time to think things through.

9. *Review your time control efforts.* Once you get a handle on using your time more effectively, don't get cocky. Like other bad habits, it's easy to slip back into the old routine. Therefore, the ultimate secret to managing your time is to remain alert for new ways to improve your efforts, as well as watching out that you don't slide back into helter-skelter patterns.

NOTE: Don't waste too much time planning your time saving efforts. Come up with a simple but effective system that works well for you. You may have to do a little experimenting before you find your best working pattern.

$$1.7$$

✦

Eleven Time Traps You Should Learn to Avoid

Managing your time effectively by using the tactics in the previous section is difficult enough, but for the most part it's something that's within your control to do. However, there are a substantial number of time traps which you have to learn to conquer, since these time-eaters can wreck your efforts to maximize your productivity. The following list contains many of the most common time-sapping culprits you will have to overcome.

- A work overload. This can result from excessive demands by a boss, or your spending too much time getting involved with details.

- Casual visitors. Give these people short shrift, or you'll never get any work done.

- Unnecessary meetings. Don't schedule them yourself, and try to beg off if they are called by someone else.

- Poor delegation. If you don't delegate, then you will be doing the work.

- Lack of organization. If you're disorganized, you will spend more time looking for things than getting them done.

- Socializing. If you're too friendly with subordinates, they will waste much of your time discussing personal matters.

- Lack of self-discipline. Get off to a good start every day, and you won't be playing catch-up all day long.

- Buck-passers. Don't let other people dump their work on you.

- Outgoing telephone calls. If you're calling someone who is talkative, call when they won't be in and leave your message. You can also keep calls brief by making them before lunch, or just before the end of the day.

- Incoming telephone calls. Screen them through your secretary if you have one. If not, at least have someone who works for you field your calls when you don't want to be interrupted.

- Internal conflict. Try to avoid getting involved in any infighting and bickering that takes place. It's both time-consuming and emotionally draining.

1.8

☙

Fourteen Useful Ways to Keep
Any Meeting Short

One of the most time-consuming functions for many supervisors the seemingly endless string of meetings that, more often than not, squander your time with little or nothing to show for it. As a result, any attempt to be more productive requires an earnest effort to reduce the time you spend in meetings. The other side of the coin is to make certain any meeting you personally schedule accomplishes its purpose. How to achieve that particular goal is covered in Section 2.10 of Chapter Two. But, for now, let's just consider how you can reduce the amount of time you spend in meetings. The steps you can take to accomplish this include:

1. The shortest meeting is the one you don't have to attend. Therefore, whenever possible try to either bow out of meetings you're asked to attend, or delegate a subordinate to attend in your place. The most obvious excuse for missing a meeting is to plead you're working on a project that can't wait. However, don't use this, or any other excuse, on a repetitive basis if you expect to be believed.

2. Whenever you are thinking about holding a meeting ask yourself the following questions.

   - Can it be justified from a cost/benefit standpoint?

   - Can it be better handled through one-on-one communication?

   - Are alternatives such as a conference call, a memo, or electronic mail, a better way to go?

   - What is the purpose for calling the meeting? Can it be accomplished by holding the meeting?

   - Who should attend this meeting?

   - When is the best time to hold the meeting so there will be minimal interference with the other duties of the participants?

   - Will you send out advance notice of the meeting telling participants what you expect to accomplish? If not, this alone can serve to prolong the meeting.

By answering these questions you may discover that a meeting isn't necessary and/or practical. Even if it is, the answers will help you lay the sort of groundwork that will keep the meeting short and well focused.

3. Limit the invitees to a meeting to the minimum necessary to accomplish the intended results. The more people there are at a meeting, the greater possibility the meeting will take longer than you planned.

4. Set time limits when you send out notice of the meeting, and reaffirm them when you start the meeting off.

5. Don't wait for late arrivals. In fact, you may want to close the door when the scheduled time for the meeting arrives. This will prevent tardy invitees from quietly sneaking in. Hopefully, the embarrassment of attracting people's attention when they open the door to walk in will encourage them to be on time in the future.

6. If you are planning to cover more than one item, start with the most important, and work toward the least significant. That way, if the preset ending time arrives before everything has been covered, at least the significant items will have been addressed.

7. Interrupt talkative people. Don't let one or two people monopolize the conversation. Not only does this slow things down, but it frequently causes the discussion to get off course.

8. Try standing up throughout a meeting. This sends a message that you don't expect it to last long. This is particularly practical with smaller groups. In fact, if it's feasible, try to hold these smaller meetings where seating isn't available. Of course, if someone volunteers to go get chairs, immediately say, "Don't bother, this isn't going to take long."

9. At larger gatherings where you are an attendee, sit at the back of the room and try to slip out unnoticed. If you're worried about potential criticism, talk to your boss beforehand about leaving early.

10. Another approach is to ask to be excused. Say something such as, "Excuse me. I think we've covered my area. If you won't be discussing anything else for which you need me, I have a top priority shipment to get out today."

11. If you can't figure a way out of a boring meeting, at least use the time constructively by unobtrusively reading material you brought along for just such a purpose. If it's impossible to do this, or you neglected to bring anything, at least try to spend the time thinking about some other problem you have to deal with.

12. If you have the choice of holding a meeting in your office or elsewhere, choose the latter. This will make it easier for you to leave if the discussion goes off on a tangent.

13. See if you can eliminate regularly scheduled meetings, especially if they aren't proving to be very productive. For example, you may be in the habit of holding a daily staff meeting to deal with employee questions and problems. If it appears that there's very little to discuss at these meetings, reduce their frequency. Do this progressively until you reach a level where the content is sufficient to justify the meeting.

    Be careful though, because this sort of meeting is a good tool for furthering two-way communication between yourself and your subordinates. What it is doing is providing an opportunity to be heard, so even though the meetings don't seem that productive, there is value in just having them. In any event, keep them short.

14. The most unsuspecting meetings are those impromptu gatherings which generally originate with someone sticking their head in the door and saying, "Can I see you for a minute?" Learn to find out right away if the purpose is that important. If not, schedule a meeting for a later time. If you have people who always do this to you, make the meeting times as inconvenient for them as is possible.

1.9

Helpful Hints on Establishing Priorities

One of the hardest things to do when you're overloaded with work is to decide what to do next. The danger is in trying to do a little bit of everything, and as a result, nothing much gets finished on time. Solving this sort of dilemma requires you to first recognize your limitations when you're overburdened with work. Obviously, you can only do so much at a performance level that satisfies your desire to do the best job possible. Unfortunately, many people fail to recognize this and continue to strive for perfection even when their workload is overwhelming them.

Therefore, the initial step in establishing priorities is to realize that some tasks won't be done as well as you would like. Learn to accept mistakes as part of the process when you're managing an increased workload. The reality is that mistakes will be made no matter how much time and energy you expend in doing anything. For this reason, when facing work pressures, you're better off doing more in less time than trying to cover all of the bases on everything coming across your desk. With this in mind, let's look at some questions you need to answer in order to decide what priority you should assign to individual projects.

1. Who wants the particular project done? Naturally, if your boss requests that something be done right away, it gets top priority. Be careful here though, since if giving your full attention to this task will cause some other critical job to fall behind schedule you may end up in a bind. So when this is a possibility, make certain your boss knows about it. And since your boss is responsible for creating the conflict, he or she should be the one to decide which project get top priority.

   Incidentally, if from your experience you work for someone who has a short memory span, try to get written commitment on which task will come first. This, of course, isn't always practical, but as a minimum write yourself a note to the file. That way, you will at least have a written record if something happens later and your boss's memory has conveniently failed. In addition, if the project being bumped involves people outside your department, be sure to let them know of your boss's decision.

2. What's the deadline for the task? Can it be changed if necessary? If a task is assigned and the completion date can't be changed, assess what if any impact it will have on other items on your priority list. If it means something else will slip, let anyone who will be impacted know about it.

3. How long will the job take? Whenever you get a new assignment which has a high priority be careful about estimating how long the work will take. Optimistic projections only end up causing panic and job juggling at a later date.

4. In determining priorities, what other tasks can be delayed in order to work on higher priority items?

5. Is assistance required from other departments, or for that matter, from outside the company to complete a project? If so, be sure to factor this into your estimated completion date.

6. What happens if you don't complete a priority task on schedule? This is worth thinking about, since the repercussions of not completing

something on schedule aren't always as traumatic as you would imagine.

7. Can this, or some other priority task, be delegated to one of your subordinates? Barring that, do you have work that can be reassigned to another group within the company? If so, bring this to your boss's attention when you are faced with too many priorities and too little time.

1.10

How to Meet, Beat, or Modify Any Deadline

One of the most frustrating aspects of a supervisor's job are the inevitable deadlines you face in completing assigned projects. To further complicate matters, special projects are usually imposed on top of your regular day-to-day duties. And as you have probably experienced in the past, any attempts at pleading a lack of time to meet seemingly impossible deadlines are generally brushed aside with comments such as, "Don't worry about anything else. This has to be finished on schedule." Of course, what goes unsaid is that you will still be held accountable if your regularly assigned work falls by the wayside.

Coping with deadline pressures is never easy, but achieving your goals can be simplified if you take the necessary action to avoid some of the commonplace bottlenecks that can impede your progress. Aside from the standard planning required for any project, some often overlooked measures to take include:

1. Try to establish deadlines for completion of assignments which give you leeway if the required performance isn't completed on time. For example, if meeting a project deadline is contingent upon some prior action of another department, give them a deadline which is in advance of the date you actually need their input. This gives you flexibility in meeting your completion date.

2. Enlist the support of everyone needed for the successful completion of the project at the outset. Even if their assistance won't be needed until some time in the future, giving everyone advance notice allows them to plan accordingly. It's also worthwhile to make it a practice to cooperate with other departments on a routine basis. This helps you get the type of rapid response needed to meet an urgent deadline.

3. You may encounter bottlenecks of one sort or another which threaten to derail your time schedule for project completion. When this happens, look for alternatives for working around the source of trouble. In some instances, you may be able to anticipate a potential bottleneck before-hand. For example, an individual and/or department may have a reputation for being uncooperative. Here, you should plan at the outset to circumvent this trouble spot.

4. Do many of the tasks involved concurrently rather than sequentially to compress the project timeframe. In addition, leave nonessentials such as routine documentation or other paperwork to be caught up with after the primary assignment has been completed.

5. Be realistic in your demands. Don't try to represent non-priority tasks as rush jobs when you need the support of other departments. Otherwise, they will tend to ignore you when a real rush job comes along.

6. When you're handed a priority project, delegate as much of your daily routine as possible to trusted subordinates.

7. Any complex project will require you to make a number of important decisions. On occasion, you won't have time to seek the counsel of those who may have expertise which would help in the decision-making process. However, aside from these unusual situations, be sure to take sufficient time to give yourself confidence that your decision is the right one.

8. As a project moves along, stay on top of situations where you can reasonably anticipate problems will arise. Obtaining feedback from those working on any project for which you have responsibility will allow you to resolve minor difficulties before they become major problems. Frequent feedback also has the advantage of allowing revision or cancellation of a project doomed to failure before extensive resources have been expended on the assignment.

9. Your enthusiasm and self-confidence can contribute substantially to expediting even the most difficult assignments. It's also important if you make a mistake to acknowledge it promptly and be explicit about what you will do to correct the error. This sort of can-do attitude will give you the credibility that encourages others to work a little harder to complete what sometimes are seen as impossible tasks.

10. Above all else, don't let deadline pressures overwhelm you. If you have done your best, don't question your decisions after the fact. This sort of thinking can lead you to overplan in the future, and in the final analysis, it's results, not the planning, that counts.

1.11

⇓

Ten Useful Rules for Supervisor/Subordinate Relations

Making better use of your time is only part of the equation for being an effective supervisor. Of even greater importance is your ability to manage your subordinates. Otherwise, you'll just end up spending your time resolving one employee problem after another. Even worse, it will be a constant struggle to maintain satisfactory levels of productivity within the group you supervise. The remaining chapters of this book will address the many detailed specifics of supervision. However, it's useful to first consider some broad rules for sound working relations with employees, since people problems can become the biggest time trap of all for a supervisor. The following guidelines will help in this regard.

1. Learn the individual strengths and weaknesses of people you supervise. This will aid you in assigning tasks on the basis of skills rather than at random.

2. However, work on developing the abilities of every employee, rather than continually making assignments based only on past performance. This will allow you to maintain a fair distribution of the workload, rather than having to go to your best workers with every difficult job.

3. Treat everyone equally. Some people are by nature more likeable than others, but as a supervisor you have to avoid even the slightest hint of favoritism.

4. Be flexible in dealing with employee concerns. Going strictly by set procedures won't always give you the flexibility you need to resolve individual problems.

   So when necessary, bending the rules a little may bring a big return in terms of work loyalty and productivity.

5. Show concern for employees. Try to look at problems from the perspective of the employee. It will help you deal with difficulties from an angle that will resolve problems permanently, rather than just postponing them.

6. Criticize with care. Try to be positive and impersonal when you criticize any aspect of an employee's performance. If you're not negative, you're less likely to receive a hostile response to constructive criticism.

7. Give simple, but specific, job directions anytime you assign a new task to a worker. And don't overlook the need to provide any necessary resources and training needed for the employee to do the job.

8. Show a continuing interest in your subordinates by providing feedback on their performance regularly, not just at performance evaluation time. Be honest and level with workers about how they're doing, whether it's good or bad. This means giving praise when it's deserved, and not giving it when it isn't.

9. Defend your subordinates against unfair criticism. Don't let other departments make your people the scapegoat for mistakes made elsewhere.

10. Be a coach—not a general. You're at work, not at war, so be loyal to your subordinates as well as the company. Include workers in the decision-making process whenever it's feasible to do so. You can also show leadership by working to obtain promotions, pay raises, and awards for deserving employees. In addition, don't minimize employee complaints. Some things that appear trivial on the surface may have major significance for employees.

Chapter Two

SHARPENING
YOUR SUPERVISORY
COMMUNICATION SKILLS

Good communication skills were undoubtedly one of the reasons you were initially selected for a supervisory position. This fact alone can lead to benign neglect of the different aspects of communication when you're thinking about ways to improve your management capabilities. Beyond that, the ability to communicate is a technique that tends to be taken for granted. Yet, as it turns out, success or failure in a supervisory role often rests upon the ability to excel at presenting your position to both subordinates and superiors.

Being convincing is a necessity, whether you're trying to motivate employees, or pitching a proposal for additional help to your boss. The lists in this chapter are focused on increasing your ability to communicate in the performance of your supervisory duties. The pointers provided may not place you in demand as an after-dinner speaker, but they should help you handle both the routine and complicated parts of your job with less difficulty.

25

2.1

The Do's and Don'ts of Being a Good Listener

One of the basic tools for supervisory success is the ability to be a good listener. This is particularly true as participative management and teamwork replace the traditional one-sided flow of direction from top to bottom within companies. Indeed, solid two-way communication is impossible unless you first master the art of being a listener.

Of course, like most other things, being a good listener must be done in moderation. The reality of being a supervisor means that you probably have more work than you can handle, especially if you give your undivided attention to everyone who seeks a hearing on matters minor or major. Therefore, being a good listener goes beyond practicing basic listening skills.

You will also have to learn to weigh the relative merits of what is being said against your time and work demands. This, of necessity, requires knowing when to tactfully bring discussions to an end. For the most part, this shouldn't be a major problem, since you can pretty well pinpoint the few people who just like to hear themselves talk.

Probably the biggest obstacle to improving your listening skills is your own view of how good a listener you are. So take the time to think through whether you're making the effort to be the best listener you can be. In doing this, the following suggestions should be helpful.

1. Don't listen on automatic pilot. It's easy to tune people out, particularly if they tend to be boring. However, listening halfheartedly can convey the wrong impression to subordinates and others. For example, if you appear distracted when employees are talking to you, they may assume you either don't care about what they're saying, or else don't want to know about it. As a result, employees may stop telling you what you need to know to supervise effectively.

2. Establish the proper setting. Show interest and offer encouragement to the speaker by establishing eye contact, and using nonverbal signals such as nodding and smiling at appropriate times. It also helps to make brief comments such as, "That's very interesting," or "I agree," to verbally relay your attentiveness. However, be certain that what you say doesn't sound phony, or it will destroy the image of being attentive which you're trying to create.

3. Try to eliminate distractions such as interruptions. In fact, if an extremely important subject is being discussed, you may want to meet somewhere other than your office. This is especially true if the topic is a complaint about another employee, or some other matter which a worker would feel more comfortable discussing in a location removed from the general work area.

4. Avoid excessive note taking. A speaker deserves your undivided attention, so avoid taking a lot of notes while someone is talking. Along with showing inattention to the speaker, it can also be self-defeating, since as you're taking notes, you may miss parts of what is being said. Get any additional information you need after the speaker is finished. This will help put the entire topic into a context you can understand and react to.

5. Exercise patience when listening, since some people take longer than others to get to the point. Try to put yourself in the position of the speaker, as this will help you concentrate on what the person is trying to say.

6. Don't jump to conclusions and interrupt speakers with a quick response. People can listen faster than they can talk, so it's tempting to form a judgement and then cut someone short before they have finished. Instead, evaluate silently what is being said, and try to sort the main ideas from the details as you listen.

7. Treat the subject seriously even if it's of little or no importance to you, since it may have a great deal of significance to the speaker. This is particularly true with minor gripes and irritants that workers sometimes complain about. Incidentally, in these situations, it sometimes helps to do a little probing, since a minor complaint may be masking a more serious grievance that the employee either doesn't want to raise, or else is doing so in a confusing manner.

8. Never interrupt just because you don't agree with what is being said. Hear the person out, since they may have other things to say that support their position. Besides, if you make a habit of interrupting people whenever you don't agree with them, workers will be less likely to discuss anything with you. This will seriously hinder your ability to manage effectively.

9. Listen for what isn't being said. Listening to what people are telling you isn't always the full story. This is particularly true when someone is pitching a project, or point of view, in which they have a vested interest. What you will hear in these situations are the advantages of the speaker's posi-

tion, but none of the disadvantages—or at best a quick glossing over of the weaknesses. On these occasions, when the speaker concludes, ask questions that focus on the unspoken arguments that rebut what the speaker has just told you. This will force the person to address these specifics. As you learn to do this, you may find that over the long term, those you supervise will be less inclined to give you only one side of the story.

10. When someone finishes talking, summarize what was said to be certain that you fully understand the speaker's position. This will also show people that you were listening to them, even though you may not agree with what they said.

2.2

✣

Painless Ways to Say "No" to Common Requests

Whether it's an employee seeking a day off during the busiest time of the year, or another supervisor asking to borrow one of your people for a week, quite frequently your answer will have to be "No." In fact, under some circumstances, you might even have to reject requests that you would ordinarily agree to.

As you know, it isn't always easy to turn people down. So if you're not careful, you may find yourself granting requests when it isn't in your best interests to do so. Another pitfall to avoid is making future promises to compensate for turning down otherwise reasonable requests that can't be honored at the present time. Here, too, you have to be careful not to commit to something in the future simply because you are saying "No."

Of course, everyone wants to be liked, but rejecting both reasonable and frivolous demands goes with your job. And although saying "No" may sometimes be difficult, there are ways to do it that can help soften the blow. Let's look at a few approaches for handling some of the more common situations where you have to stand your ground.

1. *When an employee wants to go on vacation and you can't spare him.* This sort of predicament generally arises in one of two ways. Either the worker didn't follow the rules on scheduling vacations, or the time slot requested has already been given to someone else. In the first instance, let the employee know that he didn't follow proper procedure.

However, go beyond that to state specifically why the request can't be honored.

In other words, don't leave the employee with the impression that his vacation request is being denied just because the proper procedure wasn't followed. Say something such as, "I'm sorry, Joe, but we are taking inventory that week and I can't spare anyone. You know that's why we make out a vacation schedule every January. If you remember, last January you didn't want to schedule your vacation and said you would take your chances. Ordinarily, I'd like to accommodate you, but the next two weeks are out of the question."

In some instances, the worker may be making a vacation request that's in compliance with company rules, but it conflicts with other vacations previously scheduled for the same time period. Here, you have to essentially let the worker know that it's first come, first served, so the request can't be approved. Nevertheless, you may want to give the employee an opportunity to swap with the person already scheduled for vacation in that time slot. For instance, try saying something such as, "Sorry Marilyn, but Joan has already asked for those two weeks. However, I don't have any objection if you can work something out with her."

2. *When an employee is seeking a pay raise or promotion.* One of the hardest times to say "No" is when you get inquiries from hard-working employees about the likelihood of a promotion and/or a pay raise. This is especially true when a change in the employee's status is long overdue, but budgetary constraints, poor business conditions, or other factors have prevented you from properly rewarding someone for their efforts. The best way to deal with these situations is to level with workers as to why a promotion or pay raise isn't in the cards at the present time.

When you're dealing with problems in this area, be careful to avoid making future promises that are beyond your authority to carry out. What you rightly view as a promise that's contingent on future events—such as a pickup in business which loosens budgetary constraints—a worker may see as a firm commitment. Then, if future circumstances don't allow for the promise to be carried out, you end up with an unhappy worker who blames you. You're better off telling it like it is and saying something such as, "Alan, with business off 20% from last year, top management has suspended pay raises until further notice. I know that's disappointing, and I wish I could tell you when I'll be able to put your raise through, but I don't want to make a promise that I can't carry out. Let's hope for the best and perhaps things will turn around sooner rather than later."

3. *When a worker wants to reschedule his hours because of personal problems.* Child care, commuting arrangements, and other matters may occasionally cause difficulty for workers in terms of working hours. Of course, it's good policy to be as cooperative as possible in helping employees work around temporary difficulties, but this isn't always feasible.

   How you go about turning down an employee is crucial, since an employee who feels you're not being sensitive to his or her problems is likely to look for work elsewhere. For this reason, try to be as flexible as possible in working something out. In fact, your efforts to be helpful will by themselves serve to lessen any resentment if you're forced to refuse the request after exploring all possible alternatives.

4. *When a worker wants a transfer to another department.* Naturally, if the request comes from a dud, approve it quickly and enjoy your good fortune. Of course, as fate would have it, workers you wouldn't mind losing aren't usually the ones who request transfers. More likely, it's going to be one of your most productive workers, and chances are the request will come either at the busiest time of year, or when a hiring freeze prohibits you from getting a replacement. However, don't just bluntly deny the request, since this can quickly turn a good worker into an unproductive one. Sit down and go over why the worker wants the transfer. It may be that you will uncover a situation unrelated to the work itself that has triggered the employee's request. For example, perhaps the worker is being bothered by a co-worker. There may even be some aspect of the job itself that can be adjusted to satisfy the worker. In any event, if it's a correctable situation where you can make adjustments to satisfy the worker's concerns, talking the problem out will reveal it.

   On the other hand, if your discussion doesn't turn up anything that will change the employee's mind about transferring, you will simply have to turn the request down. However, to minimize any ill feelings on the part of the worker, try to offer some glimmer of hope for the future. For example, say, "It's impossible to transfer you at this time, Peggy, but let's look at the possibility again in a couple of months." This approach not only gives you some time to consider alternatives, but it may well be that the employee's desire to transfer may change in the meantime. In any event, whatever the outcome, showing concern for the worker's transfer request will help alleviate the impact of turning the request down.

5. *When workers ask to leave early or come in late.* Generally, it isn't a big deal to let an employee leave a little early or be a little late for work on occasion. However, it's important to insist that this be done with your prior approval. Otherwise, you're likely to find workers starting to set their own working hours. Of course, the amount of flexibility you have in granting these requests will depend to a large degree upon the nature of the work operation you supervise. Some jobs—such as assembly line operations—will require fairly strict adherence to set times, since you would need to assign someone to cover for the absent worker. In other functions, such as many administrative operations, where the worker's absence doesn't have a direct impact on other jobs, it's easier to grant this type of request.

However, even in situations where there's a fair amount of flexibility in letting an employee leave a little early, there are times you will have to refuse such requests. When this happens, it's prudent to tell the employee why. Otherwise, workers may think you're either being arbitrary about giving your approval, or playing favorites within the group. You may also find you have to keep a tight rein on one or two people who try to make it a habit of coming in late or leaving early by using one excuse or another. When you see this developing, tell them that this is a privilege to be used in emergency situations, not on an everyday basis.

6. *When another department head wants to borrow an employee.* One of the trickier situations where you may have to refuse someone's request is when another supervisor wants to use one of your workers to help handle an overload of work in another department. Of course, in a spirit of teamwork this sort of request would normally be granted assuming you have someone you can spare. However, there are several things you should consider before granting such requests:

- Will this leave you shorthanded?

- Does the other supervisor help you out when you're in a bind?

- What will the reaction of the designated employee be?

- Will your other workers resist picking up the slack?

- Will your own boss think you're overstaffed, since you apparently have someone you can spare?

- What is the possibility the short-term detail will turn into a permanent assignment leaving you with one less worker?

- If you grant the request what is the likelihood of this happening again? Remember, once you say "OK," it's natural that the other supervisor will approach you again when he's in a pinch.

Even if most of your concerns are satisfied, it's not a bad idea for you to clue your boss in as to what's happening. That way, an erroneous impression won't be formed that you have more help than you need. On the other hand, if it turns out that you have valid reasons for refusing the request to borrow one of your people, how you go about turning the other supervisor down is important for several reasons. First of all, you don't want to be pegged as not being on board as a team player. In addition, you may need a favor yourself in the future, and alienating someone won't help you get it. Therefore, when you reject the request do it by implying that you want to grant it, but that under the circumstances it's just not possible to do so. Say something such as, "You know I'd really like to help you out, Paul, but I'm behind in my schedule as it is." It also helps if you suggest alternatives such as, "Why don't you ask Smythe (the boss) if you can hire a temp?" Naturally, the other supervisor may have already thought of that, but your pointing it out shows your concern and cooperative spirit.

CAUTION: When you do turn down a request to borrow a worker from another supervisor always be prepared to justify it to your boss in case it is brought to his attention. On occasion, this may happen and your boss may override you, but even then you can still come out a winner. How? If you are subsequently criticized for something going wrong, you may be able to defend it on the grounds you were missing the detailed worker. From another angle, you can use it as an argument at some later date when you need help and your peers aren't willing to let you borrow someone for a few days.

2.3

General Rules for Refusing Requests

The circumstances and subject matter which require you to reject employees' requests are of course wide and varied. Beyond the suggestions offered in the prior section for specific topics, the following general rules are helpful when you can't honor an employee's request.

1. Be as positive as possible in turning someone down. Saying something such as "I'm sorry, but we're just too busy," doesn't have the harsh tone of a blunt "No."

2. Don't let your emotions get in the way of refusing a request. Everyone's desire to be liked can sometimes cloud the ability to refuse a request. But remember, respect is a two-way street, and the person making the request should be considerate of your reasons for saying "No."

3. Hold your ground and don't start to waffle if the other person tries to persist in getting a positive response. The more you appear to back off, the greater the chances the other person will continue to pursue the issue.

4. Don't be put on the defensive. Sometimes people seeking something will try to justify it based upon some unrelated event. For example, just because someone has worked overtime consistently during the winter doesn't have any bearing on their request to worker shorter hours in the summer.

5. Don't be rushed into a decision one way or the other. If you want time to think about a request before responding, say so, but be specific about when you will get back to the employee.

6. If you use a conditional "No" such as, "You can leave early if your work is finished," be precise in setting the condition. In other words, let the employee know exactly what has to be done to meet the condition you have imposed.

2.4
⇓
How to Ask Questions That Get
the Right Answers

It's only human nature for workers to be reluctant about being forthright when something goes wrong. Therefore, the questions you ask will largely dictate the response you get when you're trying to get to the bottom of something. If you ask a vague or misleading question, this opens up an opportunity for an evasive answer, especially if a worker thinks unpleasant repercussions will result from being honest. In fact, even otherwise routine matters can turn into confusing situations if questions aren't carefully phrased. As a result, you can spend a lot more time trying to resolve problems if you don't ask questions that zero in on the problem at hand. And, of course, along with learning the knack of asking the right questions is the equally important element of adopting an attitude that doesn't put workers on the defensive. The following techniques should not only help you to get the answers you seek, but also promote a greater degree of openness in communicating with those you supervise.

1. Don't ask open-ended questions if you're looking for specific answers. For instance, if you want to know about the progress of a specific task don't say something such as, "How's everything coming along, Carl?" Instead zero in on the subject, such as by saying, "Is the Grunewald order still on schedule?"

2. If you're asking a question that doesn't seem to be eliciting the sort of information you're looking for, try asking the question in a different way. Sometimes, people simply misinterpret seemingly simple questions because they're mentally preoccupied with something else. Asking the question in a different way will tend to focus them on what you want to know.

3. Be careful about using jargon or technical language that the person you're talking with won't understand. Often, people will give you a quick "Yes" or "No" answer that may be wrong, rather than admit they didn't understand your question.

4. If you think someone is deliberately avoiding giving you the information you seek, when feasible, steer the conversation to another topic, then come back and ask the same question again. This may catch the person off-guard and elicit the information you're looking for.

5. If you want someone to do something for you, try to phrase the question so it's easier to reply positively. For example, if you are looking for volunteers to work overtime, saying, "Are you interested in working tonight?" requires only a "Yes" or "No" in reply. But, if you say, "Colin, we have overtime tonight. I know I can count on you to help out. OK if I pencil you in on my list?" It's harder for the worker to refuse, since he pretty much has to come up with an excuse for not working.

6. If you're questioning an employee about a negative matter, such as a work error or rules violation, don't start off with a hard-ball question that will put the worker on the defensive. Instead, first ask simpler questions that will ease into the subject and be more inclined to get the

employee to level with you. As an example, suppose you want to know why an employee is making an unusually large number of errors. If you say, "Linda, how come you're making so many mistakes lately?", the response is likely to be, "I'm not," which then likely will evolve into an emotional debate over the worker's performance. If, on the other hand, you start off by inquiring about any problems the worker is having, or anything you can help with, they will be more inclined to level with you about the problem.

2.5

Practical Steps That Will Generate Feedback from Workers

Your success or failure as a supervisor depends to a large extent on knowing about problems at the earliest possible moment. That way, minor matters won't become major disasters. In addition, the overall efficiency and productivity of your department is enhanced if workers are encouraged to willingly contribute their thoughts and ideas about the workplace in general and their own job in particular. This requires effective feedback from subordinates, which isn't likely to be forthcoming unless you encourage two-way communication on a daily basis by providing regular feedback to employees on all aspects of their performance. A systematic approach for doing this is as follows:

1. Observe each employee's performance on a regular basis. Sometimes, there's a tendency to let this slide, either because you're busy with other duties, and/or your employees are experienced and need minimal direct supervision. This doesn't mean you should hover over people and watch them work, but rather walk around, inquire as to their needs, and in general just be visible.

2. When an employee is doing something you don't like, give immediate feedback. Explain what's wrong, how it should be done, and why it's important to do it the way you want.

3. Don't just be negative in your feedback. Praise employees when you see them doing something that you like. When people are working hard, they appreciate it that the boss recognizes their efforts.

4. Be low-key when something goes wrong. Employees are more likely to make you aware of potential problems if they know it won't result in anger or disapproval.

5. Don't make assumptions. Just because a worker isn't keeping up with his workload doesn't mean he is lazy or incompetent. There may be underlying reasons such as equipment problems, lack of training, and so forth.

6. Be as accessible as possible in terms of having an open-door policy. Employees are reassured when they feel free to approach you with problems at any time.

7. Admit your own mistakes. If you're willing to admit your mistakes when you make them, your employees will be more likely to admit theirs.

8. Don't send mixed signals. You can't yell at people one minute and then turn around and tell them you won't get mad if they bring problems to you.

9. Encourage employees to discuss ways in which you can communicate better with them. Periodic informal gatherings are one way of encouraging good back-and-forth communication.

10. Show appreciation when an employee brings something to your attention. Say something such as, "That's good to know, Francine. I'll certainly try to get information to you quicker in the future."

2.6

Sure-Fire Tactics That Build Employee Trust

Perhaps the most crucial element in generating employee enthusiasm and loyalty is trust. If your subordinates don't trust you, then they won't be willing to confide in you to the extent that you'll get the feedback you need to be an effective supervisor. Of course, the process of building a foundation of trust can't be accomplished overnight. It requires a long-term commitment on your part, along with a considerable investment of time and energy. Adopting the following tactics will assist you in this regard.

1. Share information and allow your employees to participate in the decision-making process whenever possible. Giving your subordinates addi-

tional responsibility will not only build their confidence, but it will also increase their feeling of participation.

2. Resolve internal conflicts promptly. Whether it's a disagreement between two employees, or a squabble with another department, a quick resolution will not only prevent escalation of the difficulty, but will also minimize any disruptive impact on productivity.

3. Avoid even the slightest appearance of favoritism. It's not always easy to subdue individual likes and dislikes, but equal treatment must be practiced as well as preached to promote a framework of trust in which teamwork and cooperation will thrive.

4. Have realistic expectations about the capabilities of those you supervise. Everyone has different strengths and weaknesses, and not everyone will excel at every task you give them. Some workers will also be better at handling pressure than others, but even your best workers will have a bad day now and then.

5. Avoid being seen as indecisive. When workers sense indecision on the part of a supervisor, they tend to silently question that person's ability to supervise. For this reason, it's better to admit it when you don't have a ready answer rather than waffle or toss out a haphazard reply which lacks credibility.

6. Even though consistency is important, always remain flexible enough to consider exceptions to the general rules when employees experience problems both on and off the job.

7. Always strive to show appreciation for a job well done. In this regard, it's important to be specific and not just say, "You're doing a great job, Tracy." Tell individual workers what it is that you appreciate, and be timely in your praise. When workers do an exceptional job on something, if you let time lag before telling them, they may assume in the interim that you didn't notice and/or care about their efforts.

8. Talk one-on-one with employees on a regular basis. This is time-consuming, but it builds the sort of trust that only personal contact can bring about.

9. Always be polite, especially when work pressures are the greatest. If workers sense they're going to be criticized for making errors, they will tend to work at a slower pace, and/or avoid taking the extraordinary measures or risks that are sometimes necessary to get the job done.

10. When disagreements arise between employees don't try to gloss over the matter. Instead, ask the workers who are involved for suggestions on resolving both the immediate problem, as well as avoiding any future repetition.

2.7

The Crucial Components of Sound Decisions

"She's wishy-washy," or "He can't make a decision," are judgments that can weigh heavily on the success or failure of a supervisory career. Yet even being decisive can lead you down the fast track to frustration. After all, the effects of a bad decision can be even harder to shake than the common cold.

All in all, this places the ability to make sound decisions near the top of the list of factors that can further your career. However, as you know, there's no formula available which can guarantee that your decisions will always be the right ones.

To further complicate matters, every supervisor knows there's little time to ponder and plan major decisions, much less the dozens of routine determinations that you make on a daily basis. Nevertheless, despite the difficulties, there are some standard practices which can improve the odds that your decisions are the right ones. These include:

1. Make sure you follow the basic steps that should precede any decision that's of importance in the overall scheme of things. These consist of:

   - Identifying the problem.

   - Fact gathering.

   - Identifying alternative solutions.

   - Weighing the pros and cons of each alternative.

2. Avoid excessive reliance on information furnished by a trusted subordinate. This may lead to a bad decision due to a failure to seek out facts from other sources. That's because even the most reliable worker may unconsciously project bias when furnishing input into the decision-making process. Therefore, it's always wise to obtain information from a number of sources rather than rely on one opinion.

3. Don't let your self-confidence—or predisposed disposition—lull you into a hasty decision. When the facts overwhelmingly suggest that a certain decision is the proper one to take, don't act in haste. Take a little time to play devil's advocate and see if you can come up with any loopholes that are being overlooked.

4. On the other hand, don't fall victim to analysis paralysis when making decisions. Your instincts are important, so when time doesn't allow for extended discussions, don't be afraid to go with your gut reaction. Along the same lines, the trend toward participative management doesn't mean total consensus is necessary on every decision. It's important to let people express their opinions, but if it's your decision to make, the buck stops with you.

5. One way to make faster decisions is to stay on top of situations where you can reasonably anticipate future problems will occur. By doing this, you're able to foresee potential difficulties that may arise down the road, and can think about what action you'll take if your worst fears come true. And even if something unforeseen happens which you haven't considered, you're further along toward a solution than you might be if you ignore the matter until a crisis erupts.

6. Recognize that you will occasionally make a bad decision. Don't worry about this, since the only people who never make bad decisions are still shuffling through life without having made any decision—either good or bad. Furthermore, if you think about it, decisions can be either altered or reversed to adjust for changing conditions.

7. Don't hesitate to accept the responsibility when a decision turns sour. In fact, a willingness to admit a mistake can earn you respect that far outweighs the negative implications of the decision itself.

8. Remember that there are occasions when the best decision is no decision at all. The best example of this is when an otherwise sound decision shouldn't be made because of its impact on internal politics. It goes without saying that a good decision that will alienate the wrong people isn't a wise choice under any conditions.

9. All too frequently, making a decision is the easy part. It's making the decision stick that can be tough. This is especially true when you're the victim of subtle sabotage—or even open hostility—by those opposing your actions. The best way to counter this opposition is to exhibit con-

fidence in your decisions. Once you start to second-guess yourself, you'll quickly find others jumping on the bandwagon.

10. Avoid falling victim to the "Something has to be done about this" syndrome. There are many situations which will resolve themselves without any action being taken. Consequently, hastily jumping to judgment and taking action in these cases may not only fail to cure the problem, but may actually make matters worse. This is especially true where the potential risks from taking some form of action are greater than the possible damage from waiting to see if the problem resolves itself.

2.8

Prudent Methods for Promoting Teamwork

Teamwork is persistently touted as the cure for everything from profits to poor productivity. However, as you know, teamwork is a lot easier to preach than to practice. Part of the problem is that top management sometimes extols the virtues of teamwork without actually adopting strategies to convert pep talks into productive cooperation. In fact, careless actions are sometimes taken that work against the need for cooperation, and instead serve to further alienate employees from striving toward common goals. Be that as it may, whatever the gap between policy and reality may be within your organization, as a supervisor there is much you can do to foster teamwork within your own group. Among the measures you can take are the following:

1. *Encourage worker participation in decision-making.* Soliciting the opinions of the people you supervise is a key element in developing teamwork. However, you have to actively encourage workers to contribute their ideas. Otherwise, subordinates will sense that you're just going through the motions. And once this sense of insincerity sets in, it's not easy to overcome.

2. *Don't avoid discipline in the interests of teamwork.* Everyone isn't by nature a team player and goof-offs and other troublemakers still have to be dealt with. Nevertheless, discipline in a team-oriented workplace won't have the same disruptive impact as it might where teamwork isn't encouraged. This is because workers are more likely to sympathize with you rather than the problem employee. Actually, when a strong sense of

teamwork exists, workers themselves may exert peer pressure on shirkers to pick up the pace.

3. *Be flexible in making assignments.* Everyone doesn't have the same skills, nor is everyone capable of working at the same speed. Therefore, it's important to recognize these individual differences and assign work accordingly. In this regard, don't set goals for everyone at some arbitrary standard, such as the performance levels of a standout worker.

4. *Show appreciation for team efforts.* Be creative in devising ways to reward your group. Pay raises are periodic, and promotions are remote goals, so look for other ways to show appreciation when your group pitches in to complete a rush job and/or whittles down a backlog of work. For example, when a period of heavy workload slacks off, it helps to let people goof off a bit.

5. *Make cooperation part of performance reviews.* Many employee evaluation forms list cooperation/teamwork as one factor to be considered when giving workers their periodic reviews. However, for the most part, very little emphasis is placed on discussing this trait with individuals during their review. Often, unless the evaluating supervisor is dealing with a blatantly uncooperative worker, this factor receives little attention. To encourage greater teamwork within your group, try placing greater stress on an employee's cooperative endeavors when you sit down to do their formal evaluation. Be specific in telling people both what you like and dislike about their performance as a team player.

6. *Set the tone for teamwork by your actions.* Your own people are more likely to be inspired to be team players by observing your own approach in not only dealing with them, but also with other departments. Therefore, if workers view you as being teamwork-oriented in working with supervisors and others outside of your department, they will tend to follow your lead.

7. *Don't confuse teamwork with management by committee.* Workers want to be part of the process that determines how their job is done. However, teamwork doesn't mean a "touchy-feely" communal endeavor as it's sometimes portrayed to be. Rather, it means people want respect and the ability to contribute in determining how their work is performed. Nevertheless, they both expect and respect the fact that the boss is the one to make the final decision when all is said and done.

8. *Pay attention to details.* Minor matters, such as not keeping the office copier in good repair, or replacing worn-out tools, are irritating to employees. Making certain your subordinates have the resources to work with is essential in encouraging teamwork. Otherwise, they may sense that you don't really care about how they do their job.

9. *Make certain employees see the "big picture."* Getting employees to work together as a team requires them to know how their particular job interacts with others both within and outside your group. For this reason, familiarize each of your workers with the different jobs under your supervision. If it's feasible, try to cross-train your people to do as many tasks as possible. Not only will it give them an understanding of the difficulties others may face in doing their job, but it facilitates moving people around to prevent boredom.

10. *Show a personal interest in your employees.* Beyond anything else, any attempt to improve teamwork requires open and honest communication with employees. Yet this goes beyond holding regular meetings and handing out streams of informational memos. The real key is to show an interest in your subordinates on a personal basis. Comments such as, "Hi, Joe, how's your boy doing in Little League," and similar statements of personal concern, demonstrate that you're a supervisor who recognizes employees as people—not clock-punching robots.

2.9

The Key Elements for Boosting Morale

Keeping employee morale high isn't an easy undertaking. Furthermore, it can be complicated by matters beyond your control such as layoffs, reorganizations, and other factors. Nevertheless, irrespective of these influences, there are a wide-ranging number of actions you can take as a supervisor to maximize morale and keep employees motivated. These include:

1. Avoid needless morale busters. Sometimes, seemingly insignificant actions can needlessly damage morale. For instance, "clean desk" edicts in the office that require the removal of pictures, plants, and other links to life beyond work can arouse resentment in employees. Of course, there are limits to the extent by which work areas should be personal-

ized. After all, a desk covered with plants so that it resembles a tropical rain forest is a little much. However, these are situations that should be handled on an individual basis—not as a blanket edict that arouses the wrath of all employees.

2. Be responsive to employee complaints. Take prompt action on employee problems. Workers should be told what you're doing and why that particular course of action is being taken. This doesn't mean you have to agree with every employee demand, but at least give an explanation as to why you can't comply with the employee's request.

3. Don't make impossible demands. Assign work based upon the capabilities of each employee, so someone isn't given a task that they can't complete. When you do assign unusual and/or difficult tasks assure the employee that you recognize the difficulty and that you stand ready to provide assistance if needed.

4. Be willing to do things differently. Don't arbitrarily reject employee suggestions for doing things their way rather than yours. Make a conscious effort not to reject ideas just because they require a change in the way tasks are handled. Even when something suggested doesn't have any meaningful value, take the time to discuss the pros and cons with the worker who made the suggestion.

5. Don't neglect common courtesy. Requesting rather than demanding is far more likely to get positive results when you want workers to do something.

6. Don't use comparisons. Extolling the virtues of a star performer to other workers will create resentment. For instance, saying something such as "What's taking you so long? Stanley can do that in twenty minutes." Perhaps he can, but individuals have varying abilities so this isn't a proper motivational technique.

7. Be specific when you offer praise. Instead of a generalized comment such as, "You're doing a great job, Ellen," use specifics such as, "That was an excellent job you did for the lab yesterday." There's nothing wrong with providing general encouragement, but tying it to specifics gives the praise more meaning to the individual worker.

8. Don't treat certain jobs as less important than others. If a worker is made to feel that her job isn't as important as others in the group, then it isn't likely that she will work her hardest at it. Strive to make every worker feel like a valued contributor.

9. Practice rumor control. Nothing damages morale more than rumors that run unchecked. Do your best to keep your people informed, and try to track down answers to employee concerns no matter how trivial they may seem.

10. Lead by example. By demonstrating the importance you place on doing your job to the best of your ability you set the tone for your subordinates.

11. Keep people busy to avoid boredom. Most jobs have peaks and valleys in terms of work volume. During slow periods find other constructive tasks to keep people occupied. However, don't create "make work" projects, since this will only make matters worse.

12. Help employees work toward their goals. Encourage people to learn new skills on the job, and provide any training that will help them work toward advancement.

13. Don't just dump unpleasant assignments on workers. Explain the necessity for assigning the task, and try to spread the less desirable jobs around so individuals don't think they're always the one getting the dirty duty.

2.10

Practical Guidelines for Conducting Effective Meetings

Getting the most out of the meetings that you schedule is essential for several reasons. First of all, as noted in Chapter One, meetings can consume a big chunk of your time. This alone makes it worthwhile to try and make every meeting serve its purpose. But beyond this, a meeting that isn't planned and executed effectively can lead to confusion and misinterpretation. This tends to result in responses similar to, "I thought you said to do it this way," when something goes wrong.

Of course, sometimes this sort of reply is simply an attempt to deflect criticism by a worker who wasn't paying attention. But on other occasions, it may result from a loss of focus during a meeting which leaves the participants unsure of what is wanted. The following are some of the more common measures you can take to make every meeting you hold more productive.

1. Adequate preparation is the key ingredient for conducting successful meetings. Once you have established that a meeting is necessary, take the time to think about precisely what you want to accomplish.

2. If you will be covering several topics—or going into detail on a single complicated subject—it will help to prepare an outline of your goals for the meeting. Doing this helps you think about how to proceed during the meeting itself. If the meeting has several objectives, and will be attended by people from other departments, you may want to prepare a formal agenda and distribute it before the meeting. This helps avoid people showing up unprepared to discuss a topic and then pleading, "I didn't know we were going to cover that."

3. Try to anticipate objections and be prepared to counter them if they are brought up. If the meeting will cover a topic likely to cause conflict you may want to touch base with key participants beforehand. For example, if you and some of your people are meeting with another department head over some interdepartmental dispute, it may be worthwhile to discuss the matter with the other supervisor ahead of time. You may be able to agree on a joint solution, but even if you can't, at least you will have a solid feel for the other side's position before the meeting takes place.

4. Try to schedule meetings when people's attention spans are highest, rather than at the end of the day, or on a Friday afternoon.

5. Always start meetings at the scheduled time. Waiting for tardy attendees only aggravates those who were on time.

6. Start the meeting off by briefly describing its purpose, unless that is already obvious.

7. Take notes of who is supposed to do what as a result of the meeting. Otherwise, a future meeting may be required because someone dropped the ball.

8. Never hand out material at the beginning of a meeting. People will immediately immerse themselves in reading the material rather than paying attention to what's going on. There's nothing more aggravating then seeing people reading a handout, and ten minutes later asking questions that were answered while they were busy reading.

9. Never let meetings take precedence over more important work. If it's a meeting scheduled by someone else, send a trusted subordinate in your place. However, be sure to instruct them to take good notes, and have them brief you afterwards. Otherwise, you can get caught short if the meeting resulted in action items which you weren't told about.

10. Make sure you keep control of the meeting and don't let people go off on tangents. Ask specific questions and short circuit any irrelevant remarks by interrupting the person talking and saying something such as, "That's interesting, but let's get back to what we were discussing." There are exceptions to this rule, including those meetings you have with your group to let subordinates express their ideas, gripes, and the like.

11. If you are having a one-on-one disciplinary meeting with a worker, make sure you have it in private. It may also be a good idea to hold it in a conference room, or borrowed office, away from the work area. This is so, since even if you do close your office door, everyone in your group will have seen their co-worker being called into the office, and it won't be hard to figure out the reason why. Holding it elsewhere also prevents you from being cornered in your own office while an employee rants on about why you're being unfair. If it's somewhere else, it's easier to just walk out if you start to lose your patience.

12. As mentioned in Section 1.8 on how to keep meetings short, set time limits and limit the number of attendees to those necessary to accomplish the purpose of the meeting.

13. If you're holding a meeting with subordinates to give them information on some new company policy and procedure, don't get bogged down in a disjointed discussion because your people don't understand the changes and/or you don't have readily available answers.

    If there is written material on the change, give it out beforehand so subordinates will have a better understanding before the meeting begins. If there isn't any handout and/or you are receiving a great many questions about the new policy, have people write their questions down and give them to you later. That way, you will be able both to shorten the meeting, and avoid repetitive running around to get answers whenever another subordinate pops into your office, saying "Just one more quick question, boss."

2.11

Twelve Keys to Writing Better Memos and Reports

Writing memos and reports is a task that you may dread. However, being successful in getting your point across in writing can make your job a lot easier. After all, if you're looking for additional help and your boss says, "Put it in writing," your ability to be convincing may spell the difference between success and failure. Of course, not everything you have to write has that sort of significance. But even a relatively routine memo can cause hassles if it tends to be confusing. So it's certainly worthwhile to get it right the first time. The following tactics will help you do just that.

1. Consider whether or not a written response is the best way to go. Many times a personal meeting or phone call may be preferable. For example, sometimes rather than confronting people directly with complaints, individuals will write nasty memos. If you respond directly in writing, you pretty much either have to admit to the charges, make excuses, or completely rebut them. The first two choices can make you look bad, while refuting the complaints may ignite an internal feud.

   Generally, in this type of situation, it may be preferable to meet directly with the sender of the memo to resolve matters. Not only does it avoid documenting mistakes that may have been made within your department, but it also gives you the upper hand in resolving the matter. After all, the person who wrote the memo probably isn't expecting you to directly confront him, and may tend to back away from the complaints when you meet on a one-to-one basis.

   This example demonstrates one important point, which is that written matter is etched in stone. You don't have the opportunity to give and take that a conversation provides. Personal contact also allows for elaboration and explanation if questions are raised, or a statement is challenged. This flexibility isn't present with written communication, which is one more reason to get it right the first time if you put something in writing.

2. It can sometimes be tough getting started when you have to write a tricky memo, or a complex report. A good way to get around this is to

start by writing a rough draft of whatever comes to mind. Don't worry about grammar, editing, and so forth. Once you get your rough thoughts down on paper, it will be relatively easy to expand upon them and put them in a logical sequence.

3. In terms of writing style, decide whether you want to be formal, informal, personal, impersonal, simple and direct, or forceful. Both your audience (whom you are writing to) and the subject matter will come into play here. It's important not only to be aware of what you're writing, but also to keep in mind whom you are writing to. If possible, send replies in the style of the person you received the written message from. And when in doubt, follow the rule that simpler is better.

4. Be clear and concise in your writing, but don't waste a lot of time striving for perfection. This is particularly true with routine memos and other simple correspondence.

5. Keep your writing simple. As a general rule shorter is smarter in terms of words, sentences, and paragraphs.

6. Put your points in proper sequence, and confine your writing to telling readers what they need to know—no more or less.

7. Consider how the reader will react to what you're saying. For instance, don't let hostility creep into your writing, unless, of course, it's your intent to do so. However, even then be careful, since once you send something out it's too late to change your mind.

8. Make your writing error free. There's no excuse for words not being spelled correctly, particularly with all sorts of software spelling checkers available for computers and word processors.

9. Watch the use of acronyms, jargon, and technical language. It's easy to generalize the readership when you're hastily composing replies to business mail. This can easily lead to the use of technical terms which may be unfamiliar to the recipient of your correspondence.

   With acronyms, everyone won't necessarily know their meaning. If you do use them, spell out what they mean the first time you use them in a written communication, for instance, EDI (electronic data interchange).

10. If you're requesting some form of action, spell out precisely what it is you want the reader to do. If you're vague, there's less likelihood the desired action will be taken. Frequently, this type of request should be supported with detailed facts and figures. For example, if you're asking

your boss for additional help, be sure to spell out why you need it with facts such as (1) production has increased (2) you have made maximum use of overtime, and the like.

11. When you send out correspondence, send copies to those directly involved in the matter, as well as those who will be directly or indirectly affected. Unless your company uses a different policy, list people by their rank within the organization.

12. Last, but not least, if you expect a reply to anything you send out, be sure to ask for it. People who don't like to write, won't, unless they have to.

Chapter Three

✿

Strategies to Improve Individual Employee Performance

Whether you're supervising two employees or twenty, one of the most difficult duties of a boss is improving the performance levels of subordinates. You must deal with differences in personalities, work attitudes, skill levels, and experience just to mention a few of the hurdles. You have to handle negatives such as criticizing poor performance, as well as the positives of praising a job well done.

These tasks, as difficult as they are, can be compounded by changes in technology which place a premium on training needs, and by top management pressures for you to maximize the productivity of your group. Of course, when you seek additional resources to meet these demands the response is likely to be, "Make do with what you have." The lists in this chapter should help you stay ahead of the game in meeting these challenges.

3.1

The Proper Way to Conduct a Performance Evaluation Session

Performance evaluations are often viewed as an exercise in frustration by both supervisors and subordinates. That's natural enough since attempting to boil a year's performance into a series of check marks, or a few sentences of narrative, is at best a difficult endeavor. In addition, the burdens of daily business tend to lower the priority given to employee reviews. The net result is that supervisors don't like to do reviews, and employees often aren't happy with the results. Nevertheless, despite the many difficulties associated with any performance rating system, reviews can be effective if they are done carefully. The procedures that follow will help you do that to the ultimate benefit of both you and the employee.

1. The first hurdle to overcome in doing performance reviews may be the evaluation form itself. Quite frankly, many performance evaluation forms are poorly designed. If you find this to be true with the form currently in use within your organization, don't try to force the evaluation to fit the form. Instead, make the form conform to the evaluation. The form itself is nothing more than a tool—and not always a very good one. So don't get frustrated with the form. Learn to live with it, and work around it to give the best evaluation you can.
2. If possible, try to separate the performance review from the pay review. This allows for more open discussion with employees. Otherwise, if workers feel their comments are tied directly to the size of their potential pay raise, they are more likely to be defensive when discussing negative aspects of their performance. Of course, you will have to live within the guidelines of company policy, but even if the system you use links the pay raise with the evaluation, try to do the performance review first.
3. There's nothing worse than starting to prepare for a performance review and drawing a blank when you try to remember good and bad aspects of an employee's performance over the past year. At best, you may only be able to come up with generalizations, such as "Bob spent too much time talking at the water cooler." These broad-based statements can be hard to defend if they're challenged by the employee. On the other hand, specifics can't be easily rebutted.

The fact is that very few outstanding events of either a positive or negative nature take place over the course of a year. Most of the things an employee does that deviate from acceptable performance consist of minor achievements or minimal transgressions. As a result, for the most part, it's the sum total and trend of these pluses and minuses that you end up evaluating. However, since on an individual basis these are relatively forgettable events, they aren't always remembered weeks or months later. For this reason, it's very helpful to keep notes during the year of the minor triumphs and failures of your workers. This will give you a solid basis for discussion when performance evaluation time rolls around. You don't have to do anything that's very formal or time-consuming. Just a file folder with scribbled notes will do the trick.

4. Using the notes that you have collected, and any other relevant information, sit down and plan what you will cover in the evaluation beforehand. Don't forget to take the personality of the employee into consideration when you plan your approach. Some people are more receptive than others to a discussion of their performance, and a few may have a totally unrealistic attitude about their achievements. You may also want to think about how you will respond to questions that may be raised.

5. Let employees know several days ahead of time when their evaluation is scheduled, and suggest they think about any questions they might have. Never postpone evaluations, since this sends a signal that they're not important.

6. Take the time to do the job right. If necessary, schedule more than one meeting. This can happen if it becomes difficult to agree with the employee on goals to be achieved within the next rating period. This isn't something that should be glossed over quickly. Otherwise, when the next evaluation rolls around, you'll be trying to evaluate the worker on goals that were meaningless and/or unattainable.

7. Avoid rating people on their most recent performance. It's relatively easy to remember how well or poorly a worker has performed over the last month or two, but harder to recall what happened before that. In fact, savvy workers know this and they will tend to pick up the pace as performance evaluation time approaches. You can avoid this pitfall by taking notes as mentioned in Item # 3.

8. Work out job objectives with the employee. Take the time to do this carefully. The employee can then be measured in the future against the accomplishment of these goals.

9. Be sure to rate employees against their own goals and objectives, and not the performance of other employees. Sometimes there can be a little wishful thinking done as to why everyone should be as productive as the star employee in your group. That's OK as long as it doesn't seep into your thinking when you are rating everyone else. People have differing strengths and abilities, and should be evaluated on their own accomplishments.

10. In a related area, don't fall into the trap of rating a worker based upon any single outstanding or negative trait. Some people work fast, while others perform at a slower pace, yet are more quality-conscious. Whatever the outstanding trait may be, it is only one factor and shouldn't influence the evaluation of other aspects of the employee's performance.

11. Ask employees for suggestions as to how they think their performance can be improved, and what can be done to further their career development. This will help establish rapport and create two-way communication. If you don't get people involved in the process, they may tend to view the meeting as a lecture session, and think negatively about the whole process.

12. Use the worker's past performance as a guide to future improvement. In areas that may be subpar, ask yourself what you can do to upgrade the worker's performance. Additional training, or perhaps a realignment of duties are among the possibilities that should be considered.

13. Don't fill the evaluation form out until after your evaluation session with the employee. There may be valid reasons for some aspect of subpar performance which you're not aware of. Waiting to fill out the form gives you the chance to hear what the employee has to say. Workers will also feel they have more input into the process if it's done this way.

14. Give workers a few days to review their evaluation before signing and returning it to you. If an employee comes back with arguments about why some aspect of the evaluation should be changed, don't start to waffle, or be drawn into an argument about essentially minuscule differences of opinion. Calmly explain that the evaluation should be viewed on an overall basis, and not on the relative merits of individual ratings. Of course, if the worker presents new evidence that substantively affects the evaluation given, you should properly consider it. However, at this stage, having already undergone discussions with the employee before

the evaluation was completed, it's unlikely any changes are justified. If the worker is still dissatisfied, then he can make his own comments on the appropriate section of the form.

15. Don't use performance evaluations for the wrong reasons. It's not unknown for supervisors to give good performance reviews to duds in the hope that this will propel them to a job in another department. In the short term this may seem like an excellent way to rid yourself of a headache, but it's likely to backfire in one way or another. The reputation of duds tends to travel well, so it isn't likely their job search will be successful. This means you're stuck with them, but if you've given them a good evaluation, your chances of eventually firing them have diminished. And if through some stroke of good luck, a poor performer does land a job in another department—due in part to your good evaluation—your reputation as a supervisor will soon start to suffer. Not to mention the fact that you probably have another supervisor waiting in the wings to gain revenge for your sleight of hand.

16. Bringing employees to their full potential doesn't end with completion of the formal evaluation process. It's important to provide continuous feedback on performance throughout the year. The extent to which you do this will depend upon the employee's needs, but in any event, try to be both constructive and unobtrusive in providing the necessary guidance.

3.2

Mastering How to Criticize
Without Creating Resentment

Even though employees are making too many mistakes, you may experience a natural reluctance to criticize their poor performance. After all, criticism isn't something people enjoy, whether they are on the giving or receiving end of the advice. However, ignoring the possibility of an unpleasant confrontation won't solve the problem. In fact, if you wait too long before criticizing inferior efforts, you may eventually become so frustrated that you erupt in anger. That, of course, will make the situation even more difficult to deal with.

Although constructive criticism of inadequate work is never an easy thing to do, the following techniques will assist you in overcoming any reluctance you may have. The measures should also help minimize employees' resentment when they're spoken to about correcting some aspect of their performance.

1. As a starting point, it's important to think about the particular aspect of performance that you want to correct. Doing this gives you an opportunity to decide both what you want to say, as well as the possible choices for correcting the problem. For example, is an employee making careless errors because of his or her own negligence, or is it the result of inadequate training, or some other factor beyond their control?

2. Deciding beforehand—both what you want to say and how you want to say it—has a couple of advantages. First of all, it will help keep the conversation on track when it takes place. In addition, it will give you the opportunity to think over any potential excuses the employee might make, and allow you to prepare to counter them.

3. Keep in mind that criticism isn't constructive just because it's preceded by a qualifier such as, "I'm only trying to help make your job easier." To be truly effective, the remedial advice must be carefully thought out, and then given to the worker in a manner that will achieve the desired results.

4. Of course, corrective discussions should be conducted in private. In fact, if you use a conference room, or some site other than your office, the neutral location may serve to put the employee more at ease. This may help lessen the defensive posture that tends to arise when someone is called on the carpet. It also avoids the meeting being interrupted by other business, which can both lead the discussion off course, as well as lessen its importance in the eyes of the employee. Furthermore, interruptions allow time for the worker to think up excuses which justify his or her mistakes.

5. Don't just concentrate on the negatives during the discussion. If you provide some input on positive aspects of the employee's performance, it will help make the individual more receptive to the negative aspects of the session. After all, if the employee isn't doing anything right, then a termination interview and not a corrective meeting should be taking place.

6. Always solicit employee suggestions as to what can be done to correct the problem. This makes the worker part of the process, and a partner in resolving the difficulty.

7. Be practical when you're considering criticizing someone's subpar performance. Everyone has differing capabilities, so you have to take an individual approach to improving performance.

8. Be careful to avoid threats and personality attacks, since they only serve to lessen the willingness of the worker to cooperate.

9. Don't use humor since the employee may interpret that to mean you don't take the problem seriously. Alternatively, workers may view any attempt at humor as sarcasm and see it as a personal insult.

10. Avoid anger at all costs even if you're provoked by the worker's reactions to what you have to say. Losing your temper will only lead to losing control of the situation.

11. On some occasions, criticism may be given on the spur of the moment when a mistake is made. This usually happens when an error is observed at the time it occurs. Here, under pressure situations, is when it's most likely you will lose your temper. If this happens, it's prudent to later apologize to the worker for any anger, threats, or otherwise unjustified behavior. Nevertheless, if the criticism was itself valid, and only your method was unreasonable, don't convey the impression that the worker's mistake was acceptable. Be careful about making clear that the performance must be corrected, even though you are smoothing over your initial reaction to the error.

12. Be sensitive to non-work related factors that may be contributing to poor performance. If you know someone is having personal problems, if it's feasible to do so, you may want to wait until they subside before you talk to them. In fact, in these cases, often the performance improves when the personal crisis passes.

13. When criticizing an employee's performance, always refrain from making comparisons with other workers. The employee will not only resent this, but it weakens teamwork within your group, since workers may see this as playing favorites.

14. Since the purpose of the meeting is to correct some aspect of the worker's performance and/or behavior, it's important to be certain there are no misunderstandings about any agreements reached. For this reason, it's useful prior to the conclusion of the meeting to summarize what has been agreed to, and what the employee is expected to do to correct the problem.

15. Always follow-up to make sure that corrective actions are taking place. And above all else, be patient if the employee's performance doesn't improve immediately. It may take several attempts to improve someone's subpar performance, so don't throw up your hands in disgust and quit after one attempt.

3.3

✣

When, Where, and How to Use
Praise As a Motivator

At first glance, it would appear that offering praise to employees for a job well done is a no-brainer. After all, everyone enjoys receiving compliments and recognition for their work. In fact, perhaps because it's such an easy thing to do, praise is often doled out routinely with little thought given to its proper use. However, praising people willy-nilly for little valid reason is a useless exercise which can often do more harm than good. On the other hand, if it's done right, praise can be one of the best tools in molding a loyal and productive group. The following factors will give you a sound starting point for deciding when to use praise and when to put the compliments on hold.

1. Always show sincerity when you praise people. If you indiscriminately praise employees for little or no reason, they won't believe you when you really mean it.

2. Identify specifically the performance that the praise is being given for. For example:

   Good: "Shirley, you did a great job handling that customer complaint this morning." (You're specifying what was done well.)

   Bad: "You're doing a great job. Keep up the good work." (She takes it as a general compliment, and since she's been goofing off for the past hour, thinks you're not on top of your game.)

3. Give compliments on achievements as close as possible to the time that the event takes place. When a worker has done an outstanding job on a task, and a considerable period of time passes before you say anything, the impact of the compliment is lessened. In the meantime, the employee thinks you didn't even notice the good work that was done.

4. Whenever possible, use concrete actions to show appreciation. For instance, if someone regularly does a good job on difficult tasks, thank them, and then try and give them additional responsibility. But be sure to tie it into their superior performance. Say something such as, "You've exceeded your quota for eight straight weeks, Manny. How would you like to work on special orders?"

5. Use praise for doing a good job in one area to encourage workers to improve weaker aspects of their performance. For example: "You did a nice job on getting that rush order out today. Now let's see about reducing your overall defect rate."

6. Compliment employees you have criticized for poor performance when they show improvement. For example: "You have really improved in maintaining your work area, Carmen. Keep it up." It encourages people to try a little harder when they know you recognize their efforts.

7. Share any credit you get with any of your workers who contributed to the project. Employees really know you appreciate their efforts if they find out you were singing their praises to others.

8. Don't just use "hit and run" praise. Show an interest in exceptional efforts by spending some time with employees to discuss their achievements.

9. Use little rewards as a way of saying thanks. Buy coffee, or take an employee to lunch. Let someone leave a little early if they have just wrapped up a rush job. These types of gestures send a strong signal that you appreciate the efforts of your people.

10. Praise the entire group, as well as individual efforts, if circumstances justify it. At any of your regular meetings with your department or unit, express your appreciation for overall performance. Comments such as, "Nice going, we had our best production month ever," will help keep the competitive juices flowing.

11. *Don't* praise ordinary performance. If someone is praised for doing routine tasks in an ordinary way, they won't be motivated to do better. They may, in fact, lag in their work on the assumption you don't know how hard they're working, or else you wouldn't be praising them in the first place. On the other hand, if someone is performing menial tasks in an exceptional manner, encourage them to continue. Everyone needs a pat on the back now and then, even if they're holding down the least desirable job in the place.

12. Superior performance over an extended period of time should be rewarded with something more substantial than compliments. This means giving your high achievers promotions, interesting job assignments, and the highest pay raises. At times, you may have to battle with your boss and others to do this, but it's worth the effort, since it tells your workers that exceptional performance will be rewarded.

3.4
↓
How to Sell Cross-Training to Reluctant Workers

Top management is constantly urging supervisors to increase the productivity of the employees under their supervision. One technique that can help in this regard is to cross-train your people to do other jobs within—and in some cases outside of—your department. Cross-training, of course, is essentially nothing more than systematic on-the-job training for employees in other jobs. Naturally, people are resistant to change, some more so than others. As a result, workers won't necessarily jump at the opportunity to learn another job unless you can show them it's in their own self-interest. Fortunately, training workers to become more versatile can be beneficial to employees, so all you have to do is a little bit of a selling job. A few approaches you can take to accomplish this include:

1. The ability to perform other jobs can provide a greater sense of job security. When workers know they are of value to the company in more than one capacity, this alone can create a general sense of well-being. After all, when you look at what motivates employees best, it's hard to argue that in the final analysis it's self-interest. So along with money, job security ranks right up there in the minds of workers.

2. Many workers complain of a lack of job fulfillment in their current positions. By encouraging employees to learn other jobs, you can prevent this dissatisfaction which breeds downtime, poor performance, and high worker turnover.

3. Morale improves when workers become adept at performing a variety of jobs. By gaining a knowledge of different positions, employees gain a better knowledge of how the department—and other parts of the com-

pany—work together as a unit. This familiarity gives workers a greater sense of being part of a team, rather than feeling like isolated individuals who are being paid to do a particular job.

4. Boredom often results in poor productivity, especially in jobs that require the performance of repetitive tasks. However, by periodically assigning workers to do other jobs, some of this tedium can be avoided.

5. Every attempt should be made to tailor cross-training to the individual goals of workers. On the other hand, realism should prevail, and workers should be encouraged to learn less desirable jobs. Pointing out the increased value to the company of an employee who can perform various tasks helps to overcome employee objections.

6. Remind workers that the more jobs they know how to do, the greater their chances of securing transfers to better-paying positions.

REMINDER: If cross-training extends beyond department boundaries you may be reluctant to relinquish control of workers for cross-training in other areas. However, since cross-training will be done during periods of downtime on existing jobs, you have far more to gain than you might initially think. First of all, cross-training will increase the pool of experienced help available to assist when your department is overloaded with work. In addition, you may well be evaluated on how well you do in meeting cross-training objectives, so cooperation rather than resistance is a career advancement consideration. Furthermore, if some of the jobs in your department have sharp fluctuations in workload, it's far better to have workers being cross-trained than you having to create make-work projects.

3.5

Sensible Methods for Introducing
New Equipment

A major hope of every supervisor when new equipment is introduced is that it will increase workers' efficiency. Unfortunately, new technology doesn't always perform up to expectations. When this happens, the assumption is often made that the problems being experienced are caused by the inadequacies of the equipment. There are, of course, times when this is true. Yet even when considerable care is taken to match new equipment to the needs of a particular department or operation, the hoped-for productivity gains never materialize.

More often than is realized, the fault isn't with the equipment, but is instead the failure to both convince employees to accept the new equipment, and to train them properly in its use. These are not mutually exclusive goals, since the best training in the world will be to no avail if employees resist adopting the new technology. The following measures will help overcome the hurdles of new equipment introductions.

1. Determine the job impact of new equipment beforehand. How will new equipment affect workload, both in the short term, as well as after the workers using the equipment have become skilled in its use? It's important not to underestimate the initial negative results, such as lower production rates, inferior quality, and so forth, as employees go through the learning curve on new equipment. Sometimes those responsible for procuring equipment don't adequately discuss the pros and cons with the potential users beforehand. As a result, the opportunity for conflict is present the minute the equipment arrives. What happens is that whoever bought the equipment is under pressure to show results, while workers may be reluctant to even use it.

2. Get employees involved in the process before the equipment is purchased. Try to plan the introduction of new machinery and equipment from an employee perspective. It helps significantly to have your workers contribute their ideas from the beginning when new equipment purchases are under consideration. This will not only encourage acceptance of any new technology, but it will also provide valuable input as to what equipment will best meet the intended purposes.

3. Let workers know they aren't going to be automated out of a job. Any significant introduction of new technology always has workers thinking they're going to be replaced by a machine. Explain how the new equipment will make workers' jobs easier to do, eliminate boring tasks, and allow them to learn new skills.

4. Try to introduce new technology gradually. This keeps employees from being technologically overwhelmed.

5. Don't expect instant productivity gains. The learning process will involve a lot of trial and error, no matter how sophisticated the formal training is. A willingness on your part to accept the inevitable glitches associated with new equipment instructions will encourage your employees to overcome the fear of change associated with new technology.

6. Training should be carefully targeted, both in terms of who does the training, as well as the level of training that's appropriate to the need of individual workers. On the one hand, everyone doesn't have to know everything about a particular piece of equipment. However, it's equally ineffective to fail to teach the required skills to someone who will make costly errors because of a failure to be adequately trained.

7. Beyond the initial formal training that may be provided by the vendor or internal training specialists, appoint one of your people to be the department expert. Their job will be to handle ongoing implementation questions as they are raised. Doing this yourself has a couple of pitfalls. First of all, your supervisory duties will keep you from giving the type of hands-on assistance that's required. In addition, some workers may be reluctant to ask you questions for fear of displaying a lack of knowledge. For these reasons, it's best to designate a training troubleshooter who is both knowledgeable about the equipment, and also has the patience to help other workers when called upon.

NOTE: It's not the way it's supposed to work, but in reality there will be times when you're given little or no notice of new equipment being bought for your department. On other occasions, you may be told in advance, but neither you or your subordinates will be given an opportunity to contribute your suggestions. Whenever you do hear of the prospect of new equipment being considered that will affect the way your department functions, bring it to the attention of your boss that worker input will assist in buying the proper equipment, as well as smooth the transition when it arrives. Even if your advice is ignored, don't consider it to be a worthless exercise. If it subsequently turns out that the equipment wasn't all it was cracked up to be, you're on record as recommending worker input. In short, when the buzzards start circling to look for someone to blame, you will be able to say, "Don't blame me, I told you we needed input from the people who have to use the equipment."

3.6

ᴪ

A Dozen Doable Shortcuts for Conducting On-the-Job Training

There are any number of on-the-job training requirements that every supervisor must handle. These range from the rather extensive effort required to assimilate new hires into your operation, to relatively minor changes in how a particular task will be performed. Some training will require the participation of your entire group, while other instruction will involve only individual workers. Unfortunately, these time-consuming responsibilities have to be performed amid the hustle and bustle of your normal workload. Where practical and feasible, your burden can be lightened by assigning some of these tasks to subordinates. Others, such as working with an employee who just isn't cutting the mustard, you will have to deal with yourself. The suggestions that follow are aimed at helping you stay on top of your training requirements without being overwhelmed by them.

1. Be cooperative and not negative when providing on-the-job training. When a worker isn't meeting performance standards, show your interest in working with the employee, and his or her response is likely to be positive. Most people want to do their best, but they can become frustrated when they experience difficulty, and/or receive negative feedback rather than positive advice on how to correct the problem.

2. If a worker is performing below expectations, try eliminating or changing some aspect of the job to make it easier to do.

3. Always keep in mind that some people do certain tasks better than others. Sometimes, reassignment to a different job may be the answer when an employee isn't working out on their present assignment. Of course, this alternative assumes that training hasn't corrected the problem.

4. Look for an easier way to do the same task. Often, the methods for doing a job become ingrained and are passed on from one worker to the next. However, with a little thought, sometimes an easier way can be found to do the same task.

5. Look for basic skills shortfalls that may be hampering performance. For example, a worker may be having difficulty understanding written

instructions. If so, try to simplify them, and/or resolve the problem by showing the employee how to do the task on a repetitive basis until she learns to do it by rote.

Incidentally, if you run into one of these situations, encourage the worker to enroll in courses to learn the necessary basic skills. Most of the time, employees will follow your advice once they see that their lack of skills is hindering their job performance.

6. If you are going to teach some aspect of job performance to several workers, it's logical to instruct them all at the same time. However, follow up individually, since the slower learners and/or less attentive workers will undoubtedly require additional individual attention.

7. Recognize that people have a natural reluctance to change the way they do things. For this reason, you may encounter some initial resistance when any new method of doing a job is introduced. Try to counter this attitude by pointing out the advantages of the new approach for the worker. For instance, it saves the worker time, requires less physical exertion, and so forth.

8. On occasion, learning a job or new technique can be easier if on-the-job training is combined with formal classroom instruction. So use your initiative in looking for courses that may help workers improve in areas where they are deficient.

9. Use learning aids whenever possible to facilitate your on-the-job training. Video cassette tapes, flip charts, pre-packaged training programs on computer software, and books, are just a few of the potential resources you can use in training your employees.

10. Always carefully research the reasons behind inferior performance, since training alone may not be what is needed. The inadequate performance may result from other factors such as a lack of resources to do the job. These can range from the wrong equipment and tools, to problems with the working environment such as inadequate lighting or ventilation.

11. Training is an on-going process, so continually search for new ways to do old chores, and update equipment whenever possible.

12. Be alert for the "bad habits" syndrome. It's easy for workers, particularly those doing repetitive tasks, to lapse into doing tasks the wrong way. This may be inadvertent, or even intentional as a way to relieve boredom.

Always get people back on the right course quickly, since one bad habit can lead to another with the end result being deteriorating performance.

3.7

How to Select Someone to Train
Other Employees

Whether it's on-the-job training in a new method, the use of a new piece of equipment, or training someone new to your group, you won't always have the time to get involved to the degree necessary to do this task yourself. Nevertheless, this is an extremely difficult assignment that just can't be randomly given to the first employee you see. Of course, different employees may be designated to train others according to the particular purpose of the training, as well as the individual skills possessed by your workers. However, anyone you select should have certain characteristics in order to ensure that the training is conducted properly. These requirements include:

- *Knowledge of the subject.* It's obvious that the person should have command of the subject matter they are going to instruct someone else on. What isn't so obvious is that this basic requirement often leads to assigning the most experienced and/or skilled person to be designated as the trainer. However, this shouldn't be the sole basis in making such a decision. It's not knowledge or skills that are paramount, but rather the ability to easily communicate this information to someone else. For this reason, you may find that someone less technically skilled than others may be better suited to be an instructor.

- *Show and tell skills.* In the selection of a subordinate as a trainer, perhaps nothing is quite as critical as the person's ability to clearly explain the subject matter to others. All of the knowledge of the job is of little avail if it can't be communicated in a clear and concise matter.

- *A willingness to listen.* People being trained will have any number of questions to be answered. Many aspects of any job become routine to an experienced person, while remaining confusing for a novice. As a result, basic questions will be asked and often repeated by those being trained. Therefore, the ability to listen carefully to questions that may not at first make sense is essential for a trainer.

- *Plenty of patience.* Everyone doesn't learn at the same pace, so a great deal of patience may be needed in training some people. This is especially true with workers who may have language barriers, and therefore have to deal with not only the details of what is being taught, but also the basics of understanding what is being said.

- *Enjoys working with other people.* Since anyone you designate as a trainer will have to deal with the varying personalities of others, it's best to appoint people who tend to get along with everyone.

- *Willingness to assume responsibility.* You may find that one or more logical choices as trainers are hesitant to assume the role. The reasons, of course, may vary, but suffice it to say, that anyone reluctant to fill the role isn't likely to show the kind of enthusiasm for the job that is conducive to doing it successfully.

- *Has your trust and confidence.* Anyone you select to train other employees is being delegated an important duty for which you are ultimately responsible. Therefore, avoid appointing someone otherwise qualified if they have some other quirk that gives you pause. For example, you may have an excellent worker who tends toward a negative attitude on matters large and small. Assigning new hires to be trained by such a person is likely to leave some trainees wondering if they made a bad decision when they accepted the job.

3.8

Crucial Components
for Employee Development

Improving the performance of people you supervise requires close attention to developing their existing skills, as well as encouraging them to learn new ones. Sometimes this tends to get sidetracked by other priorities, the most common being workload pressures. Unfortunately, in many situations, there never seems to be an ideal time to schedule training. Yet, a failure to develop employee skills is a two-edged sword. On the one hand, improving skill levels will help increase productivity, both on an individual and group basis. The flip side of neglecting training is that it tends to send a subtle message that you have no interest in seeing workers develop their individual abilities.

Needless to say, this isn't likely to motivate workers to excel. For these reasons, it's wise to make every effort to further the individual development of those who work for you. In doing that, several considerations should be kept in mind. These are:

1. Work jointly with each employee to develop future goals. This is generally done in a formal way as part of the person's formal performance evaluation. However, don't limit this to a once-a-year exercise. Continually look for areas where existing skills can be improved, and new skills learned. Incidentally, whenever training is planned as part of the annual review, make every effort to see that the training is provided before the next performance rating period rolls around. Otherwise, employees will tend to view the entire evaluation process as a meaningless exercise.

2. Try to develop both short- and long-term goals. First, agree on what sort of training is needed to improve the worker's skills in the short run. Then, work on developing the employee's long-range career goals.

3. Agree with the worker on what measures have to be taken to achieve the goals. These can include on-site and off-site formal training, on-the-job training, and cross-training. Any off-site training at schools or colleges can be either company-sponsored and reimbursed, or initiated and paid for by the employee. This will primarily depend on company training policy, and whether or not the training is job-related.

4. The goals that are established don't have to be elaborate. Some people don't have any career goals, and for one reason or another, are quite happy with what they're doing. They pretty much want to maintain the status quo, which means doing their job and picking up their check on payday. Therefore, for some workers, training development goals may not go much beyond basic measures to improve deficient aspects of their job performance. Others, even though they're in menial jobs, will seek any training that will help them increase their ability to perform more meaningful and financially rewarding jobs. If you happen to be supervising workers in low-skill positions, it's important to recognize the difference when you're working with employees to develop their goals.

5. Some workers go through the motions in setting goals. You probably have one or more workers who will readily tell you they want to receive some form of training, but have no intention of following through on it. One reason employees do this is to disguise their lack of initiative, since they feel compelled to give some form of positive nod toward training. You can discourage this tactic by making sure workers' goals are attainable, and by scheduling the training and making sure workers attend. At the least, it should minimize this practice once employees recognize you aren't just giving lip service to training needs.

6. Monitor the progress of employees' training needs. Don't just go from one performance review period to another without discussing training with employees. Follow up constantly to make sure that training is scheduled and attended. After training is finished, get the employee's input as to its usefulness.

7. Revise training goals as necessary. Both people and organizations change, so today's goals may not be valid tomorrow. Workers' needs and interests will shift, so be flexible about changing employee development goals to reflect this fact.

8. Be selective when scheduling formal training. Both on-site and off-site courses are expensive in terms of both time and money. Therefore, only send people to these courses who will benefit from them. Another useful approach is to send one person and have them brief others on the course afterwards. If you do this, be certain the person attending the course has the communication skills necessary to adequately relay what they learned.

9. Make use of peer skills training. Many of your workers will excel at one or more aspects of their job. Use these people on a regular basis to impart their skills to others within your group. Often, it's a lot easier to learn from those you work with than from taking more formalized training.

10. Let workers know you care about their career development needs. Display enthusiasm about training, and take the time to show an interest in each worker's personal development. At the same time, an equal burden is placed on workers to take advantage of the training offered, so don't hesitate to let them know this.

3.9
※

Workable Ways to Give Job-Specific Instructions to Workers

One of the most irritating aspects of supervision is to discover that mistakes were made because someone working for you didn't follow directions. If this happens repeatedly, you may start to think twice before you delegate anything more than the simplest tasks to certain subordinates. Of course, that approach will just serve to increase the burden on other employees. It will also create resentment on the part of those workers who have no difficulty in completing assignments in accordance with your instructions.

Therefore, rather than avoiding the problem, the solution lies in figuring out why a few people don't seem to understand even the simplest directions. Most likely, the reason is either in the way the instructions were given, or the ability and/or the temperament of the person receiving the guidance. Even though you're confident the problem doesn't have anything to do with how you give directions, don't overlook the fact that instructions have to be customized to account for the differences in experience, learning ability, and personality of individual employees. For this reason, a two-part approach is required to be effective in giving directions to workers. The first part requires following some fundamentals when giving directions, while the second element calls for recognizing employee differences that may require modifying the basic rules. In terms of the basics of giving instructions, the guidelines are fairly simple and include:

- Always take the time to give complete instructions on how a task is to be performed. Sometimes directions are given in haste, particularly when there are other more urgent matters to be dealt with. This is the time when carelessness is most likely to creep into the process.

- If the project being assigned is unusual in any way, you may want to sketch out the instructions beforehand to make certain everything is being covered properly.

- When the instructions are lengthy and/or complex, put them in writing so the worker has something to refer to along the way. However, you should still go over them with the worker to make sure they are understood.

- Encourage workers to ask questions when they are given instructions. Otherwise, they will tend to operate on a trial and error basis.

- Have the employee repeat the instructions back to you so that you're certain everything is understood.

The second aspect of giving instructions is trickier, and involves an understanding of the ability of individuals to both understand and react to what you tell them. For many workers the rules outlined above will be sufficient. However, with some employees you may have to modify your approach to be successful. A few general categories of workers that will require greater care in giving instructions are as follows.

1. *The non-listener.* Some people just don't listen very well. If you are issuing directions to a worker who falls in this category, always be sure to give the instructions as slowly and clearly as possible. It's also useful to have them repeat them back to you to be sure they understand them.

2. *The slow learner.* People are able to learn at differing rates of speed, and absorb material of various levels of difficulty. With anyone who is a slow learner, in addition to using the same approach as with a non-listener, you should avoid giving them difficult assignments, and follow up more carefully as tasks are carried out.

3. *The pro.* This represents your experienced workers who always perform at an above-average level. What you want to do here is only provide the minimum of direction necessary to state what you want to be done. The danger here is in overdoing your guidance so you create the impression you don't have confidence in the pro's ability to operate independently.

4. *The novice.* With inexperienced workers you want to explain everything in greater detail, since it is probably their first time doing even the most basic aspects of the assignment. Spending the time to carefully instruct them will ensure that they learn the correct way to do things without going through a lot of trial-and-error to learn the ropes. It also helps to gradually lessen the detailed directions you give initially as they gain experience. Otherwise, they may never be weaned from the need for excessive supervision.

5. *The know-it-all.* This type of individual will be likely to interrupt you when you're telling them what to do by saying something such as, "I

already know how to do that." Unfortunately, they often don't, and mistakes result. If you have people who fit this pattern, don't be dissuaded from carefully giving them guidance. If they object, don't be shy about reminding them of the last time they didn't want to listen, and then went ahead and fouled something up. Naturally, you want to be diplomatic, even though you may be silently seething. To do this, emphasize the importance of the task if someone tries to cut your directions short. Try saying something such as, "I realize you may understand how to do this, but it's extremely important that it be done right, so why don't you tell me how you're going to handle it." Then, if they don't know the instructions, you can tell them again.

6. *The perpetual excuse machine.* You may have the misfortune to have one or more workers who continually blunder and then have a truckload of excuses to cover every mishap. With these people, it may be worthwhile to commit anything beyond the simplest instructions to writing. That way, you can at least avoid the alibis that center around the notion that they either weren't told, or misinterpreted what you said. This has a secondary benefit of documenting persistent mistakes that may eventually result in disciplinary action and even dismissal.

3.10

Tested Methods for Conducting Follow-Up on Job Assignments

No matter how careful you are in giving directions on how assignments are to be completed, you can never be sure that the job is being carried out successfully unless you consistently follow up to see that satisfactory progress is being made. All sorts of things can go wrong, and some workers will be hesitant about bringing problems to your attention. So the only guarantee you have that everything is going smoothly is to do a little bit of periodic checking.

Perhaps the greatest challenge in the area of follow-up is to achieve the proper balance. Both looking over people's shoulders, or alternatively, neglecting them completely, can cause trouble. Both the individual and the task have to be considered in determining how much or how little follow-up is needed. The following measures will help in doing that.

1. In general, the amount of follow-up you perform should be based upon the assigned task, with more difficult jobs receiving greater scrutiny. There are exceptions to this rule, such as a relatively minor task which takes on added significance because it has been given a high priority for one reason or another.

2. Some workers desire and/or require more guidance than others. The level of follow-up should reflect the differing needs of individual workers.

3. Don't overdue it. Competent workers will resent it if you appear to doubt their capabilities to complete assignments with a minimum of supervision.

4. Act like an advisor—not a boss. Be supportive, rather than critical, when mistakes are made. Otherwise, workers aren't as likely to openly admit potential problems. As a result, they may not be discovered until they become severe.

5. Encourage workers to solve problems themselves by asking questions rather than just giving them the answer. This will build self-confidence and encourage subordinates to think things through to completion.

6. Don't get behind the wheel yourself. With people who lack initiative, don't let them off the hook by doing the job for them. Steer them in the right direction, but let them do the work.

7. Offer to interact with other departments if a worker is encountering bottlenecks or a lack of cooperation.

8. Don't be vague about checking the progress of a project. Ask specifically how the job is progressing and don't settle for wishy-washy answers which may just be an attempt to disguise difficulties.

9. Always ask if anything is needed in the way of assistance. Frequently, workers are reluctant to ask for help on the assumption you will interpret it as a failure on their part.

10. With new employees try to practice a policy of lessening the degree of follow-up as they gain experience and confidence.

11. Don't let your personality get in the way of effective follow-up. Some supervisors tend to delegate a task and then forget about it, while others don't have much confidence in anything they aren't doing them-

selves. If you fall into either extreme, try to condition yourself to work toward a middle-of-the-road approach to follow-up.

3.11

❦

Eight Proven Ways to Assign Non-Routine Tasks to Subordinates

Assigning unusual or difficult tasks can present a whole array of problems. Some workers will consider them a burden that interferes with their regular assignments. A few employees may lack the ambition and/or skills to carry out any duties much beyond the scope of their job. Other laments that may be expressed—although not directly to you—include a sense of unfairness and a feeling of being overworked. Beyond that, anyone tapped for non-routine tasks may well adopt an attitude of "What's in it for me?"

Aside from the personal reactions of anyone you may select for a special assignment are the practical considerations of picking the right person for the job. Workload, qualifications, and the temperament of potential candidates can't be ignored. In addition, the office politics aspects of such assignments come into play, since you don't want to be perceived as assigning these duties as forms of either reward or punishment. A few strategies that will help you overcome these and other obstacles include:

1. Exercise care in making difficult assignments. Try to give assignments that will occasionally challenge workers to go beyond their usual level of performance. However, avoid giving someone a project that is doomed to fail from the start due to their lack of experience and/or qualifications.

2. Explain the importance of the assignment, but don't overdue it in an attempt to convince someone that you have confidence in them.

3. Some non-routine tasks may be just time-consuming and/or thankless. With these, try to parcel them out equitably so no employee gets stuck with more than their fair share.

4. When it's feasible to do so, try to give the employee a say in accepting or rejecting the assignment. This is particularly true where the assignment would be viewed as a choice one by workers and you have more than one person qualified to handle it. Some people prefer to avoid any-

thing that's different, so it makes little sense to give a plum assignment to someone who doesn't want it. They will only complain to co-workers, who will resent the fact you didn't give the project to someone else.

5. Explain to employees why they are being selected for non-routine tasks. Being realistic, you selection may be based on something as simple as current workload. However, telling it like it is won't always be wise. For example, someone who works more quickly than others won't appreciate getting stuck with a dirty job because of their hard work. Therefore, at times you may have to use a little creativity in explaining why the person was selected. Incidentally, it helps to keep an informal record of whom you assign unpleasant tasks to, so everyone gets their fair share.

6. Let workers know how much authority they have when you assign an unusual task. Actually, giving workers authority they may not usually have can help overcome reluctance at being selected for a project. After all, everyone wants to be a boss—at least until they become one.

7. With complex assignments, you may want to establish reporting milestones that are either time-based (Ex: once a week), or dependent on completion of part of the project. By having the worker report to you periodically, you can check on the progress of the assignment and make any necessary adjustments.

8. Whenever possible, provide rewards and recognition to workers who successfully complete difficult assignments. Even something as simple as a memo to the worker thanking him or her for the job they did can do wonders for morale. Obviously, you will thank people personally, but putting it in writing provides an additional boost. Don't do this routinely though, or it will lose its significance.

Chapter Four

TACTICS TO IMPROVE YOUR GROUP'S PRODUCTIVITY

One of the hardest jobs you face as a supervisor is to constantly improve the overall efficiency of the group of people you supervise. As the person charged with this responsibility, you may sometimes think that top management expects too much in terms of your group's productivity. At other times, you may wonder if every incompetent employee in the company has been placed under your supervision. All things considered, there's little question that improving productivity isn't easy to do.

For one thing, it frequently requires changing the way jobs have been done in the past. This alone can be tough to sell to workers who may be perfectly satisfied with leaving things as they are. Of course, additional resources in the form of equipment and people are often needed to keep abreast of your workload. As you know, selling this to a boss can be even harder than convincing employees to do their jobs more efficiently.

Beyond these major hurdles are a number of other factors that have an impact on your group's performance. These include controlling worker downtime, scheduling overtime, working conditions, and for some supervisors, union-related problems. All in all, these issues must be dealt with before

77

you can make your unit as productive as possible. The topics in this chapter explore ways to do this.

4.1
⇓

Strategies for Implementing Changes Within Your Unit

Change of any sort is difficult, since even though some people tend to be adventurous, most of us to a large degree are creatures of habit. Consequently, any sort of change in our lives can sometimes be unsettling. This is particularly true when changes take place that are beyond our control, and/or alter something we don't want to be changed. For these reasons, employees tend to be reluctant when changes take place at work that affect their jobs. This gut-reaction hostility can occur even when work-related changes offer visible benefits to the employee.

Therefore, whenever you plan to make changes, ranging from the way a single task is performed, to a reorganization of your unit, it's necessary to think about how you will implement it. Doing this will help generate worker acceptance of changes, which will go a long way toward guaranteeing successful implementation. Issues to be considered when you plan to make changes that affect subordinates include:

1. Look for all the possible consequences of any change beforehand. Frequently, what seems to be a relatively minor revision of the way something is done is put into effect without realizing the fallout that will result. For example, a simple time-saving revision in the way a worker performs a task may at first glance seem to be foolproof. Only later will it be discovered that the change causes other problems such as worker dissatisfaction, product defects, and so forth. To prevent these unintended results, it's necessary to carefully think through all of the potential positives and negatives of changes before they're implemented.

2. Get your workers involved in planning changes. They may pinpoint problems that weren't thought about, and/or suggest creative solutions in terms of alternatives.

3. Workers generally will look at changes from a "What's in it for me" perspective. To counter this sort of attitude, it's important to sell the change beforehand.

4. To sell the benefits of change to your subordinates, try to use a "show and tell" approach. For instance, tell them and show them how a change will save time, make their job easier, and so forth. Naturally, this won't always be possible, but with some thought you can even offer justification for sweeping changes imposed by top management.

   For example, if your group is part of a general reorganization to improve the companies' competitiveness, you can't offer direct evidence that the change will work. However, with a little thought you can reasonably argue that making the company more efficient will preserve jobs. Furthermore, you can use real life examples of other companies that have been in the news for doing this successfully. Of course, it's naive to assume that every worker will buy into this sort of reasoning. On the other hand, if workers know inefficiencies exist, they may not openly welcome a reorganization, but will silently recognize that something has to be done. If that happens, you will at least avoid major resistance to the change.

5. Rely upon feedback from workers to let you know how changes are being accepted. If you have always had open lines of communication with your employees, they will be sure to let you know of any adverse impact a change is having. However, take it a step further and actively solicit opinions on the pros and cons of how a change is working.

6. If a change is meeting resistance, try to identify the cause or causes, and then work to overcome them. Encourage workers to express their feelings, and don't overlook tapping into the rumor mill. Sometimes workers won't want to openly express dissatisfaction with a change, so the rumor mill can fill this void.

7. Some changes may require you to delegate responsibility to subordinates. In doing this, workers may make mistakes. However, coaching will work better than criticism in getting a worker to accept newly delegated duties.

8. Just telling workers what to do in terms of a change in how they do their jobs won't get the best results. More often than not, there's a tendency to lapse back into the old way of doing things. Therefore, follow-up is important to make sure old habits don't reappear.

9. Your own attitude toward a change will help to either sell it, or sink it. This is particularly true with changes that are originated by top management. Your workers aren't likely to accept them unless they are convinced that you earnestly back the change.

10. Perhaps surmounting all of the other difficulties in implementing major changes is the need to recognize there are no shortcuts to success. Solutions may appear to be easy on the surface, but the task of implementing changes is loaded with pitfalls that only patience and perseverance will overcome.

4.2

**Shrewd Ways to Use Worker Downtime
for Other Purposes**

Every job has periods when workers may be idle for some length of time. In some jobs, where work fluctuations are high, this may be relatively frequent, while in other positions it may be less common. The causes can also vary, including everything from a general business slowdown, to a poorly designed job that leaves a worker with extended periods with little or nothing to do. Actually, in some situations, due to the nature of the work, the downtime may be unavoidable. Whatever the cause, it's imperative to keep workers busy during these idle intervals. Otherwise, you may find your boss deciding that your department is overstaffed. So although you don't want to schedule every idle moment, and/or engage your people in make-work projects, there are many constructive ways to deal with downtime including:

1. The most practical use of downtime is to use these idle intervals for training purposes. This can be for additional training on the worker's own job, or in cross-training to perform other duties. Most employees will welcome the chance to increase their skills, especially if you point out that the additional versatility will give them greater job security.

2. Sometimes, especially where the workload has peaks and valleys, workers experience idle periods. If this is a problem for you, try to find other tasks for your people to perform. Otherwise, workers will become conditioned to long periods of time without anything to do.

3. Eliminate distractions that encourage idle time on the part of workers. For example, people wandering through your work area can be distracting as it tends to encourage interruptions and idle conversation. When feasible, rearrange the area to alter foot traffic through your department.

4. Make your presence known. Nothing discourages idle workers more than knowing the boss is nearby. Make yourself seen frequently, but don't establish a consistent pattern of making an appearance at set intervals. Otherwise, shrewd workers will time their goofing off to your scheduled tours of the area.

5. Be upfront with employees about downtime. If it's a problem, let your people know about it.

6. Shift workers to different assignments periodically to keep them from being bored, since boredom alone will lead to downtime.

7. Plan ahead so workers will have something to do if you can anticipate idle periods. You have to be on top of scheduling, since workers won't come running when they don't have anything to do.

8. Be reasonable. Don't expect employees to work from dawn to dusk without taking a breather. If people think you're being too tough about keeping them busy, they will quickly learn how to go through the motions.

9. Be consistent in your actions. For instance, practices such as taking extended lunch hours, and conducting personal business at work should be uniformly enforced. Put a lid on these practices right away, or you will send a signal that you condone them.

4.3

Sensible Policies for Scheduling Overtime

Scheduling overtime can be a two-edged sword with some workers scrambling to get all of the overtime they can, while others want no part of working beyond their regularly scheduled hours. Workers complain when there's too much overtime, and when there's too little. There are also the inevitable hassles that erupt when overtime is scheduled for holidays and long summer weekends when even the most ardent overtime enthusiasts are reluctant to work. Beyond these worker-related difficulties are issues such as whether overtime is being used as a temporary expedient to meet a heavy workload, or is instead compensating for a permanently understaffed department. A few measures which can help deal with these problems are as follows:

1. Don't schedule overtime on a regular basis unless it's unavoidable. Otherwise, some workers will start to think of overtime pay as a regular part of their paychecks. As a result, when overtime finally gets cut back, they will look upon it as an enforced reduction in their wages.

2. Overtime shouldn't be used as a convenient substitute for failing to complete work during regularly scheduled hours. When overtime is used, you have to be alert for employees who will drag their feet during the day so they'll be able to work overtime.

3. Before scheduling overtime, look for other alternatives such as borrowing workers from other areas to meet intermittent peaks in workload. Hiring temporary employees is another possibility that should be explored. These other options are especially valuable if you encounter difficulty in filling overtime demands on a voluntary basis from within your own group.

4. Rotate overtime assignments on a regular basis, so all employees are offered the same opportunities to work.

5. If overtime is fairly frequent in your operation, keep an overtime assignment roster. Usually, some employees will want to get as much overtime as they can, while others won't ever want to work. Rather than arbitrarily forcing people to work, go to the next person on your list until you fill your quota.

6. If certain jobs under your supervision require overtime more than others, try to train as many people as you can in these areas. That way, you will have a sufficient pool of available help for overtime assignments.

7. Try to avoid mandatory overtime. However, if it becomes necessary, be flexible in granting waivers from working. It's important to recognize that workers have other responsibilities that may conflict with working overtime. Continually insisting that people work extra hours when they object to doing so will damage morale and encourage workers to seek employment elsewhere.

8. If overtime is a regular requirement of the job, be sure to point this out when you interview candidates for open positions.

9. Always try to notify workers of the need to work overtime at the earliest possible time so they can juggle their personal schedules to meet this need.

10. If there is a certain amount of flexibility in terms of when overtime is scheduled, consult with workers to determine the most convenient times for them to work.

11. If the unit you supervise is regularly working overtime due to understaffing, make sure your boss recognizes this dilemma. Otherwise, higher management may assume it's lagging productivity in your department that is causing the overtime to be scheduled.

4.4

Basic Guidelines for Defending Unpopular Company Rules

One of the hardest jobs you may have to do is justify new company policies and procedures which may be unpopular with your subordinates. This becomes even more difficult when you don't necessarily agree with the rules yourself. Nonetheless, it's still your responsibility to work at gaining their acceptance by the people in your group. It may not be fair, but it goes with the job, and it may not be easy, but it can be done. Here are a few tips that should help in this regard:

1. You attitude is important, since if you're openly negative toward a policy you don't agree with, you are actively encouraging subordinates to do likewise.

2. Just as you don't expect subordinates to ignore your rules if they disagree with them, you shouldn't advocate workers ignoring company policies you don't like.

3. Get your own questions answered by your boss when you are implementing a policy or procedure that is likely to be unpopular. Unless you fully understand the basis for a new policy, it becomes even more difficult to defend when employees voice their objections.

4. If you have serious objections to a new policy or practice, make your thoughts known to your boss. There may be valid reasons which you haven't been made aware of. Nevertheless, whether you ultimately change you opinion or not, as a manager, it's your job to do the best you can to see that the new policy is implemented.

5. When employees question a new practice, you can sometimes counter their arguments by putting the impact of the change in perspective. On occasion, even though a new policy may have widespread unpopularity, it's actual impact may be minimal. When this happens, your ability to respond with a "So what, it doesn't affect us," argument will defuse most of the opposition.

6. Just as there are two sides to every coin, most new policies and procedures have both advantages and disadvantages. Therefore, one way to overcome negative reaction is to show the objecting employee how the advantages of the new policy outweigh the liabilities. This isn't always as hard to do as it might seem, since often objections are based on initial emotions without taking into account the positive aspects of a change.

7. Whenever possible, try to be prepared for negative reaction to a change in policy beforehand. Having the facts to answer questions upfront will keep the rumor mill from blowing something out of proportion.

8. Try for a consensus when new rules are implemented, but don't expect everyone to be converted. A few people are likely to take exception to almost anything. As long as you convince most of your people of the wisdom associated with a new policy, you will be able to neutralize any opposition that remains.

9. Once you have done the best job you can in selling the wisdom of a new policy, don't waste a lot of time in trying to win converts for an unpopular rule. Let your boss know of the negative reaction, and as long as there's no impact on operations, just let the matter drop.

10. Always keep in mind that most resistance to a new policy will quickly fade. Alternatively, on those few occasions where widespread opposition doesn't subside, upper management will usually rethink and revise the policy.

4.5

How to Encourage Suggestions That Improve Productivity

Increasing the productivity of your department is a lot easier to do when subordinates are active participants in offering suggestions on improving operations. However, it's not an easy task to encourage workers to willingly offer suggestions on realigning the way they do their work. A good formal suggestion system can help if it's easy to understand, isn't time-consuming, provides rapid responses, and furnishes suitable rewards. Of course, even in the absence of a good company-wide suggestion system, you can use your own informal system to encourage employees to suggest ways to improve operations. Try the following approach to do this:

- Be considerate when employees disagree with you. No one will suggest anything if they're going to risk being ridiculed by doing so.

- Give all suggestions a fair hearing. Don't quickly disregard something just because you don't agree with it.

- Get to know the details of how workers perform their jobs. This will give you a better understanding of what they want to accomplish when suggestions are brought to your attention.

- Whenever possible, work with employees to make their suggestions usable.

- Be a good listener. Some people have more trouble than others in saying what they mean. If you cut people short, you may miss out on some good ideas.

- Don't ignore suggestions just because they don't show a definite quantitative or qualitative benefit. Sometimes a minor change in the way a task is performed will have indirect benefits such as improving a worker's morale.

- Workers want to see their suggestions implemented. Otherwise, they will adopt an attitude of, "Why bother making suggestions, since they are never used?" For this reason, when a suggestion can't be adopted, take the time to explain the reasons why to the employee.

- Give conditional approvals whether it's feasible to do so. Let workers try out an idea for a week or two to see how it pans out.

- Don't shoot for the moon. Suggestions on how to make minor changes are what matter most. Seldom—if ever—will anyone suggest a far-reaching change that will have a significant impact on productivity. Instead, it will be the cumulative impact of many minor changes that will have long-lasting results.

4.6

❦

Dealing with the Nuts and Bolts of the Working Environment

Problems large and small can arise around such simple matters as whether it's too hot or cold in the work area, or even the arrangement of machinery or equipment. Handling these matters may sometimes seem to be relatively unimportant. But if they're not dealt with in a timely manner, they can cause anger and lessened productivity on the part of affected workers. Some of the working environment issues you may be able to resolve yourself. In other instances, you will have to refer them to upper management for possible resolution. A few of the difficulties that can commonly arise, and reasonable ways of dealing with them are as follows:

1. Inefficient layout of the working area. Whether you work in an office, a warehouse, or on the floor in a manufacturing environment, the layout can impact upon the operating efficiency of your unit. When you have space limitations and other constraints that are beyond your control, there's little you can do here other than to bring this matter to upper management's attention. However, there are many aspects of work area layout that are relatively easy to do something about. These include minor rearrangements to eliminate distractions such as people tracking through the work area, or to make things easy to reach.

2. Consider future needs in terms of equipment. Plan ahead so you will be able to requisition new equipment as needed to keep your people supplied with the necessary tools to do their job.

3. Keep track of routine supplies so they can be replenished before they run out.

4. Make sure that broken, lost, and/or stolen tools are replaced promptly.

5. Make a serious effort to respond to employees complaints about the work area. A few of the gripes supervisors routinely hear are:

   - It's too hot.

   - It's too cold.

   - It's too noisy.

   - The work area isn't big enough.

   - The work area is dirty.

   - Copiers or other frequently used equipment are always breaking down.

   Actually, this list could go on and on, and undoubtedly you could add several more items that your people complain about. Some gripes may be legitimate, while others may amount to nothing more than unreasonable expectations on the part of workers. Furthermore, even in the case of legitimate complaints, there may be little you can do.

   This is particularly true in situations involving facility management issues, such as temperature control, where a large area may be controlled by one thermostat. Here, you may frequently find one or more workers complaining about the temperature. The best you can usually do with this sort of dilemma is to explain that there is only one thermostat. Just listening to the employee's gripe will often help solve the problem.

   Of course, if there is a serious facilities problem in areas such as heating, cooling, or lighting which is bothering everyone and hampering job performance, bring the matter to the attention of top management. Whether anything is, or can be done, the fact that your subordinates know you aren't ignoring the problem will avoid you being thought of as a non-caring boss.

6. Don't overlook minor factors which can improve the working environment. For instance, having coffee available in the area can reduce extended coffee breaks.

7. Always keep in mind that improving the working environment will help improve productivity and/or prevent it from getting worse. Perhaps of

even greater importance is that if you stay on top of working environment issues, it will send a signal to workers that you care about their well-being.

4.7
ψ
Sound Ways to Deal with Workplace Health and Safety Issues

Health and safety in the workplace may not be issues that you are constantly confronted with unless you happen to supervise an operation that's inherently dangerous. However, even in a modern office environment, health and safety matters arise which have to be dealt with. For instance, smoking in the workplace is a health issue which is generally covered by a company policy. Yet, within the constraints of that policy you still have to cope with the problem of enforcing it. And even in what appears to be a relatively hazard-free working environment, accidents can happen if certain basic practices aren't followed. The following suggestions will help in dealing with the more common problems that may arise concerning health and safety and their impact on your department.

1. Make sure you enforce any formal health and safety regulations your company has implemented. These include not only dealing with major job-related hazards, but also relatively routine rules on smoking and food in work areas.

2. Hold regular meetings to emphasize the importance of safety. Risk management starts with awareness, so constant reinforcement of safety rules will keep your employees conscious of safety requirements.

3. Emphasize safety-conscious habits. Frequently, accidents happen because people are rushing to get something done, and/or fail to seek assistance when doing a task that requires more than one person.

4. Encourage safety improvement suggestions from your subordinates. This is a simple, but effective, accident prevention technique, since no one knows the potential hazards of a job better than the person doing it.

5. Make certain that any safety equipment required for a job, such as safety glasses is or protective clothing, worn as required.

6. Avoid overworking people so that fatigue sets in which will make them more injury-prone. This is especially significant if long stretches of over-time work are required.

7. Try to alternate any tasks that require heavy-duty physical effort with those requiring less exertion, so no individual employee performs these tasks for extended periods of time.

8. Keep work areas clean and obstacle-free. If maintenance and janitorial services are inadequate, bring these to the attention of upper management before—not after—an accident.

9. Show concern for injured workers. Consistent with company policy, encourage injured workers to return to work as soon as possible.

10. Look at the cause of any injury on the job to see what can be done to prevent a repetition.

11. Whenever possible, transfer workers who consistently violate safety rules to jobs where safety is less of a concern.

4.8

Strategies for Maintaining
Good Union Relations

If you're working for a company where your employees are union members, good union relations will go a long way toward making your job easier. Of course, as a supervisor, you have to operate within the constraints of any union agreement with the company, as well as the reality of the company/union relationship itself. However, even if the company and union are extremely hostile in their dealings, you can still maintain good working relations with the union as it relates to your activities.

Of course, it can be extremely frustrating and time-consuming to find yourself constantly confronted with complaints from a union steward relative to grievances of union members you supervise. Sometimes, these are just unavoidable, but for the most part you can minimize the number of complaints with a little bit of foresight in handling these headaches. Some sensible practices that will contribute to lessening this sort of difficulty are as follows:

1. Sometimes, one or two workers may create most of the problems with union-related complaints. They may well assert that you're the problem—not their lack of performance. When feasible, see if a job transfer can be worked out. It gets them off your hands, and if they continue to non-perform elsewhere, it will add substantiation to ultimately justify their termination. If this course of action isn't practical, then ultimately you may have to proceed with formal disciplinary action.

   Other workers know who is playing the game for all it's worth, so you should encounter no resentment when action is taken. And even though a union steward will formally defend the culprits, here too, your relationship shouldn't be damaged. After all, no one likes people who consistently cause problems, even though they have to defend them.

2. Try to separate the person from the position when dealing with union officials. Just as you have a job to do, so do they. Keep any disagreements at a professional level, since this will go a long way toward maintaining a reasonable working relationship. In short, don't take remarks personally.

3. Never criticize the company and/or company policy in trying to resolve a dispute. In the same vein, don't criticize the union and/or the employee. Instead, try to use a problem-solving discussion that looks for workable ways to deal with the issue that's in dispute.

4. Know the provisions of the union contract. When necessary, get guidance from your industrial relations department, or other knowledgeable source, on any provisions you don't understand. It's a lot easier to deal with union matters when you have a command of the facts. Furthermore, being informed will help prevent minor misunderstandings from needlessly escalating into something more serious.

5. Create a cooperative work environment. If workers view you as being reasonable and objective, they will be less inclined to adopt an "us against them" mentality in dealing with you.

6. Always keep control of your emotions. Once you lose control, not only will it cloud your thinking, but it may also carry over into future dealings. Of course, it's natural that you may get angry in a particularly testy situation, but when things cool down, make an effort to apologize for losing your temper. However, be sure to make it clear that your apology is for getting angry, and in no way changes your opinion on the matter which evoked your anger.

7. Always encourage workers and/or the union steward to offer their suggestions as to how a problem can be resolved. Obviously, they may start off with something that is totally unacceptable. Nevertheless, you may be able to move from this position to a more common ground for resolution with subsequent discussions. The important point is to sit down and talk matters out until an agreement can be reached. This may not always work, but even if it fails, you then can take whatever action is necessary with a full understanding of the union position on the matter.

8. Be reasonable with the shop steward in trying to informally resolve disputes. In many instances, there will be some merit to both sides of an argument. Don't always try to prevail on all points when you are in one of these situations. Otherwise, you will be at continual odds with the shop steward and unable to resolve anything informally. By making concessions on one issue, you can get concessions on others.

9. Whenever possible, try to trade off disagreements you may be having with the shop steward before they escalate into formal grievances. Going through the formal grievance procedure can be time-consuming, and you can't reasonably expect to always win on every issue. Taking this fact into consideration, it's sometimes preferable to trade off minor issues to resolve them, even when you are convinced of your position.

10. Never make overt or veiled threats of disciplinary action as a means of retaliation. It will only serve to solidify resistance from both workers and the shop steward.

4.9

✤

Using Two-Way Communication to Promote Productivity

Whether it's in the office, or on the factory floor, employee productivity is a constant concern. Part of the problem is that supervisors and their subordinates have differing points of view when it comes to productivity. As a boss, you may sometimes think that your employees don't work hard enough. On the other hand, workers may think you're pushing them too hard. Breaking through this barrier of misunderstanding requires effective two-way communication. Several elements that are necessary to create the sort of rapport with workers which will encourage them to do their best are:

1. First of all, supervisor–employee interaction must take place within an environment that encourages the open exchange of ideas. This takes time to establish, and quick-fix gimmicks won't do the trick. After all, every employee has individual priorities they place upon how hard and how efficiently they work. Some workers will always do their best without any encouragement. Other people don't seem to respond to either pleading or pressure. It takes time to figure out the proper way to motivate each worker to bring forth their best efforts.

2. You must recognize that employees seek to benefit themselves—not an employer. Therefore, if what you want someone to do doesn't jibe with their desires, it will only frustrate both you and the employee. You can overcome this conflict by encouraging workers to share their opinions on how their work should be done.

3. Encourage workers to voice their concerns without fear of overt or covert retribution. No matter how understanding a supervisor may be, there is always a natural reluctance by workers to express grievances.

4. Getting employees to voice their concerns goes hand-in-hand with taking prompt action on any employee problems. Workers should be told what is being done to resolve a problem, and why that particular course of action is being taken. This, of course, doesn't mean that every employee demand has to be agreed to. However, to preserve good two-way communication, explanations should be given when you can't comply with employee requests.

5. An atmosphere of open communication will provide an environment where differing viewpoints can be discussed and resolved without hostility, even when the outcome isn't what an employee wanted.

6. Effective two-way communication also places responsibility with employees. They should be expected to perform their duties to the best of their abilities. You should be not only fair, but also firm when necessary, in carrying out your supervisory duties. This includes letting workers know when they're not meeting standards.

7. You should take disciplinary action when it's called for. Workers who do their jobs suffer along with any supervisor who condones shirkers. For

example, there's very little motivation for any worker to observe time and attendance policies if persistent violators aren't dealt with. Furthermore, everyone resents having to be burdened with the duties of a malingerer who is allowed to coast along without being called on the carpet by a boss.

8. Be practical in working at increasing the productivity of your group. Know each worker's abilities, and learn to recognize when performance limits have been reached. Pushing people too hard will only turn out to be counter-productive.

9. Be willing to stand your ground if your boss insists on striving for unrealistic productivity from your group. Have arguments ready to prove your point. If at all possible, try to refer to facts and figures that support your position. For instance, "We have the lowest absenteeism record in the company," or, "My group has worked more overtime in the last three months than any other department."

4.10

Ten Ways to Request and Get Additional Help

One of the hardest selling jobs you may ever have is when you go to your boss seeking to add positions within your unit. Most companies are increasingly emphasizing the need to control expenses, and labor costs are frequently one of the prime targets. So no matter how overworked your group may be, it may require some ingenuity on your part to hire additional workers. In fact, you may even encounter problems in trying to fill the position of someone who leaves. Some methods you can use to overcome resistance to hiring from your superiors include:

1. Timing is sometimes crucial. When business is good your chances of success in hiring additional help will improve. Conversely, no matter how badly understaffed your department is, when times are tough you aren't likely to meet with much success.

2. Plan your hiring needs in advance. Try to foresee future staffing requirements to allow plenty of time, not only to gain approval to hire, but also to make allowances for the period needed to go through the actual hiring process.

3. Weaken resistance with persistence. You have to be tough-skinned enough not to quit trying when you get an initial refusal from your boss. Allow a reasonable period of time to elapse and then ask again. But whenever you make subsequent requests, try to approach the subject from a different perspective. For example, a boss may not bite on a plea that your people are overworked, but will give the go-ahead if you can show product quality is suffering. The point is to keep making pitches from every conceivable angle until you finally succeed.

4. Take advantage of opportunities when they present themselves. For instance, if your boss complains about how your department isn't keeping up with its workload, that's the time to make your pitch for help.

5. Use excessive amounts of overtime as justification for hiring another person. It helps if you can quantify your argument by showing how money can be saved by adding a position and reducing overtime pay.

6. If you can justify it, compare the output of your group with comparable departments in terms of output per worker. If you can prove your unit is more productive, even if you don't get help right away, you stand a better chance of getting the first crack at adding someone to the payroll in the future.

7. Show how the workload of your group has increased significantly without adding any people for a period of time. Be careful here, since a savvy boss will come back with a statement such as, "Well, if you've been able to do it up until now without any more help, let's just keep up the good work." If that happens, be ready to counter with something such as, "The workload is continuing to increase, and I've now reached the limit in terms of how far I can go in squeezing any more work out of my people."

8. Look for anything that may have increased the workload of your department indirectly, such as compliance with new government regulations, or corporate policy changes.

9. If all else fails, and you're unable to get hiring approval, try to get someone permanently transferred from another department. Failing that, you can go for assigning someone on a temporary basis. Sometimes, when someone is working on detail to a group for long enough, they become permanently assigned by default.

CAUTION: Be careful if someone is assigned to you internally. If you don't have any say in the person selected, the supervisor who is loaning the worker may well use the opportunity to get rid of a dud. If this happens, you may discover that additional help can sometimes mean less rather than more.

10. Another way around not getting approval for a full-time position is to lobby for a part-timer. Then, after the person is working for a few months, attempt to get the position upgraded to full-time. It's sometimes easier to do it this way, since you then have a known quantity on board and can argue how valuable they have become. Of course, another advantage of doing it this way is that it gives you a chance to evaluate the person before you even attempt to hire them on a full-time basis.

4.11

Sensible Tips on How to Justify New Equipment

Along with seeking additional help for your department, trying to get new equipment can also be a long, and sometimes futile, process. This is especially true if the equipment you are looking to purchase is expensive, and isn't simply replacing an item that is no longer usable. Nevertheless there are techniques you can use that will help overcome resistance to your request. These are:

1. Lobby for new equipment on the basis that it will eliminate the need to hire additional help. Be careful here though, since this approach can come back to haunt you at a later date when you're trying to get a hiring request approved. A shrewd boss may also use this against you even if you're only trying to replace a departing worker. You may well hear something such as, "Fred, since we just spent $40,000 for that equipment you wanted, let's see if we can get by without filling this vacancy.

2. Hard facts are the best evidence in support of any expensive expenditure request. Show how the equipment will (1) cut costs, (2) raise revenues, (3) increase efficiency, (4) improve customer service, or (5) meet some other basic goal.

3. Another tactic is to make your appeal on the basis that the purchase will help employees to do their jobs better by eliminating errors.

4. In some cases you may be able to justify a purchase by showing how the new equipment will improve product quality. Incidentally, in this situation and others it will help your cause if you can get other managers and department heads to support your request. In this particular case, the support of the quality control manager would add weight to your argument.

5. For some equipment requests, you may be able to prove that the new equipment will reduce maintenance and repair requests. This is particularly effective if you are trying to replace older items that are frequently breaking down. If it's practical, relate the costs of employee downtime while older equipment is being repaired to the cost of the new equipment which will cure that problem.

6. Sometimes you can support a purchase request by proving that the new equipment is easier to operate and can be used by lower-skilled (and lower-paid) workers.

7. On occasion, you may be able to show that a competitor is updating to the equipment you want to get. A "keeping up with the Jones's" pitch works best when you are in a highly competitive industry where the slightest advantage can spell the difference between success or failure.

8. When feasible, show how what you want to purchase will help overcome some persistent problem that your boss, and perhaps other higher level managers, have expressed concern about in the past.

9. Not every piece of equipment you want to purchase can be justified in terms of cost savings and/or increased productivity. It may just be necessary to eliminate an administrative headache of one form or another. The important point is to know the specific reason for the expenditure, and not try to justify something because it has a few more "bells and whistles" than the equipment you're now using.

10. No matter what the merits of your request for new equipment may be, the best route to quick approval is to get your boss to adopt the idea as his or her own suggestion. This requires some thought—and a little bit of luck won't hurt either. The specifics for doing this will vary with each individual situation. The key is to plant the seed in your boss's mind to suggest buying the particular equipment you need. You may be able to

do this by approaching the subject in a general way, or else asking your boss for advice on the equipment in question. If possible, do this in terms of resolving a particular problem your boss is aware of.

The advantage of this approach is that if final approval at higher levels is needed, a boss will fight harder to get the go-ahead for something they think is their idea. So what if they get the credit for a good idea? You score twice. You get the equipment you want, and you also make your boss look good, which certainly can't hurt your career prospects.

Chapter Five

COPING WITH
PROBLEM EMPLOYEES
AND EMPLOYEE PROBLEMS

Perhaps nothing can be quite so frustrating as some of the employee-related problems you have to handle. Both the scope of the difficulties that can develop, and the potential for conflict, make this an area that's loaded with land mines. If that's not bad enough in itself, the sheer creativity of workers when it comes to making excuses, conceiving complaints, and causing conflicts, can keep your mind working overtime in trying to cope. Among the subjects that will be covered in this chapter are typical personnel problems such as tardiness, absenteeism, and employee complaints, to more difficult topics such as sexual harassment, employee theft, and alcohol and drug abuse.

Beyond these, there are other topics that can test your temperament that will be discussed, ranging from office gossip to dealing with goof-offs. And since no discussion of these subjects can avoid the need to take firm measures to resolve many of these problems, effective steps for dishing out discipline can't be ignored. In fact, that's the first topic to be addressed, so that you know what to do if other efforts fail to resolve and/or prevent problems that call for disciplinary measures.

5.1

Ten Simple Steps for Holding
a Discipline Session

Taking disciplinary action isn't something that any supervisor looks forward to. On the other hand, there are times when it becomes necessary, and when that happens, how it is handled will influence whether it helps correct the offending employee's behavior and/or job performance. The ultimate disciplinary action is, of course, firing an employee. If you eventually face that decision, the proper procedures to follow are covered in Chapter Seven. Here, the focus is on less severe measures you can use that will hopefully encourage a worker to get on—and stay on—the right track. You may not always succeed, but most of the time sitting an employee down and telling it like it is will turn the tide. The following measures will help correct most situations.

1. Consider what you're going to say to the employee beforehand. You want to be able to state succinctly what has to be corrected without having to fumble around deciding what to say next when the meeting takes place.

2. Think about any possible rebuttals or excuses you may get from the employee and be ready to counter them.

3. Hold the session in private. In fact, an office or conference room removed from the immediate work area is preferable. That way, other employees won't be able to overhear the conversation, especially if the worker being disciplined gets loud. Furthermore, when it's held in your office, it isn't too hard for other workers to figure out what's going on. And the boldest ones will ask the worker why he or she was in your office the minute they exit.

4. Be sure to follow the formalities of the company policy on administering discipline. Most procedures follow a pattern of progressive discipline with an informal oral warning, a formal oral warning, a written warning, suspension, and then termination. Serious offenses such as theft or physical assaults may be dealt with by eliminating the initial steps, and having an immediate suspension or termination.

It should be noted that some companies use alternative approaches, such as positive discipline, which rather than suspending an employee without pay, gives them a day off with pay to think things over. Still others provide for a peer review. Whatever the process is, the important point is to adhere to the procedure, and document your actions accordingly.

5. If an employee gets emotional, wait until they calm down before you proceed. However, that doesn't mean you have to endure a fifteen minute diatribe. If the worker's reaction gets to be too intense, try settling things down, and if that doesn't work state that the discussion will be continued at another time. Then, if the employee continues, get up and leave.

6. Be specific about what the employee did wrong. If you're vague or general in discussing what is wrong, the worker may later assert you didn't really pinpoint the problem, and that's why it wasn't corrected. Of course, a worker may do this anyway, but if you have been clear about the matter there will be no room for misinterpretation.

7. Try to combine good aspects of the employee's performance with the negative if it's feasible to do so. Doing this will keep workers from rationalizing that it won't do them any good to correct what they did wrong. Sometimes workers being disciplined adopt an attitude that they're just being set up to be fired, so why bother to change. Therefore, any form of positive encouragement can be helpful in this regard.

8. Always be flexible in listening to what an employee has to say. Sometimes there may be a personal problem which contributed to the disciplinary situation. Bringing this out into the open may in itself help to resolve matters.

9. Even though you want to hear what an employee has to say, you can't let the worker sidetrack you by bringing up unrelated issues. Some people are experts at always being able to find something or someone to pin the responsibility for their own mistakes on.

10. At the close of the session, summarize any actions you expect the employee to take, as well as any agreements you reach with the worker. This will guarantee that any extended discussion didn't confuse the specific changes you want the employee to make in performance and/or behavior.

5.2

✤

Effective Methods for Handling a Grievance

Employee grievances can cause a great deal of grief for both you and those you supervise if they're not handled properly. Nonetheless, there are steps that you can take to deal with these matters which will often serve to resolve any controversy with a minimum of conflict. These are as follows:

1. If you are dealing with a grievance by a union member, follow the formal procedure established by union/management negotiations to handle the complaint. In these situations you will frequently have to consult with your own industrial relations personnel, and the employee will be represented by the union steward. But apart from these restrictions, the general rules which follow essentially apply to any employee grievance in both union and non-union environments.

2. Listen carefully to what the employee is saying, since what someone is complaining about may not always be what is really bothering them. There are any number of reasons for this. For example, a worker may not want to identify a co-worker who may be the cause of a particular problem. As a result, the complaint will be phrased in generalities. Whenever you're not sure the worker is leveling about the problem, ask specific questions that will help you zero in on what's wrong.

3. Always let employees express themselves freely. Sometimes just being able to talk openly about their feelings will go a long way toward resolving the difficulty. At times, you may be tempted to interrupt when an employee appears to be going in circles. However, this is to be expected, especially if the employee is highly emotional. Be patient and eventually the worker will pause, which will give you the opportunity to ask questions in an attempt to pinpoint the problem. Conversely, if you start quizzing an employee right away, this may trigger a defensive posture by the worker which will make it all the more difficult to get to the point.

4. Incidentally, if an employee is initially angry, first work at calming them down before you even begin to discuss the grievance in detail. Very little of substance can be accomplished when either party to a discussion is angry. In fact, if the employee's anger doesn't subside, you are better off

asking them to come back and see you after they have had a chance to cool down.

5. In some situations that are brought to your attention, you may sense that a worker is uncomfortable discussing the grievance with you. In other instances, even though the employee doesn't appear to be uneasy, you may independently conclude that the worker would be better served in airing their grievance to someone else. When this happens, suggest an appropriate alternative such as someone in the human resources department and/or your boss. Do this in such a way that (1) the employee doesn't feel you're just bouncing them around, and (2) the employee has no objection to the person you recommend.

6. Never be rushed into resolving a grievance that you want time to think about, and/or do a little research to verify that you have all of the facts. However, always let the employee know when you will get back to them with an answer.

7. Under some conditions you may want to ask the employee to recommend what can be done to resolve the problem. Actually, the more an employee participates in coming up with a solution, the greater the odds that the grievance will be settled to the worker's satisfaction.

8. Always determine if the employee with the grievance is contributing to the problem. This is especially true if the grievance involves some form of complaint about another worker. When necessary, get both sides of the story before attempting to resolve the matter. In some cases, a complaint about another worker may represent nothing more significant than a personality conflict. If this is so, perhaps something as simple as changing their respective work locations to lessen the amount of personal contact will alleviate the situation.

9. When an employee comes to you with a grievance about another worker, never jump to conclusions based upon the relative job performance of the two workers. Things aren't always what they seem to be, and good workers can be hard to deal with, while a goof-off can be charming and pleasant.

10. Sometimes an employee will come to you with a gripe which isn't yours to settle. For example, two workers may just not like each other, and one of them may decide to level some form of charge as a matter of spite. When you see this developing, let both employees know that how they

get along is their business—not yours. All you care about is that their conflict doesn't interfere with the operations of the department. You have enough to do without being called upon to referee grudge matches.

5.3

Seven Basic Guidelines for Preventing Sexual Harassment

As a supervisor you are the first line of defense in preventing sexual harassment in the workplace. To properly carry out this responsibility, it is necessary to go beyond taking action when complaints are brought to your attention. After all, if the allegations are true, then sexual harassment has already happened. What you want to do is prevent it from taking place not merely rely on responding when it occurs. A few practical guidelines for prevention are:

1. Know the company policy and regulations on sexual harassment. If you have any doubt as to what constitutes sexual harassment, you should consult with the person within your company who is designated as the appropriate authority on the subject.

2. It's good practice to periodically brief your employees on sexual harassment guidelines to continually reinforce the fact that it won't be tolerated.

3. You should make certain that any new hires are made aware of the rules in this area. It's also prudent to do the same thing with transfers to your department from other parts of the company. After all, other bosses may not be as diligent in promoting awareness.

4. Posting a policy, and even regular briefings, aren't going to serve as prevention in and of themselves. The most important way for you to prevent sexual harassment is to let your employees know that you won't tolerate anything even remotely resembling offensive conduct.

5. Discourage even any remarks that don't seem to be objectionable to the recipient. In the first place, they may be considered offensive, but the person may not feel comfortable objecting. Second, they may be dis-

comfiting to someone else who overhears them. Perhaps most important of all, tolerating these remarks tends to encourage this sort of behavior on an indiscriminate basis.

6. Your company policy may provide for sexual harassment complaints to be made either to you or some other designated representative within the company. Even if it doesn't, you may want to let employees know that if they feel uncomfortable making a complaint to you, they can do so with someone in the human resources department. Of course, you should coordinate this beforehand through channels, so you can give workers a specific individual to contact. This is a helpful, since someone working for you may feel uneasy about coming to you with the complaint.

7. When anyone does come to you with a complaint, it should be acted on both quickly and fairly in the interests of everyone involved.

5.4

Six Smart Ways to Control Tardiness

A common headache for every supervisor is to start work in the morning by having workers arrive late with excuses that are probably true ("I overslept"), to those that are suspect ("I fell asleep on the bus and missed my stop"). Valid excuses or not, controlling tardiness is crucial, since laxity in enforcement of working hours encourages an even greater degree of noncompliance by habitually tardy workers. It also can create resentment on the part of punctual employees, who make the necessary effort to report on time.

On the other hand, there are sound reasons why strictly following a firm policy on working hours isn't the answer. First of all, there are times when being late is unavoidable. For example, with working parents it's only reasonable to expect that a last-minute household crisis will cause an employee to be late on occasion. Even something as simple as the daily commute can cause difficulty when a parent has to drop a child off at school or day care. So even though tardiness has to be controlled, it's important to be flexible in responding to justifiable problems that make it difficult for workers to be on time. The following guidelines will help in this regard.

1. Holding periodic meetings about tardiness isn't likely to be the answer. Frequently, it will only cure the problem temporarily. For a week or two, everyone will tend to arrive on time, but you will soon find workers slipping back into the habit of coming in late. Therefore, deal directly with those people who are tardy. Expect to be told why they were late, and what will be done to cure the problem in the future.

2. Don't be negative when you confront employees who are late. Some people are hesitant about speaking to a boss about some personal circumstance that's causing them to be late for work. Say something such as, "Art, you've always been one of my reliable people, but for the past few days you have been late every morning. Is there some problem causing this that we need to talk about?" This gives the worker an opening to level with you about the reason for the tardiness. Then, you can jointly reach agreement on what can be done to avoid being late in the future.

3. Workers should be told how exceptions to the established time and attendance policy will be handled. This will prevent resentment from other workers whenever a temporary exception is made to accommodate an employee who is having a problem. Of course, if workers are going to be allowed to deviate from normal working hours on a regular basis, it's best to have these provisions in the formal company policy. Otherwise, it may be viewed as favoritism or special treatment for some and not for others.

4. Even though you may work longer hours than any of your subordinates, try to set the standard by being punctual in the morning. Workers tend to take cues from their boss, and if the boss comes in late, they will soon follow suit.

5. Be practical in dealing with tardiness issues. For example, someone who works late consistently shouldn't be criticized for occasional tardiness. However, someone who arbitrarily adjusts their own hours by working late and coming in late is setting a pattern for other workers to follow in establishing their own schedule. This, of course, shouldn't be condoned.

6. Above all else, it's important to be realistic in dealing with tardiness, since the reasons can vary widely. For instance, some younger workers may be tardy for no better reason than simply not knowing and observing the basic responsibilities associated with employment.

5.5

⍦

Seven Workable Tools to Reduce Unscheduled Absences

Absenteeism is a little bit like the common cold. You can't prevent it, but there are measures you can take to control it. There are obviously emergencies and sudden illnesses which will cause an employee to be absent without advance notice. So it certainly is necessary for you to be reasonable in recognizing this. On the other hand, a few culprits will occasionally attempt to take advantage of the situation. And, if they are allowed to succeed, then like the common cold, the practice will spread quickly. To prevent this from happening try a few of the following techniques:

- Know your company policy on unscheduled absence, let your people know what it is, and follow it in dealing with absences. If you don't apply it across-the-board you can run into trouble when you try to use it to discipline a habitual offender.

- Make the most of any company incentives for good attendance. Measures such as bonuses and cash awards can be a big help to you in this area.

- Insist that people contact you directly and don't just leave a message when they call in. At least if they have to talk to you, they're forced to come up with a good excuse.

- Motivate people to come to work by letting them know they're needed. For example, when someone returns to work, say something such as, "Good to see you back, Jack." It not only makes people feel appreciated, but it also lets them know their absence didn't go unnoticed.

- Watch for patterns in unscheduled absences. Mondays, Fridays, and the days before and after a holiday are when most unjustified absences are taken. Then again, a savvy employee may avoid taking the days that are most suspect, so you won't always find a pattern.

- Make a point of asking if everyone will be in the day before a holiday. People may assume it's alright to extend the weekend if you tend to tolerate the practice.

- Concentrate your efforts on the one or two people who tend to be the habitual offenders in calling with one excuse after another. These are the people who will cause the most problems.

5.6

♥

Ways to Deal with Vacation Schedule Hassles

The joys of summer are accompanied by a recurring headache for many supervisors, which is how to keep productivity up during a season which inspires vacations, long weekends, and more than a few shoddy excuses for not being at work. The risks of being shorthanded during the summer months can range from just being a minor annoyance to a major problem. It can leave you anxiously awaiting Labor Day while everyone else is seemingly enjoying sunshine, sand, surf, fishing, and fun on the fairway. However, rather than stew about this injustice on hot summer days, you're better off doing what you can to cope with any shorthanded situation you may have. Several measures that can help in this regard are:

1. The first step in dealing with summer downtime involves nothing more elaborate than recognizing that people just may not be as productive in the summer months. So to some degree, you have to recognize and cater to this tendency.

2. If it's practical, try to implement some form of summer schedule that will allow employees to take advantage of the good weather. The possibilities include working an extra hour on Monday through Thursday and having Friday off, or an extra half-hour the first four days of the week with work ending at noon on Friday. Of course, this may not be a doable alternative where you work, and unless it's done company-wide, you probably can't implement it within your own group. Nevertheless, it's still helpful to be as flexible as possible in granting time off on an individual basis.

3. Avoid overtime work whenever it's possible to do so. Let your people know that overtime won't be scheduled if work requirements can be completed during normal working hours. This will encourage them to be as productive as possible in order to avoid working extra hours.

4. Look for little things you can do to make work a little more bearable during the summer months. If feasible, adopting casual dress codes, and/or allowing longer lunch hours are just a couple of the many tactics you can use.

5. Vacation time is a subject that can cause a great deal of unnecessary conflict. For this reason alone, vacation schedules should be prepared as early in the year as possible to allow people to plan ahead.

6. Inevitably, more than one person will want the same two weeks for vacation, when you can just let one of them go. To avoid these hassles, it's best to provide for first choice to be based upon seniority, or some other set criteria. You can also modify this arrangement to provide that when a conflict exists, the person who loses out this year will have first choice the following year.

7. Of course, you're limited in what you can do about scheduling vacations by the overall company policy. But whatever is done, make sure it's as fair as possible, and understood by everyone. After all, many people plan their vacations well ahead of time, while others face problems in coordinating vacations with a working spouse. It's probably impossible to plan for every potential scheduling problem that may arise, but a formal yet flexible procedure can help.

8. Sometimes carelessness in scheduling vacations can cause unnecessary problems. Take the case of a boss who hired a new employee in April, and as part of the hiring process promised the person the first two weeks in July for vacation. Having made this commitment, he subsequently came up shorthanded when another employee quit in June. As a result, he rejected the vacation request of someone who had been with the company for several years. Needless to say, this employee was less than pleased at having to reschedule vacations plans, while the new hire got the time off.

9. Even your own vacation can cause job-related anxiety if you spend it worrying about work. Therefore, appoint someone to fill in for you while you're gone, and get away and relax. Incidentally, avoid the urge to check in to see how things are going, since this will only get you involved on a long-distance basis. If you feel it's absolutely necessary, then leave a number where you can be reached.

5.7

ψ

Seven Helpful Hints on Dealing with Alcohol and Drugs

Dealing with substance abuse isn't an easy thing to do, as any expert in the field will attest. When you have an employee with an alcohol or drug problem, there's a natural tendency to mind your own business. However, when the employee's performance is deteriorating, just as with any other work-related problem, you have to take some action. Even though it may be distasteful for you to do so, when you confront employees with these problems, it forces them to seek assistance rather than lose their job. So as unpleasant as it may be, you may well be doing the worker a favor, even though it may not be viewed as such at the time. The proper way to deal with this delicate situation is:

1. First of all, know the details of your company procedures for dealing with alcohol and drug abuse problems. Many companies have formal employee assistance programs in this area. The larger organizations will provide internal counseling, while others will refer workers to outside agencies specializing in this area. Some companies will also grant a leave of absence to employees who need it. Whatever the case may be, always follow the company's written policy which will detail what is expected of workers in the area of alcohol and drugs, and what will happen if the policy is violated.

2. Learn to watch for the warning signs that may indicate an employee is having a problem with alcohol and/or drugs. These include:

   • A decline in the quality and/or quantity of work.

   • Changes in personality and physical appearance such as mood swings and/or energy levels.

   • Excessive tardiness and absenteeism.

   • The employee is frequently absent from the work area for unexplained reasons.

   • The worker is involved in careless accidents and/or suffers job-related injuries.

   • Company property is disappearing, which may be resulting from theft.

3. Keep notes of specific job-related deficiencies when you suspect an employee may be having an alcohol or drug problem. However, never

accuse an employee of having a substance abuse problem, since something else, such as personal or financial difficulties, could be affecting a worker's job performance.

4. Timing is important in confronting the employee. Even though you shouldn't jump to conclusions, you can't let the situation drag on forever in the hope that it will go away. If anything, it will just get worse.

5. Once you're sure the employee's poor performance is a continuing problem, discuss the inadequate job performance factors with the worker. Ask the employee for explanations as to why errors are being made and what can be done about them. Frequently, the employee will deny there is a problem, which is where your previous note-taking will come into play.

6. Agree on solutions to the work-related problems and set a time-frame for correcting them. Schedule a follow-up meeting at a later date. If the worker's performance hasn't improved, refer them for counseling in the employee assistance program. By this time, the employee's lack of adequate performance will be such that you should insist on the worker entering the program as a condition of continued employment.

7. As the boss of a long-time loyal employee, it's often difficult to recognize the possibility that the employee may have an alcohol and/or drug problem. However, your other workers don't want an employee with a substance abuse problem threatening their safety, or goofing off and forcing them to carry the extra workload.

CAUTION: Never attempt to diagnose the worker's problem, and/or offer counseling on how to handle it. This is a job for experts in the field. Confine yourself to taking action on having the employee seek help. If the employee refuses to comply, and job performance remains subpar, then the appropriate recourse may ultimately be termination of the worker in accordance with company procedure.

5.8

The ABC's of Controlling Employee Theft

If there's one hassle you don't need, it's trying to track down a thief within your department. Fortunately, even if you had the time—which you don't—that's a job best left to the experts. However, as with many other things, prevention is critical when it comes to controlling employee theft. And it's in this area that you can be a major influence by adopting measures that will discourage theft before it becomes a reality. Here are a number of actions you can take in this regard:

1. The first step in controlling theft is to recognize its importance. This can extend beyond the actual dollar loss to the company. For example, workers can spend valuable time looking for tools they assume were misplaced, which were actually stolen. Similarly, office supplies can be depleted before a scheduled reordering date because employees are taking them home for personal use.

2. Adopt a theft prevention attitude. There is a natural tendency to assume that your workers wouldn't engage in theft. That may or may not be true, but it's important to keep in mind that the most successful thief is often the person one would least suspect.

3. Let the people you supervise know that you will not tolerate theft within your unit.

4. Employees don't ordinarily think of things such as taking office supplies home, or making personal long-distance phone calls from work as theft. Therefore, it's necessary for you to let them know that this is indeed stealing. Be careful that you're consistent with company policy in this area, since some businesses condone such practices. Hopefully, your company doesn't, since a casual approach that tolerates minor abuses can set the stage for more serious forms of theft.

5. One of the best methods of theft prevention is the careful screening of new hires through reference and background checks. The extent to which this is done may be largely beyond your control. However, you can look for subtle signs during the interview process that may alert you to potential trouble. For instance, if a job candidate mentions he likes to gamble, then that should raise a red flag in your mind. Of course, someone who gambles isn't necessarily a potential thief. However, it is a risk factor that you should weigh, particularly if you supervise in an area where theft is a prevalent concern.

6. Establish a good control system for supplies and equipment which will (1) limit access, and/or (2) record the usage.

7. With items such as hand tools, it's a good practice to require the old one to be turned in when a replacement is sought.

8. If computers are used in your unit, it's useful to give out passwords that will only allow workers to access information that is required to do their jobs.

9. If you are in a position where periodic inventories are conducted, look for signs that signal something isn't right, such as significantly lower inventories during a period when they should have increased.

10. A common form of theft is expense account padding. If this is a potential problem in your department, require prompt submission of expense vouchers, and make a habit of disallowing questionable items to encourage employees to follow company travel policy.

5.9

Six Sure-Fire Techniques to Combat Excuses

Other than dandruff, the one thing almost certain to leave you scratching your head are some of the excuses you hear from workers. And even though on occasion some of the alibis offered by creative employees may make you want to laugh, for the most part they can have you wishing you were in some other line of work. Whatever your reaction may be, it's necessary to be able to counter excuses effectively. Otherwise, you will never be able to hold the perpetrators responsible for their actions, which is exactly what they're hoping will happen. A few approaches that are helpful in outwitting even the most clever alibi artists are:

1. Ignore the excuse completely, and shift the discussion to whatever went wrong that resulted in the employee making the excuse. After all, what matters is correcting the situation so it doesn't happen again, excuse or no excuse.

2. State that the excuse is irrelevant if it's one in a long line of excuses you get from the same individual time and time again. For example, if the person is late for work and gives you an alibi, say something such as, "Chris, anything that causes you to be late is your responsibility—not mine." If the excuses are used continually to cover the same type of transgression, let the employee know that disciplinary action will have to be taken if the situation isn't corrected. Once persistent excuse-makers

are put on notice that alibis won't fly, they know that they either have to perform, or face the consequences.

3. You may have a good worker who always makes excuses whenever anything goes wrong. This may just result from a lack of confidence. If you suspect this to be the case, try reassuring such a worker that he is doing a good job. You may find that over a period of time this will boost the employee's performance to the point where excuses become fewer and farther between.

4. Conditionally recognize the excuse. If an employee who usually doesn't make excuses gives you one, you may want to accept it. Nevertheless, you may want to let the person tactfully know that you won't be as receptive the next time. If so, try something such as, "That can happen to anyone once." If the excuse is unusual you may want to say, "Don't worry about it. That's a once-in-a-lifetime happening."

5. Don't intentionally hook yourself on an excuse-maker's line. Sometimes employees will preface their excuse by saying something such as, "You're not going to believe this, but..." When alibi artists do this, cut them short at the pass by saying, "If I'm not going to believe it, there's no point in telling me." Then, start discussing the issue that the excuse is aimed at.

6. When an excuse appears to represent a potential continuing problem for a worker, go beyond the excuse to discuss what can be done to address the difficulty. For instance, an employee may tell you she was late because the school bus wasn't on time to pick her children up. This is the sort of difficulty that can be expected to repeat itself, so it may be worthwhile to jointly agree on how the problem can be handled in the future. This will not only spare the employee the embarrassment of having to repetitively tell you the same thing time and time again, but it will help the employee's morale to know that you are willing to be reasonable about a justifiable problem.

5.10

Strategies for Overcoming Petty Complaints

Earlier in this chapter there was a discussion on how to deal with grievances of a more or less serious nature. A lesser problem you may have to deal with are the petty gripes generated by one or two constant complainers. These people can drive you up a wall if you let them. Who knows, that may even be their secret goal. To make matters worse, some of these whiners can even present a pretty good case to justify their moaning and groaning. The fortunate part is that since they are habitually griping, you will soon recognize that their complaints are seldom if ever substantive. Therefore, what you have to do is quickly verify that the current complaint is trivial, and then end the discussion. Otherwise, you'll become a captive audience for this type of pest. Here are a few tactics you can try to make these sessions short:

1. Listen long enough to make sure the complaint isn't a valid one that requires you to take some action. Even habitual whiners may have a legitimate beef now and then.

2. Never let a constant complainer get the best of you. Some gripers can persist until they succeed in causing you to respond in anger. They may then leave, but only after accusing you of being unreasonable. Even worse, it may inspire future encounters once they know their actions are getting under your skin.

3. Don't do any griping of your own to a subordinate. There may be occasions when you generally agree with a complaint, but don't let a constant complainer know it. It may give them satisfaction on this particular issue, but the complainer may think he has a soulmate and will be back repeatedly with an assortment of other gripes.

4. When someone continually complains about something that isn't going to change, let the person know that time and energy are being wasted on the subject. Say something such as, "Marion, I know you don't like the new working hours but they aren't going to change, so you may as well try to get used to them."

5. Some complainers may only be seeking attention. You may have someone working for you who lacks self-confidence and is looking for reassurance. If you sense this to be true, then try praising this person more frequently and you may see the griping come to an end.

6. Give them the facts. Some people tend to be unrealistic about their performance. As a result, they continually complain about being overworked and underpaid. Inevitably, with this type of griper, you eventually have to just tell it like it is, which is that a pay raise or promotion isn't in the cards. If they persist, politely suggest that they try to achieve their objectives in the marketplace. In fact, the poorer the quality of

their work, the more helpful you may want to be in assisting these types in getting a job somewhere else.

7. With some types of complaints a good way to discourage gripers is to ask them to give their complaint some further thought and then submit it to you in writing. The odds are slim that you will ever see a memo on the subject.

8. Some constant complainers can be reformed, or at least discouraged from bothering you further, by referring them elsewhere with their pet peeve. For example, if they complain about the heat, send them to talk with someone in maintenance. If you're lucky, sometimes you can get a little bit of revenge, particularly if you refer the griper to someone you know is particularly nasty to deal with.

9. Make it unpleasant for chronic complainers to visit you. If you have one or two workers who persist in bothering you, try discouraging them by either giving them an unwelcome task, or asking hardball questions about their work.

10. A lot of petty complaints are of the type you have heard time and time again. With these, the quickest and best tactic is to thank the person for bringing it to your attention. Then tell them the very same complaint has been raised in the past and there is nothing further that can be done.

5.11

How to Put a Lid on Employee Conflicts

You may not have been hired to be a referee, but you will find yourself in that unenviable position if you aren't careful in handling employee conflicts. Disputes of one sort or another happen regularly within the workplace. One reason is no more complicated than the competition that arises for pay raises and promotions. This is in theory supposed to motivate people to work harder, but inevitably it encourages a few workers to try for success by back-stabbing their co-workers.

Then, you will always have the inevitable disagreements that occur because of personality differences, jealousy, and every other matter that can cause people to dislike one another. Whatever the cause, you have to control these conflicts, since they are both unproductive and damaging to the overall morale of your department. Here are a few methods for dealing with these problems:

1. A few troublemakers may try to use you as a pawn to get even with a co-worker for some real or perceived wrong. To do this, they come to you with a complaint about another worker, usually with an opening remark similar to, "I really don't want to tell you this, and I hope you will keep it confidential but..." They then go on to skewer a co-worker with a smugness that sometimes shows through.

   Of course, if the complaint is an obvious attempt to make a co-worker look bad, then the best approach is to quickly dismiss it by telling the backstabber you aren't interested in idle gossip, and don't expect the person to be wasting valuable working time in creating rumors—with you or anyone else within the department.

   However, if it's a complaint which would normally require you to take some action, simply acknowledge what was said in a noncommittal manner, and check it out independently. If it turns out to be false, you have the option of doing nothing, or telling the troublemaker there was no substance to the complaint. This is a flip of the coin choice, since you may not be certain whether it was an honest error or a deliberate attempt to get another worker in trouble.

   By not having any further discussion with the troublemaker, you will leave the impression you saw through his scheme from the start. This may dissuade the person from trying this tactic again. On the other hand, if you choose to pursue the matter with the instigator, it's worth telling him that you won't tolerate rumors about others workers. Try saying something such as, "I know this was an honest mistake, Louie, but be more careful in the future, since I won't allow false accusations about anyone in my department."

2. Make your attitude toward conflict clear. Your own actions can set the tone for your employees. For example, if you feud with other supervisors, your workers will take this as a cue that arguments and disputes are an acceptable course of action.

3. Poor communication can also cause misunderstandings that can lead to disputes. Try holding regular meetings with workers, since open discussions can resolve many problems that might lead to bickering.

4. It's also important not to bypass individuals when giving out information within the department, since some workers will see this as favoritism. This will inevitably result in the sort of resentment that will trigger feuding.

5. Job rotation can be useful in giving people a better understanding of what other workers do. This will avoid the type of bickering which results when workers see others as having easier assignments.

6. Use tact when dealing with issues that you know are sensitive to employees. It helps in this regard to use a positive approach to criticism. For example, if you want changes in something an employee has prepared, say something such as, "This report is very good Brian, but I think we have to include next month's production schedules." This is far preferable to criticizing the employee for not including the schedules in the first place.

7. Look for hidden agendas in employee conflicts. Sometimes, worker conflicts arise from jealousy over assignments, promotions, and other perceived injustices. You can prevent this to some degree by letting everyone know where they stand in terms of their performance, and what they have to do to improve it.

8. Naturally, serious conflicts such as fighting are grounds for disciplinary action. But even lesser disagreements should be dealt with once you see them as interfering in the smooth operations of the unit. If necessary, sit the perpetrators down and tell them you aren't going to tolerate their quarreling.

9. If bickering continues after you have admonished the participants, you may eventually have to transfer and/or terminate one or both of the people involved.

5.12

Prudent Ways to Outwit Gossips

One of the most common irritants facing every supervisor is having to deal with a constant flow of chatter circulating through the gossip circuit. The easy approach, of course, is to grin and bear it, since office gossip is both difficult to control and impossible to eliminate. However, ignoring gossips can create an environment where rumors will flourish to the extent that they hinder productivity and undermine morale. In addition, when workers are gossiping, they're not doing their jobs. Therefore, simply letting office gossips operate at will can create more problems then trying to deal with them. Several tactics that will help control workplace gossip and/or minimize its ill effects are as follows:

1. A lot of office gossip is of little consequence and can be ignored. However, when one or more individuals spend too much of their time gossiping instead of working, find additional work for them which will give them less time to engage in idle chatter.

2. If you have a very productive worker who also manages to specialize in starting damaging rumors, assigning additional work may not be the answer. Here, you can try talking to the employee about how disruptive work-related rumors can be. Suggest that in the future, the employee contact you to verify any rumors. This will not only put the employee on notice that you're aware of his rumor-spreading tendencies, but also that you expect him to verify with you anything he hears. This often tends to either quiet the rumormonger down, and/or force him to gossip about trivia unrelated to work.

3. Prevention is a necessary measure to control gossips. To do this successfully, it's necessary to create an atmosphere of open communication with your employees. This will allow you to serve as a sounding board to confirm or deny the more serious types of rumors which can be disruptive in their impact on workers. Keeping open lines of communication will allow you to knock down many of the most damaging rumors before they begin to take on a life of their own.

4. Be careful about talking in speculative terms with workers, since some people aren't very good at separating fact from opinion. For example, a comment such as, "I don't think we're going to have any job cutbacks this year, since business has picked up," may be a valid assumption based upon what you know. However, some workers will accept that as a statement of fact that there will be no future job cuts. Then, if reductions do take place, either because of changed conditions or some other circumstance, your credibility will be damaged. Therefore, whenever workers ask you about future plans, it's better to just say, "I don't know," rather than give an off-the-cuff answer.

5. Along the same line, if you avoid speculation concerning work-related matters, it will encourage your employees to do the same. Even though

it's natural to offer opinions, there are plenty of harmless subjects to concentrate on, such as sports teams, politics, and even next weekend's weather. At least topics such as these won't make your job more difficult.

6. Whenever possible, once you hear a rumor, counter it with the truth. If you're not sure if the rumor has any foundation in fact, check with those sources within the company who would be privy to the correct information before you respond. The key point is to take prompt action, since if you don't deny rumors right away, they will continue to spread, making it even harder to put them to rest.

7. It's always a good practice to discuss forthcoming actions such as reorganizations, work force reductions, and fringe benefit changes with employees as soon as possible. This will prevent unnecessary speculation which can quickly generate rumors far worse than the reality of what is to take place.

8. When you hear a negative rumor, deal directly with those employees who are spreading the erroneous information. Tell them why the rumor is incorrect, but don't stop there. Instruct them on the harmful impact of rumors and the damage they can cause. In addition, let them know that spreading rumors is contrary to the open lines of communication you want within your group.

9. Most workers will respect your request not to spread rumors, and will seek you out for the facts when they hear one. Nevertheless, you may have a confirmed gossip or two in your group who will continue to operate on the sly. Don't lose any sleep over these people, since what they have to say is probably not accepted for fact by any but the most gullible of their co-workers.

10. Despite the headaches office gossip and rumors can create, the office grapevine isn't all bad. In fact, you can use it as a source of information you may not be in the loop to receive. For instance, unions often receive information from top management before it filters down through management levels within the company. As a result, you may hear information from union members before you get the work officially.

Naturally, be sure you have a good idea as to the reliability of your sources when you get news through the grapevine. You can also check the accuracy of what you hear with other sources, and/or relate the information to other events which will tend to confirm or deny its truthfulness.

11. Above all else, communicating openly will minimize the negative impact of office gossip and rumors. So even though you can't completely eliminate it, at least you will be able to control it before it gets out of hand. Once you have mastered damage control techniques, you may even be able to chuckle about some of the more bizarre rumors that come your way.

5.13

Practical Measures for Putting Goof-Offs to Work

Everyone who supervises people for any length of time inevitably has to deal with goof-offs who seemingly make a career out of doing as little as possible. Some of these people are actually quite productive when they actually concentrate on doing their job, rather than trying to avoid it.

At first glance, the easiest way to rid yourself of these nuisances would be to fire them. However, that's not necessarily the case for a number of reasons. First of all, terminating someone is a last resort, and even then it can be a cumbersome project. Beyond that, many goof-offs have perfected their art to the point where they do just enough work to avoid any offer that they take their act elsewhere. Also, since it isn't always easy to hire a replacement, someone working half-speed is often the best alternative. Therefore, you may want to try some of the following measures if you have any goof-offs working for you. If you don't, keep this book handy, because your turn to deal with one may be just around the corner.

1. If possible, try pairing off a slow worker with one of your more productive employees. It may force the slowpoke to pick up the pace.

2. Assign projects with deadlines, establish quotas, and use other specific time-related goals, so that goof-offs have targets to meet.

3. Study the work habits of goof-offs so you can figure out where they're wasting time. This will give you insight into what can be done to keep them moving.

4. Review the worker's duties on an overall basis. Perhaps a change of assignments is what is needed. Sometimes it's not so much that a work-

er is goofing off, as an inability to handle the assigned job. Everyone has differing skills, so reassignment to another position may sometimes solve the problem.

5. Assess the performance of goof-offs on a regular basis, so that they know you're closely monitoring their performance.

6. If group gatherings around the water cooler, or somewhere else, are getting out of hand, try joining the gathering. Then, after a few minutes say something such as, "Well, I guess it's time to get back to work." Then, walk away and your employees will likely do the same.

7. Don't let one or two people slack off just because other workers are carrying the load. This creates resentment, along with the risk that they too will start to under-perform.

8. Although you want to limit the amount of goofing off that takes place, don't go overboard. Work breaks and a little bit of socializing allow workers to blow off steam, so don't be so productivity conscious that you overdo it.

9. When nothing else works in getting a goof-off in line, you may have to take disciplinary action. Sometimes a verbal or written warning will send a wake-up call to a worker.

Chapter Six

❦

WHEELING AND DEALING WITH YOUR BOSS AND OTHERS

It's a difficult enough job just to manage the people you supervise, but your responsibilities also require working with a wide range of people outside of your own department. And sometimes getting the job done will require going well beyond just keeping a good working relationship with peers and bosses. For example, in some situations, you may find yourself having to work around bottleneck people, or cut through a thicket of other obstacles, to meet the demands and deadlines of your job.

The topics in this chapter cover the range of interests you will have to satisfy, as well as the fundamental techniques for doing so. These include knowing how to sell your ideas, and how to bargain to get what you need to do your job. Probably the most common role you will have to play is learning how to be successful in securing the cooperation of other departments, so let's look at how this can be done.

123

6.1

⚘

Shrewd Ways to Get Cooperation
from Other Departments

In order to succeed as a supervisor, it's frequently necessary to secure the cooperation of people who don't report to you, such as staff personnel and the supervisors of other groups. This can be a challenging assignment, not only because of varying workloads, but also due to differences in personalities. Some people are just plain easier to deal with than others, but most of the time you won't have the luxury of picking and choosing which ones you work with.

To further complicate matters, your work agenda may not necessarily coincide with theirs. For example, a project which you consider to be top priority may be of little importance to the supervisor of another department whose assistance you need to get the job done. For these reasons, you may, at times, have to use everything from humor to playing hardball to get the cooperation you need. Some of the strategies you can benefit from using include:

1. Develop good working relationships. People are more willing to help those they like. Therefore, always try to be pleasant even when you have to deal with unpleasant people.

2. Always show respect for the other person's viewpoint. Never offend anyone, including employees you don't usually interact with on business, since you never know when you will need their assistance. Furthermore, people get reassigned due to promotions, job transfers, and reorganizations, and ultimately may be in a position to help or hinder your ability to do your job.

3. Learn to recognize the personality quirks of those people you deal with on a regular basis. Some people handle pressure well, others blow off steam and then cooperate willingly, and there are those who will "Yes" you to death but never come through in the clutch. Recognizing these general traits will help you in learning ways to work around them.

4. Respect other people's priorities just as you expect them to respect yours. Whenever possible, try to fit your requirements into the less demanding parts of their schedule. Not only does this improve the chances that the assistance you require will be provided, but it also earns

the gratitude of your peers. This will help when you have a "rush" job that just can't wait.

5. Never overstate your requirements. If you make a habit of labeling everything as a priority project, those you deal with will soon start to treat everything you come to them with as routine.

6. Learn to bargain with people whose cooperation you need on a fairly regular basis. For example, perhaps on occasion you can modify the requirements of what you need, or alter the deadline for completion. By doing this, you are better able to secure assistance when you most need it. In short, doing favors will get favors done for you.

7. Schedule ahead whenever you can. Whenever possible, build some flexibility into the due date of your requirements. One of the standard responses used by people when you need something in a hurry is some variation of, "I'm busy, I can't do that right now." Depending upon what the work consists of, they will then offer to complete what you want, hours, days, or weeks after the date you request. To counter this tendency, make your completion requirements an earlier time than is actually the case. For instance, if you need something in three weeks, give the person you're dealing with a deadline of two weeks. This gives you some leeway, not only with people who instinctively object to deadline dates, but also in the event of a possible glitch somewhere along the way.

8. Learn how to counter routine objections. No one likes to see more work arrive when they are already busy. As a result, the possibilities of resistance are far more likely than a positive response. Develop as many individual approaches as you can to avoid negative replies when you ask for someone's help. For example, giving someone plenty of advance notice doesn't put you in the position of being the person coming in the door with unexpected and unwelcome requirements. You may also want to look for ways you can help other people out so they will feel indebted to you when you need assistance. The specifics will vary widely in accordance with the particular requirements of your job, but the important point is to always be on the lookout for creative ways to gain the cooperation you need from others.

NOTE: These tactics are aimed at gaining cooperation from other departments and groups within your own company. However, they are equally useful in working with subcontractors, suppliers, and others that you have to deal with on a regular basis.

6.2

♯

How to Work Around Bottleneck People

No matter how successful you are in getting cooperation from other groups you work with, there may still be a few people you encounter who are dyed-in-the-wool bottlenecks. These are individuals, who for one reason or another, always seem to slow things down. These bottlenecks can include people who are just plain indecisive, as well as others who attempt to justify their existence by questioning anything and everything that comes along. And in rare instances you may even run into someone whose apparent career goal is to make life miserable for everyone they come into contact with. Whatever the reason, here are a few ways to work around these types:

1. Hound them into taking action. It's not particularly pleasant pestering people to get the job done. However, with some folks it's the only tactic that works.

2. Look for ways to eliminate them from the loop. Are there ways to get the work done without having to deal with the bottleneck? For instance, can you avoid having the bottleneck's department involved, or if it can't be avoided, can you work with a subordinate in the other department?

3. Try to pinpoint the reason why the person is always an obstacle to getting things done. Do they appear to be insecure and afraid of making a mistake, or are they basically indecisive? If you can figure out why they procrastinate, then perhaps you can find a way to make it easier for them to give you what you want.

4. Tell the bottleneck that higher management is tracking the progress of the project. This can often goad a reluctant participant into action. Be careful here though, particularly if top management hasn't expressed an interest in the task you want accomplished. If so, say it in such a way that the implication can be drawn without actually asserting it as fact. Perhaps something such as "Tom Evans (a senior manager) won't be happy if this isn't completed on time." Even though no one told you this directly, you're not actually lying, since every manager wants projects completed on schedule. Furthermore, anyone you tell this to isn't likely to do any checking to see if top management has actually expressed an interest in the project. Even a diehard bottleneck isn't that

foolhardy, since checking to see if upper management is interested is a sure-fire way to arouse interest—even where none previously existed.

5. If necessary, put third-party pressure on the bottleneck. Have your own boss contact the bottleneck's boss to get what you want. Try to do this as discretely as possible, since it will be resented, which will make future dealings even more difficult.

6. Put the burden of responsibility on the other person if they fail to act. If someone drags their feet in doing what needs to be done, let them know they will be held responsible. Say something such as, "If you don't get this finished by..., the deadline will be missed, and you will be responsible."

6.3

Proven Methods for Making Written Presentations

On occasion, you will be called upon to make written presentations, either as part of a work review process, or as a proposal in support of some position you are advocating, such as the purchase of new equipment. Often, these will be relatively brief, while at other times the effort will be much more extensive. In general, the higher the management level, the greater the degree of formality that will be required for the presentation. Nevertheless, whatever the level of effort that may be necessary, the important point is to be successful in making your case. Several pointers that will help in this regard are:

1. Direct the focus of your writing to the ultimate decision maker. This is an important consideration that's often overlooked when people prepare proposals and other written presentations. To do this successfully, several factors should be considered, such as:

   Format—Individuals have preferences in how they want things presented to them. Many people like lots of detail, others just want summary presentations. Charts, graphs, and numbers are preferred by some folks, and viewed as mind-numbing by others. So if you don't know the preference of the recipient, find out before you start. After all, yours isn't the first presentation made to that person, so other supervisors should be able to clue you in if this is a first-time pitch to someone.

Length—Generally, the higher the level of management, the less they want to be involved in dotting the i's, and crossing the t's type of detail. Give 'em the facts, the alternatives, and a recommended course of action. However, at lower levels a greater amount of detail is generally expected. In any event, never make any presentation longer than it has to be, since you run the risk of boring the reader. And boring isn't convincing, so whatever the merits of your presentation, it isn't likely to get a fair reading.

Position—What functional position does the person who will be the ultimate decision maker hold within the organization? For example, if you're making a pitch to financial types relative to buying new equipment, your major focus might be on the cost-saving benefits, while a pitch to engineering might emphasize the technical benefits. This isn't insignificant, since people tend to view things from their own perspective, often with little regard for the concerns of other job functions or disciplines.

2. Be clear about the subject matter. It's easy to get so submerged in details to support your position that ultimately the message gets lost in the clutter.

3. Don't ask for it and you won't get it. If you want approval of something, then ask for it. Don't leave people guessing as to what you want.

4. Support your argument with specifics, rather than opinions. It's hard to argue with specifics, but anyone can have a different opinion.

5. Don't ignore opposing viewpoints. If there are pros and cons, address them both. If you answer a question before it is raised, then you've answered it on your terms, not on someone else's.

NOTE: Many of the details of writing memos and reports outlined in Section 2.11 of Chapter Two apply equally to more detailed presentations, so you may want to refer to them for tips on style, sequence, and other writing basics.

6.4

Confidential Advice on Cutting Bureaucratic Red Tape

If there's one thing you don't need in life, your choice may well be the endless policies and procedures that seem to be strewn in your path when you're trying to get a job done. Every business has its share of red tape, some more so than others. And even though you don't always think so, some of what appears to be an unending stream of rules, regulations, and approvals may even be necessary. The problem for you is that they may be necessary for the "big picture," but in terms of what you have to do, they are only one more roadblock to overcome. And overcome them you must, or you'll be forever facing a backlog of work, and a boss asking you what the problem is. Since you can't very well plead that there's too much red tape, here are a few ways to avoid it, minimize it, or comply without getting bogged down by it.

1. Know which policies and procedures have to be followed. Many directives are written with a certain objective in mind, and are not intended to be applied across-the-board. Others are just so wordy and confusing that they are often misinterpreted. This can often lead to situations where someone will erroneously assume that a cumbersome procedure applies when in fact it doesn't. By understanding the fine points of those procedures that hinder the productive output of your group, you will be able to show how and why they don't apply.

    Very few people take the time to understand the more complex directives, preferring instead to accept someone else's judgment as to whether they apply or not. Actually, this is a pretty practical approach for run-of-the-mill situations, since it's both time-consuming and frustrating to labor over the intent and meaning of many cumbersome procedures. However, it's time well-spent to completely understand any directive that you find to be burdensome in doing your job. In addition, since you will then become one of the few people who really know certain procedures, people will accept your judgment when you tell them a particular procedure doesn't apply in a given situation.

2. You may find instances where procedures are vague enough so an argument could be made one way or another as to the application of the procedure to a given situation. Take the practical route and claim it doesn't apply. This puts the burden on someone else to either accept your assertion, or immerse themselves in trying to show where you're wrong.

3. Get approval to deviate and/or partially comply. If a requirement contains several provisions that must be met, try to secure approval for partial compliance. Agree to meet the provisions that will cause you the least difficulty, while avoiding the one or two that will cause you the most trouble.

4. Show how compliance with the directive will be detrimental to the company. If you are able to prove that following a directive will incur excessive costs, endanger production schedules, or in some other way have a negative impact, the odds are you will be easily able to secure permission to ignore it.

5. If a procedure will cause severe problems if you comply, and/or it is relatively obscure, you may choose to simply ignore it. If you're subsequently challenged, simply plead ignorance of the existence of the procedure, or its application to what you were doing. Naturally, before you use this approach you have to weigh the pros and cons of failing to comply. If, on balance, the negative impact of getting caught is heavily outweighed by the advantages of ignoring the procedure, then you might as well take the risk.

6. Ignore obsolete procedures. Corporate procedures tend to be like government programs. They never get eliminated once they are approved, even when they're outdated and no longer serve any useful purpose. Many procedures can be ignored simply because they no longer serve the purpose for which they were intended.

7. Work around burdensome procedures. Even when you have to comply with directives, you can simplify matters by looking for shortcuts in meeting the requirements. The longer a directive or procedure is, the more loopholes there are likely to be in terms of complying with it. By opting to minimally comply, you will lessen your burden considerably.

8. Put the job before the process. Many times you will find that the burden of red tape can be minimized by doing it concurrently or after the fact. Often, such things as routine sign-offs and approvals can be obtained later, by justifying your request for after-the-fact approval based on the need to get the job done right away. In fact, sometimes you may have your boss or upper-level management say, "I don't care how it's done, as long as it is." Even when this isn't openly expressed, it's often a silent agenda to be followed. When it comes to the choice of getting the work accomplished, or following every policy, procedure, and directive, down to the most insignificant detail, you'll seldom be criticized too severely for cutting red tape.

NOTE: There are certain policies, rules, regulations, and directives that should always be closely observed. These include those involving compliance with federal and state laws, local ordinances, as well as internal directives involving health, safety, and other personnel matters. The recommendations in this section apply basically to internal operating procedures, which tend to be universally applied within an organization even though they don't have across-the-board relevance. As a result, they pose an undue burden where they don't apply which is an impediment to the productive performance of your duties.

6.5

How to Cope with Unreasonable Demands on Your Department

No matter how productive your department is, there will always be added pressure to do just a little bit more. Sometimes, you will even be asked to do more with fewer people, just as though you possessed a magical wand to transform reasonable requests into instant compliance. These requests may come from your boss, or perhaps from some other department which your group supports. Whatever the source, when the request is unreasonable you have to know how to respond. There are any number of ways this can be done, including:

- *Don't set yourself up.* Always keep your people busy, even during periods of relative quiet. If necessary, conduct training sessions, or other activities, rather than letting employees sit idle. Otherwise, you're a sitting duck for more work.

- *Plead an overload.* One of the best ways to avoid getting stuck with additional duties is to be able to say you're already too busy. Naturally, you should be in a position to prove this assertion if you're challenged to do so. It helps if you have the facts and figures to support your contention. It's even better when these can be used to show workload on a favorable comparative basis with other groups doing similar work within the company.

- *Just say "No."* You may be cooperative by nature, and it's an admirable trait, but there is a limit to this, as with everything else in life. So learn when to say, "I'd like to help you out, but I'm just too busy."

Otherwise, you'll end up being everyone's dumping ground. Naturally, this tactic won't work with your boss, but it's entirely appropriate to do this with those peers who are always looking for a soft-hearted sucker to bail them out.

- *Ask for more help.* It's always useful to ask for additional help when you need it, even though you know you will be refused due to budgetary constraints or other reasons. Your boss is less likely to ask you to assume additional responsibilities if it means once again listening to your pleas for more people.

- *Get concessions.* You know that dreaded weekly report, or some similar distasteful task that you hate to do? If your boss starts to overload you with work, ask for some form of concession. Say something such as, "I could probably handle that, if I didn't have to spend so much time on these weekly reports." Bingo, the boss gives them to someone else, or even does them himself.

- *Make trade-offs.* This works especially well where there are fluctuating workloads. Have your people help in another department in exchange for them helping you when you need it.

- *Give an unacceptable alternative.* If your boss wants to give you an additional assignment, say something such as, "I won't be able to complete the priority projects if I have to do this." If what you're complaining about is an essential and/or highly visible task, the odds are your boss will seek out someone else. But even if he still gives you additional duties, if the priority project isn't finished on schedule, he's on the hook, not you.

- *Do something dramatic.* Appear visibly upset, or state the unfairness of asking you to assume any more duties than you already have. This will work, especially if you have built a reputation as a team player who is always willing to pitch in and help. The natural reaction of a boss is to think, "Gee, I guess I've overloaded Jane with work. I'll have to see who else I can get."

- *Change and cope.* Sometimes you will just have to accept additional work, even though it's straining your ability to handle it. When this happens, look for ways to take shortcuts and otherwise minimize the impact.

6.6

Several Easy Ways to Overcome Skeptics and Critics

There's no faster way to frustrate your willingness to make suggestions than to have one idea after another rejected. A natural resistance to change, office politics, and the self-interest of others, are just a few of the reasons why solid suggestions are often criticized by others. However, the major obstacle to gaining acceptance of your ideas may just be a failure to think about the right approach toward converting all of the skeptics to supporters.

This is a hurdle that can be overlooked, especially when an idea is simple to understand, promises tangible benefits, and is easy to implement. Unfortunately, proponents of practical ideas often discover that suggesting solutions without first planning how to counter objections, opens the door for critics and skeptics. To avoid this hazard, the first step in gaining acceptance of your views is to be prepared to counter criticism. Here's how it can be done:

1. The initial step in preparing to offer a suggestion for change is to be your own critic. First of all, decide who must be convinced in order for your idea to be adopted. The greater the number of people in the approval process, the greater the likelihood that you will encounter objections.

2. Don't overlook steps in the approval process that can lead to defeat by default. For example, one particular person may appear to be the sole authority required for approval, but other people may play intermediate roles in the approval process. Therefore, it's not just a case of convincing the final authority, since intervening reviewers may shoot your suggestion down before it ever gets that far. In fact, the larger your company is, the greater the number of people who may be wired into the decision-making loop.

3. Avoid the trap of picking the people who must be sold on an idea by simply relying on where people are on the organization chart. Every company has people who possess power above and beyond their official capacity. The reasons can range from expertise in a given area, to personal friendship with the decision-maker. For these reasons, it pays to be

aware of anyone who may have out-of-the-loop power to influence the decision on your suggestion.

4. Once you identify the individuals that will have a say in passing judgment on your suggestion, the next step is to decide whether they will be supporters or detractors. This is guesswork to some extent, but you can frequently pinpoint obvious supporters and opponents based upon the content of your suggestion, as well as its potential impact on particular individuals and groups within the company.

5. If it appears that your idea will meet heavy opposition, it may be helpful to seek a behind-the-scenes consensus on an informal basis. This simply requires kicking your suggestion around with potential supporters and opponents to try and determine the prospects for success if you decide to proceed.

6. Always be willing to modify your recommendations to accommodate suggestions made by people you hold discussions with. Incorporating the thoughts of others gives them a vested interest in seeing your idea adopted. This will solidify support and give you active allies to help further your cause.

7. Be generous in giving credit to others for their contributions when you seek formal approval. This can spell the difference between approval and rejection.

8. If it's feasible to do so, always ask for more than you expect to get. This will give you room to make concessions to critics.

9. Always try to present your ideas in person. A personal approach is less likely to be rejected. and it will give you the opportunity to counter objections the minute they arise. Written requests for approval tend to move slower, which, among other things, gives opponents time to organize their thoughts in opposition.

10. Be as assertive as possible without alienating anyone when you pitch an idea. Let your enthusiasm show, and communicate your ideas in a positive manner. Sell the benefits of accepting your suggestion, particularly any advantages that will accrue to those whose approval you seek.

11. Whenever it's practical to do so, always have a fallback position. That way, if you lose the battle on an idea, an alternative may be easier to sell.

12. Naturally, the extent of the planning done to sell an idea should be commensurate with its importance. However, even routine suggestions should be well thought out. Otherwise, you may face a credibility gap on those rare occasions when you pitch your most important recommendations.

6.7

⇓

Tested Tips for Managing Your Boss

As a supervisor your primary focus is on efficiently managing the employees you supervise in the performance of their duties. Yet one of the fundamentals for your success that may get overlooked is the need to manage up, or in other words, effectively deal with your boss and other upper-level managers. But if you can't successfully manage up, then doing a good job at managing your department will just leave you wondering why your talents aren't recognized and rewarded.

What most people tend to forget is that dealing with a boss's individual personality is crucial to their future. Furthermore, getting a boss to appreciate your efforts isn't something that can be accomplished quickly, since it's a slow process to build a boss's confidence in your abilities. A few tactics for doing this are:

1. Know what your boss expects. One neglected method for maintaining good relations with a boss is to key on his or her work-related tendencies. One boss may want to be kept informed about everything, while another only wants to be consulted when a serious problem arises. Some people are detail-oriented, while others just look for results. When a boss has one tendency and a subordinate has the other, unnecessary friction can result. To avoid this, make a conscious effort to do things in terms of the boss's focus, rather than battling over different means to the same end. It's often this sort of personality clash over inconsequential matters that can stall your career at the starting gate.

2. When you're criticized by your boss, avoid being argumentative, even though you think you're right. Instead say something such as, "I see what you're saying and I'll attempt to change. The reason I was doing it that way was..." and go on to explain your reasoning. This type of

approach works well because your boss is probably tense and expecting an argument.

Just as you are reluctant to criticize your subordinates, your boss is just as hesitant about saying something critical to you. Consequently, your boss will be relieved when you don't react negatively. In fact, your positive response to criticism will characterize you as someone who listens and accepts advice. And as you know from dealing with your own employees, that sort of reaction is appreciated by a boss.

3. Don't conceal problems. It's often easier to avoid calling the boss's attention to problems and hope that they aren't noticed. However, no one likes surprises, and if your boss gets caught unawares because you didn't keep him posted, you won't be trusted in the future.

4. Whenever possible, bring your boss solutions—not just problems. Otherwise, your boss may well think he's being asked to do your job for you. Offer possible alternatives for solving the problem along with the pros and cons of each possible solution. If feasible, recommend what you consider to be the best alternative. However, whether or not you make a specific recommendation should reflect your boss's preferences. If he's the type that wants to make decisions without any suggestion as to which way to go, then defer to his judgment.

5. When you're the bearer of bad news, always have answers as to what went wrong, as well as what will be done to correct the situation. If the problem is the fault of your department, admit it, and be ready to tell your boss what you've done about it. If the problem lies elsewhere, be prepared with evidence to support your contention.

6. Don't take chances that will put your boss on the spot unless you have made him aware of the risks beforehand. This is particularly true for any action which would put your boss in the position of having to answer for something going wrong when he wasn't involved in the initial decision-making.

7. Make your boss look good in the eyes of others, and you'll look good in the eyes of your boss. You may feel cheated at having your boss get the credit for your accomplishments, but a good boss will always acknowledge the efforts of those who work for him. And even in instances where a boss doesn't do this, it still works to your advantage. After all, it's your immediate boss who controls your destiny, and even a boss who hogs the limelight will at least recognize your contribution

through the form of good performance reviews and pay raises. Beyond that, if you're consistently making a boss look better than is otherwise the case, it will be known to others where the good work is originating from.

8. Cover for your boss when something goes wrong. If your boss goofs, a good way to display loyalty is to divert attention from this by making the mistake an organizational one rather than leaving your boss to take the blame. How this is done will vary with the specifics of given situations. The main point is to always protect your boss from criticism whenever it's possible to do so. After all, everyone makes mistakes, and your boss will not only appreciate your support, but may also take the heat for you when you make an attention-getting error.

9. Don't make petty comparisons about your boss's actions to peers and/or subordinates. For example, if everyone is under pressure to work long hours, but your boss comes in late and leaves early, don't create resentment over this. Even if you dislike it, keep it to yourself. Who knows? Perhaps the boss is working long hours at home. And even if he isn't, it may be bad for morale, but it isn't your job to question it. That's what his boss is for.

10. Always try to predict your boss's reaction to decisions that you make. Thinking things through from your boss's perspective will help you to perform your job in a manner that's consistent with what your boss expects.

6.8

How to Deal with a New Boss

Although it's not an everyday event, periodically during your career you will be working for a new boss. Sometimes, it will result from your own initiative in changing jobs. On other occasions, it will be dictated by organizational changes, either beyond your control, or resulting from your promotion to a new position. Whatever the reason, the first few weeks will set the tone for this new working relationship to succeed or fail. Of course, if you get off on the wrong foot, you may be able to eventually turn matters around, but it takes much longer to do so. Therefore, it makes sense to invest the time and energy at the start to ensure that things run smoothly from the beginning.

Among the considerations to take into account when you have a new boss are the following:

1. Watch carefully to see what sort of management style the new boss uses. Some managers like to be briefed on everything, while others will essentially let you go it alone. Be careful here though, since even if your boss appears to be a hands-off manager, initially at least, he may tend to get more heavily involved in detail until he has a better idea of how everything functions. So on balance, it's better at the beginning to keep the boss posted on anything of significance.

2. Sometimes when a new boss arrives, there's a tendency for people to besiege them with every outstanding problem large or small. Naturally, anything urgent should be brought to the boss's attention, but beyond that, avoid trying to get approval for every minor matter that has been on the back burner. For problems that need to be considered by a new boss, always try to point out the pros and cons of the situation, as well as any hidden minefields that could cause trouble in the future.

3. You may have to temporarily adjust your working hours, since new bosses often work long hours, at least until they get a handle on their new job. It's prudent for you to do likewise, since even though it may be inconvenient, the payoff will be worthwhile. This is especially true if other supervisors stick with their normal schedule, since you will probably have opportunities for discussions with the new boss after everyone else has left for the day. And the more you talk to your new boss, the sooner a good working relationship will develop.

4. Never circumvent a new boss by going over or around him for any approvals required by higher-level managers. Even if this was standard practice in the past, avoid it, and run everything through your own boss first. Doing otherwise, even though it's well-intentioned, can send a signal that you're trying to undermine your boss's authority.

5. Look for ways to make a new boss look good from the start. Doing this will enhance your reputation as a team player, and also assure the boss that you want him to succeed.

6. Go the extra mile in covering the details of work that you discuss with a new boss. What is routine to an experienced hand may be unfamiliar to someone new to the operation.

7. Don't show your new boss up in front of others. Avoid correcting what a new boss may say, or interrupting to respond when it appears your boss doesn't have the answer to questions.

8. Let a boss know about your accomplishments and abilities, but do so without appearing to be bragging.

9. Don't be critical of others to a new boss, since it may label you as a back-stabber. The boss will quickly form judgments of people, and attempting to influence his opinion may backfire if he decides you were being unfairly critical of someone.

10. Support a new boss in discussions with your own subordinates. How you feel about a boss will influence the attitudes of your employees, so emphasize the positive right from the beginning.

6.9

Prudent Ways to Deal with a Difficult Boss

If you have a great boss, you may be inclined to pass up reading this particular section. However, don't be too quick to jump to jump to judgment, since appearances aren't always what they seem to be. In fact, your seemingly super boss may be undermining you in ways you're not aware of. So even if it's just for reassurance, you may want to read on. After all, both times and bosses change, and even if you're in good hands now, you may not fare so well with a future boss.

On the other hand, you may be silently suffering at the present time from trying to work with a boss who is impossible to deal with. That's unfortunate, but unless you adopt a strategy to cope with it the situation may get worse before it gets better. So let's look at some tactics for coping when you've been dealt a bad hand in terms of a boss.

1. If your boss doesn't like you, take a look at the traits of those he favors. You may discover some clues on ways you can adjust your actions to more closely match the demands of your boss.

2. If your boss dumps difficult assignments on you without giving any instructions, you're being set up to take the blame if anything goes wrong. When this happens, try to get the boss's input as you proceed

and document everything he tells you. Even if he rebuffs your attempts to get him involved, whenever possible, put requests in writing that offer alternatives on how to proceed and ask for his guidance. If this fails, at least pepper him with memos on the progress of projects. That way, if push comes to shove, he can't say he didn't know what was going on.

3. Unlike a boss who avoids giving guidance, you may have a boss who insists upon making every decision to the extent that your work is often delayed while you wait for his response. A good way to cope with this isn't to resist these demands, but rather to flood your boss with details. He will then come to assume that you are just as detail-conscious as he is. As a result, he won't monitor your compliance with his demands as closely as any of your peers who choose to resist his efforts.

    This will help you avoid the boss's meddling when it would threaten getting a project completed on schedule. The chances are the boss won't notice, since you are usually so conscientious about keeping him posted. But even if he does, plead forgetfulness by saying something such as, "Gee, I don't know how I forgot that, Jim. I've never done that before." Since you're probably the only one that doesn't show resentment at not being allowed any free rein, it's unlikely you will be severely criticized.

4. If your boss likes to bully and badger people, stand your ground without losing your cool. Never get involved in arguing with a bully, but calmly let it be known that you won't be intimidated. This usually works, since bullies tend to concentrate their efforts on those who are easily manipulated by this type of behavior.

5. Your boss may be difficult to deal with simply because of incompetence. Many bosses are promoted into management positions because they were good workers or followers. Unfortunately, that doesn't mean they are automatically good leaders. Your boss may belittle people as a defense mechanism to cover up his inadequacies. If you resist being intimidated, the odds are that you will not be the target of an insecure boss's tirades.

    Basically, stand your ground and let the anger run. Then, calmly resume the discussion as if nothing had happened. A major problem with incompetent bosses is a tendency to place the blame for everything on their subordinates. As a result, disciplinary actions become a favorite weapon with warnings and job dismissals being dispensed as frequently as paychecks. The reason for this is simple. This type of boss uses employees as scapegoats for his own lack of knowledge. If you have this type of boss, it's important to document your actions and work well with others to get your talents recognized. Otherwise, you will be a sitting duck on the boss's firing line.

6. Another breed of difficult bosses are workaholics who insist that everyone work sixty or more hours a week just because they do. If you're facing this predicament, you may have to sit down and explain your situation to the boss. Tell him that you're certainly a team player and want to do your part, but that you also have responsibilities beyond work to contend with. Try to offer some form of compromise and/or accommodation. For example, suggest that you're willing to take work home, or perhaps offer changes in the way work is done that will lighten your load. Be careful to avoid being accusatory such as implying or stating that, "You're working us like robots." Instead, focus the conversation on your intent to cooperate, but within the constraints of other responsibilities.

7. Never openly criticize an incompetent boss to his superior, since in most cases, that's probably the person who selected your boss for his position. Very few people win the battle by going over a boss's head. It can be done, but the odds don't favor it. Sooner or later, incompetent bosses are often discovered and eased out of their positions. If not, you can always bide your time until you see an opportunity open up, either within your own company, or elsewhere.

8. Try to use timing in dealing with a difficult boss. Even miserable people have an occasional good moment. Look for days when things have been going well for your boss to approach him on something that is controversial. Also look for certain times of the day that are more favorable for meeting with your boss. For instance, you may discover that the boss who is an ogre during regular working hours is easy to talk to when everyone else has left the office for the day.

6.10

What to Do When You Work
for Foreign Bosses

Working for a foreign boss isn't necessarily better or worse than reporting to any other boss—it's just different. What's more, the differences may be so subtle they're not even recognizable unless you're looking for them.

However, they can exist, since cultural differences can involve everything from management style to promotion prospects. Therefore, it's crucial to be able to recognize and cope with these differences when they exist. Otherwise, you may find yourself bewildered at why your apparent successes aren't always looked upon as such. Here are several elements you should learn to adjust to if you work for a foreign boss:

1. Many foreign bosses work long hours and may expect you to do likewise. One reason for longer hours is that it may be part of the cultural work ethic of the foreigner. For example, the Japanese are noted for working long days. In other instances, a foreign boss may have fewer outside interests when working in this country, and may therefore substitute work for forgone social and leisure activities. In still other situations, a foreign boss assigned to a position in this country is likely to be more career-focused due to the desire to succeed in a foreign assignment.

2. You may find it advantageous if you expect to have a foreign boss for any length of time to learn his or her native language. This will not only impress the boss, but it will also give you a distinct advantage over other supervisors who don't make this sort of commitment.

3. Always make an extra effort to be polite when dealing with a foreign boss. Every culture has its differences, and until you learn them, it's best to be cautious in both what you say, and how you say it.

4. Try to learn the fine points of how your foreign boss tends to operate. For instance, you may not receive on-the-spot decisions as you might expect from an American boss. Learning subtle differences in the style of managing will avoid drawing the wrong conclusion from the actions of a foreign boss.

5. You may not be able to operate as independently as you would like, since some foreign bosses may value consensus above individual initiative.

6. In some cultures it isn't considered polite to directly offer criticism as it's done in this country. Therefore, you may have to look for other signals to show that a boss is displeased with something you did. In the same vein, you may not always receive positive feedback such as praise.

7. Don't be hesitant about letting your boss know that you want to learn about managing people in accordance with his customs. You may also be able to pick up pointers from other supervisors who have worked for a foreign boss in the past.

8. If it appears feasible to do so, you may want to establish a social relationship with your boss. This sort of gesture is generally welcomed, and in addition to the job-related benefits, it will broaden your own education, as well as any of your family members who participate in social activities.

9. If the new boss has just recently arrived in the community, offer to be of whatever assistance you can in providing information on local resources such as shopping, recreational activities, and anything else which may be of interest. It's easy to assume that someone is taking care of these matters, but even if they are, there are continuing questions that arise whenever someone moves to a new community from a foreign country. Even if your assistance isn't sought, the fact that you reached out to help will be appreciated.

10. Above all else, if your foreign boss doesn't speak fluent English, make sure you understand any directions you are given. Don't hesitate to ask for clarification if necessary. Conversely, try speaking more slowly and clearly if your new boss has trouble understanding what you say.

11. It helps to practice being patient when you have a foreign boss. What at first may seem strange to you will quickly become routine once you learn how to bridge the culture gap which may exist initially.

6.11

Several Rules for Scoring Points with Superiors

The ability to keep your boss and other top-level managers satisfied with your performance depends, of course, on how well you do your job. However, satisfactory performance alone isn't always enough to get you selected for the next promotion that comes along. That's one main reason why many supervisors year after year are evaluated as "promotable," yet never actually get promoted. This often leads to grumbling about office politics and favoritism, but unfortunately griping won't help fatten a paycheck, while knowing how to score points with superiors will.

Many supervisors adopt an attitude of, "My performance, not my personality, should be what counts." That may be true in an ideal world, but it doesn't always work in the real world. It also tends to overlook the fact that in most cases there is very little difference in the job performance of people being considered for promotion. Except for blatant examples of favoritism, most candidates for promotion are doing a good job. This narrows the choice for promotions down to more subjective factors such as whom the person doing the selecting prefers to work with.

Even if a future promotion doesn't interest you, it's still worth the effort to get along well with superiors. Otherwise, you may find yourself having to panhandle for people and mooch for materials to keep your department running smoothly. The end result is that you have to learn how to make yourself look good to your bosses, rather than taking it for granted that your performance will speak for itself. Here are some tactics for doing just that.

1. Show initiative. Don't worry about whether something that needs to be done is your responsibility or not. A "can do" attitude by someone who is willing to take on assignments without quibbling over whether or not it's their responsibility is a trait that is always appreciated by superiors.

2. Look for projects that will gain you exposure throughout the company. Making your talents known to a wide range of higher-level managers will increase the number of people who can exert a positive influence on your career.

3. Don't ignore volunteer activities that give you the opportunity to get to know top executives. This may be nothing more significant than serving on the committee that is in charge of the annual company picnic.

4. Work at doing what is valued most by superiors, rather than what you consider to be most important. For example, keeping inventories low may be of great significance to top management, while higher inventory levels may make it easier for you to do your job.

   Frequently, the tendency is to concentrate on the job at hand, while ignoring higher-level policy until it becomes an issue. But by that time, it's usually too late to do anything about it except to take corrective action. The supervisor who ultimately looks good from upper management's perspective is the one who had the foresight to see what top management's priorities were and to act accordingly. In the inventory example, it's the supervisor with low inventories when top management decides to check inventory levels that scores the points.

5. Don't attempt to coast along on your past accomplishments. You may be a veteran supervisor with a superior record of achievement, but never forget that performance is viewed from a "What have you done for me

lately?" perspective. For this reason, it's important not to rest on your laurels, or up-and-coming go-getters will quickly pass you by.

6. Don't overlook the little things when it comes to impressing superiors. People tend to be praised for only major accomplishments, but they are sometimes viewed critically for relatively minor matters. As a result, something such as being pegged as having an unpleasant personality can override your skills at getting the job done. Consequently, deviating from the mainstream in terms of appearance or personality can over-shadow your accomplishments. This is especially true with superiors you don't deal with on a regular basis, who are less likely to be familiar with your work ethic.

6.12

Basic Practices for Coping with Customer Complaints

Your job may require you to deal with customers in the traditional sense of someone who is buying a product or service. But even if you don't, you still have customers for whatever function your department performs, at least in the sense that the output of your unit is of value to someone. It may be no further away than the next step in an assembly process, but nevertheless the quality and service you provide is of real concern to the recipient of your out-put. As a result, you will receive complaints in one form or another if there is any dissatisfaction—either real or perceived. And how you handle these com-plaints will to a large extent determine how your performance is judged by those you serve. So whatever the source of complaints may be, let's look at some useful practices for dealing with them effectively.

1. Don't immediately disagree with someone who has a complaint. Remain calm even if you're right. After all, an argument won't solve anything.

2. Let people with complaints express their thoughts and listen carefully to what they have to say. You may discover what they are complaining about isn't really the problem at all. For instance, another supervisor may come to you complaining about the shoddy work done by one of your people. However, as he discusses the problem it becomes evident that instead of workmanship, his real complaint is that he feels your employee was rude to him.

3. Never interrupt people with complaints even if you already know the solution to their problem. When people complain they are often looking for satisfaction as well as a solution. Solving complaints that leave a customer unhappy only sets the stage for further complaints in the future.

4. Train your subordinates how to respond to complaints, and give them the authority to take action when necessary. To encourage employees to take this responsibility seriously, you may want to include this as a performance evaluation factor if the nature of the work you supervise is subject to a large number of complaints.

5. If the same people consistently complain, try to take measures to improve the quality of the work done for them.

6. If there has been an obvious mistake made by your department, readily admit it, apologize, and explain what action will be taken to prevent it from happening again. People with complaints aren't willing to accept excuses, but they will generally calm down when they see your readiness to accept blame.

7. Emphasize what you can do for people when a mistake has been made. Don't start off a reply with a response such as, "I can't get those reworked today..." Instead say, "I will have those reworked by tomorrow." Pointing out what you can't do will only encourage the other party to ask, "Why not?" This sort of back and forth can quickly dissolve into a heated disagreement.

8. When feasible, it's useful to offer alternative solutions to resolve complaints. This makes it easier for you, and it makes the person complaining part of the decision-making process. Therefore, they are less likely to think they are being offered a "Take it or leave it" response to what will be done about their complaint.

9. Look for ways that can speed up the process for resolving complaints. The sooner complaints are dealt with the less irritated the complaining party is going to be.

10. Don't look upon complaints just from their negative aspect. They also serve as a means of identifying recurring problems that need to be addressed.

11. The introduction of new equipment and/or procedures is likely to initially result in an increase in errors which may bring about complaints.

Explain to your customers about the new equipment, and ask for feedback on errors to determine if they can be pinpointed to a particular function and/or individual.

12. Continually solicit comments from your customers on the performance of work being performed by your department. This can help head off problems before they become serious.

6.13

The Basic Steps for Bargaining with Anyone

You may not have to bargain with people on an everyday basis, but on occasion you may have to bargain with a boss or other department to get what you want. You can call it bargaining, negotiating, haggling, or wheeling and dealing. What it's called doesn't matter. What does count is your ability to use bargaining techniques to get the best deal you can in a variety of circumstances. In fact, you may bargain more frequently than you sometimes realize. For example, if the boss asks you to do something and you say you can't do it because of other work commitments, it's likely the two of you will reach some agreement as to what gets done and what doesn't. On other occasions you may make deals to trade supplies, or lend or borrow personnel with another department head. The advantage of knowing some simple bargaining techniques is that it will give you the edge in getting what you want from others. Here are a few tactics that will help you accomplish this.

1. Don't be hesitant about bargaining with your boss and others. Naturally, everything you're asked to do doesn't call for making trade-offs. Nevertheless, there are times when a little bit of bargaining is appropriate and if you're hesitant about making the attempt you end up with nothing. Since that's where you'll be even if you try and fail, why not at least make the effort?

2. Probably the most common failure to bargain with a boss concerns an overload of work. Frequently, people take on more work than they can handle, and then when they fall behind the boss is told about it. Usually, at this stage of the game, the boss will likely tell them to do the best they can. Meanwhile, the boss may be wondering to himself if the person is overworked or just isn't keeping up the pace.

On the other hand, if a boss approaches you with more work and you then try to bargain for some form of relief, you are immediately putting the boss on notice that you're overburdened. This leaves the boss with one of several choices:

- Give you more help.

- Transfer some of your work elsewhere.

- Find someone else to do the new assignment he is trying to give you.

Even if he doesn't budge and hands you the new assignment anyway, at least he's on notice that you're overworked. Therefore, if something serious such as a deadline is missed, you're still in a better position than you would have been if you didn't try to bargain your way out of the hole.

3. When you bargain with people, always try to present them with the alternative of agreeing with what you want, or accepting something which is less satisfactory. For example, "I think this order should be delayed. If we do it now, we'll miss our production quotas for the month. You know how top management goes berserk when that happens."

4. Try to bargain to get future commitments. For instance, if you aren't happy with your latest pay raise, try to have your boss set specific goals for you to achieve, with the understanding that your next pay raise will be higher. This tactic can be used for any number of things, such as getting additional help for your department. If your request is turned down initially, bargain for a specific commitment in the future.

5. Bargain for more than you want, so you can settle for less. This gives the other person a feeling of victory, since they didn't give you precisely what you wanted. For example, if you need more help, ask for two or three people, and you may get the one you need.

6. Always be prepared to support any position you're taking with facts. Otherwise, you won't get very far if what you're asking for is challenged.

7. Always have the other person's viewpoint in mind when you bargain. What are they likely to settle for? What is the best approach to take with this particular person?

8. Look for simple keys that will give you an advantage in bargaining to get what you want. Approaching people when they're in the right frame of mind is one such factor, while timing is another.

9. Always look for and be ready to point out the advantage to the other party of giving you what you want.

6.14

✤

Ten Methods for Getting Others to Agree to Your Requests

No matter how major or minor the topic, getting people to respond positively to your requests makes your job a lot easier. Of course, you can't expect total agreement on everything you ask for, but increasing the number of affirmative replies is possible. Largely, it's a function of using the best methods for getting favorable replies. Here are a few you can try:

1. Be confident about what you're asking for. If you're not convinced of the validity of your request, you can't expect to be able to convince the other person. At the same time, don't be overbearing about pushing to get agreement on your request. This, in the absence of anything else, may be just the reason someone needs to say "No."

2. Provide sufficient information to make it easy for someone to agree with your request. By the same token, don't overdo it, since the easier it is to understand what you want, the more likely that you'll get prompt agreement.

3. Whenever possible, make it worthwhile for the other person to agree to your request. For example, suppose you want another supervisor to work for you next Saturday. They may not be particularly enthusiastic, but might agree if you say you'll cover for them the next two Saturdays they're scheduled to work.

4. If it can be done, always make your requests directly to the person who has the authority to act on your request. This isn't always possible, of course, since some decisions you seek will require multiple approvals from people at various levels of the organizational structure.

5. Try to make requests more palatable by incorporating the thoughts and suggestions of the person you are making the request to.

6. Get other people to support your requests. In some situations this is mandatory, especially where approval is needed from upper management

or other departments. Normally, in many of these situations, your boss, and possibly others, will have to give their concurrence.

7. Lay the groundwork beforehand. If you're planning on making a significant request, such as one requiring the expenditure of corporate funds, it helps to sound out people before you actually make a formal request. Not only will this give you a chance to further your cause, but it may also give you some clues as to the best way to proceed.

8. If someone is going to refuse a request, if it's practical, try to get them to agree on a conditional basis. Say something similar to "Let's do it and see how it works. We can make any adjustments later." It isn't right, but sometimes people just like to exercise their power by rejecting requests. Using a conditional approach gives them that opportunity, without completely sidetracking what you want to do.

9. Never become argumentative if you're turned down on a request. Instead, regroup and refocus your request to overcome any objections that have been raised.

10. Don't give up when a request that matters to you is turned down. The more you pursue something, the better the odds that you'll ultimately be successful.

Chapter Seven

HANDLING HIRING, FIRING, AND OTHER PERSONNEL MATTERS

The range of personnel issues you have to deal with as a supervisor cover the spectrum from hiring new employees to firing those who for one reason or another don't work out. Then, there are the many day-to-day issues such as dealing with promotions, requests for time off, and the need to reward good workers for their efforts.

Since you're the number one information resource for the people you supervise, these activities have to cover everything from getting a new worker settled into the job, to explaining salary and fringe benefit questions workers may have. Then, you have sensitive areas to deal with such as how to handle the situation when an employee has a personal problem.

Along with these specific areas, there are any number of other issues you have to cope with, including the use of part-time and temporary help within your unit. All in all, some very challenging tasks which can spell either success or failure for both you and your subordinates. The pointers in this chapter will help guide you in managing these essential aspects of your supervisory responsibilities.

151

❦

Six Proven Ways to Finesse Salary-Related Questions

One of the more sensitive subjects that you have to deal with is worker requests for pay increases, and other associated salary complaints. Some of these inquiries may be valid, while others originate from rumors implying that justice isn't being served. A typical example would be something such as, "Mary earns thirty dollars a week more than Joe for doing the same job," which quickly brings Joe into your office when he hears this piece of gossip. Other major sources of salary gripes include comparisons with what other companies pay, along with a tendency for workers to assume they're under-paid—even when their job performance may leave you wondering why they're being paid at all.

Whether questions on wages are valid or invalid, it's a touchy subject to deal with. This means a great deal of diplomacy has to be combined with a dose of reality when you're trying to dispense with these inquiries. Several tactics that may prove useful in this regard are:

1. *Refer to company policy.* As you have probably experienced, employees will give all kinds of reasons as to why they deserve more money than they're making. It isn't stretching the truth too much to say that just showing up for work is a good enough reason for some workers to appear at your office door seeking a boost in pay. Many request for a pay raise—or a protest over what the employee considers to be an inade-quate salary increase—can be quickly disposed of by referring to the company policy on pay increases.

   For instance, if Joe Greedy received a 5% increase which was in line with corporate salary recommendations, and he complains about not getting a higher raise, point out that the increase complies with salary guide-lines. Very few employees will argue further, since they assume there is nothing you can do even if you did agree to their request.

2. *Use non-salary arguments.* Either because your company tends to pay lower than competitors, or you have an outstanding worker who deserves a bigger raise than you're able to grant, you may have to go beyond money itself to make your case. This can be done by pointing out the non-financial advantages of the job which the worker doesn't

realize, or chooses to ignore, until you bring them out. These can include everything from outstanding fringe benefits to steady employment. Try to do this in such a way that it relates specifically to the individual worker.

For instance, if your company has on-site day care which you know the employee uses, mention this. Refer to both the expense of this benefit to the company, and the amount of money the worker would have to spend for such care elsewhere—along with the convenience and emotional benefits of having the on-site facility.

If it so happens that your company has a history of steady employment, this too is a telling argument to convince employees that salary alone isn't the most important issue. They may, of course, know this to be true, but that won't deter some people from seeking a higher pay raise at least until you refresh their memory.

In individual cases there may be other personal benefits which are compensating factors for a below-average salary. These can range from an easy commute to flexible working hours. The point is that with a little thought you can often convince employees unhappy with their earnings that the grass elsewhere isn't as green as it looks.

3. *Show the fairness of the person's salary.* Some employees suffer from misconceptions about the earnings for their type of job. They hear from a friend, who supposedly knows someone doing the same type of work elsewhere, and is getting paid $5,000.00 more a year. Many of these tales are accepted as fact when they often are little more than cocktail lounge gossip, with the salary figures going up equally as fast as the drinks go down. The best way to quickly put these to rest is by being able to show what comparable salaries are for the job in question. If you do a little research, you shouldn't have any problem obtaining this type of information. In fact, you may not have to go any further than your own human resources department, since companies of any size keep close tabs on what competitors pay for different types of jobs. Once you're able to show the unhappy worker that salary levels in the company are pretty much the same as elsewhere, the discussion should wind down quickly.

An offshoot of people trying to compare their earnings with jobs at other companies is the frequent attempt to make comparisons with other workers within their own department. Whenever someone starts to do this, quickly state that what anyone else earns is totally irrelevant, and insist that the conversation be limited to the worker's own salary.

4. *Counter claims of superior performance.* One of the trickiest arguments that can be made by a worker seeking a pay raise is a claim of superior job performance. This is particularly true when the employee is really doing a far better job than his or her co-workers. You don't want to stifle someone's initiative to excel, so you have to turn down the worker's request with reasons that have some validity. Your reasoning may only be reluctantly accepted, but if you handle it right, the worker will continue to meet high standards of performance.

Whenever workers argue that their performance merits a higher pay raise, ask for the facts that support their claims. If employees try to rationalize their performance levels with little or no evidence to support their position, you can fairly readily resolve the matter. What you want to do is agree that their performance is good, but not as good as they claim. Essentially, you want to disagree, but in a non-critical way with a response such as this: "I agree that you're doing a decent job, Martha, but you're very talented and I think there's room for you to do even better. Don't you agree?" The answer you will most likely get is some form of "Yes, but...", since very few people will argue very hard when they tell them they're even better than they think.

Of course, since they also want more money, their response will probably be some variation of agreeing with you about their abilities, but asserting that their performance is still good enough to deserve a pay boost. At this point, if they don't have any firm evidence to support their position, you can say something similar to this: "What we're really talking about here, Martha, is a difference of opinion. Let's do this. Over the next review period, why don't you make notes showing where you have done anything significant. That way, we will have something to work with when we sit down to talk. It will also help me, since as you know, I need higher approval for pay raises that exceed certain levels." Some variation of this approach should send most people away determined to prove to you when the next pay review rolls around that they do deserve a better raise.

The toughest case to deal with in this area is someone who really has excelled, knows it, and knows that you know it. However, pay constraints may prohibit you from rewarding the worker. The best thing to do here is to more or less tell it like it is. It also helps if you can find some other non-monetary means of rewarding the individual. Perhaps additional responsibilities, or a better job assignment can be used to ease the pain. Another possibility is to see if you can get the person transferred to a higher-paying position in another department. Obviously, you will lose a good employee, but that might happen anyway if they decide to look elsewhere for a job.

5. *Use lack of qualifications.* Sometimes when a worker pushes for a pay hike, you can justify turning it down based on a lack of qualifications. Frequently, workers assume they are able to perform the duties of a more complex job simply because they work in close proximity to people holding those positions. This is most common where employees work in a support function to the job they aspire to.

One such example might be a clerk who performs clerical duties for one or more buyers. By virtue of observing what the buyers do over a period of time, the reasoning becomes, "Hey, that's not hard. I can do that." Perhaps they could, although whether they could do so at a satisfactory level of performance is a different question entirely. After all, anyone can hit a golf ball, but very few people can do it well enough to become a professional golfer.

This "I can do it" reasoning is a common human trait which we all may use at one time or another. In fact, it's admirable to be ambitious and to aspire to bettering ourselves. The problem is that while some people do what is necessary to gain the experience and/or education to reach their goals, others lack the motivation, energy, and/or ability to progress beyond their present job. Some folks accept this, others continue to daydream, and a few decide that they're qualified for a higher-paid position even though they may not be performing well in the job they currently hold. And it's these workers that will urge you to upgrade their job.

Fending off an unqualified worker who is seeking a pay raise is fairly easy when you can simply cite a qualification for the job that they don't have. These requirements are generally in the formal job description, which you should show to the employee. This not only adds emphasis to what you say, but it also helps prevent resentment by a worker who otherwise might think you're making excuses.

It gets a little trickier if there are already one or more employees presently holding the position who don't meet the formal qualifications. This happens when outstanding workers are selected for a position even though they may not meet the minimal requirements. A savvy worker may mention this when you use the lack of qualifications argument with a response such as this: "Miriam doesn't meet the minimum education requirements and she's a senior clerk." Here, you first of all have to state clearly that comparisons with other workers aren't relevant. Then, go on to point out that only extraordinary performance and extensive experience would be accepted as a basis for an exception to the minimum qualifications. Tactfully point out that the employee's performance and/or experience don't meet the criteria. Since you're not dealing with a superstar, if the worker persists, it should be easy to pinpoint areas where the worker's performance needs improvement.

6. *Counter employee contentions in a reasonable way.* Whenever you turn down a request for a pay raise, it's essential to do so without giving the appearance of being unreasonable. Most workers will tacitly accept your reasoning if it's carefully explained. On the other hand, don't let yourself be swayed by emotional appeals such as, "I'm being threatened with foreclosure by my bank." Personal needs aren't a consideration for giving raises, so focus of the duties on the job and don't be led astray by pleas of desperation.

7.2

How to Fend Off Promotion
Requests from Workers

It's certainly appropriate to encourage employees to strive for future promotional opportunities. However, in doing so, there are a number of problems you will have to confront. First of all, the positions you supervise may not offer much of a chance for advancement. As a result, many workers may recognize this and not bother you with questions related to career advancement. However, there may be a few who view their current job as a stepping stone to another position within the company. Therefore, the necessity of dealing with inquiries about promotional possibilities will exist to some degree even where you supervise people in what are essentially dead-end jobs.

Where the opportunity for promotion is available, you may find yourself faced with problems ranging from counseling employees on how they can improve their promotion prospects, to fending off promotion requests from duds who aren't even doing their present job right. Let's consider some of the different types of individuals who think they deserve a promotion and look at how to deal with them:

1. *The hot shot.* This is the type of character who wants to run the company from the minute they are hired. They will perpetually tell you what's wrong with the organization and what should be done about it. They have little interest in working their way up the career ladder, preferring instead to figure a way to catapult to the top. The ego of this breed of go-getter matches their ambition to the extent that they will never admit to making a mistake. They prefer to blame things on others and spend more time playing politics than doing their job.

   These characters can be a supervisor's nightmare, since they're not at all above back-stabbing their boss. Hot shots generally come looking for a promotion before they are ready for one. When this happens, they aren't inclined to be easily dissuaded. The best overall approach is to let them spout off about their perceived virtues, and then quietly state that although they have the potential for promotion, they are still lacking in experience. Your contention isn't likely to be accepted, but avoid getting angry and/or involved in a debate. Instead, let hot shots prove how good they really are by giving them the most difficult assignments you can come up with. If they fail, you succeed in poking a hole in their ego—at least temporarily. On the other hand, if they do a good job, keep dishing out the tough tasks until they deserve the promotion they sought prematurely.

   Incidentally, hot shots will typically react to this approach in one of two ways. They will either plunge into the task you assign with a determination to prove how good they are, or will go off sulking to look for a job somewhere else. You win either way, since if they do decide to take a hike it will make your days a little happier.

2. *The self-proclaimed genius.* This type of individual is a first cousin of the hot shot, the major difference being that while hot shots can excel if they put their mind to it, the self-proclaimed genius can't hack it, but unfortunately doesn't know it. This kind of character will claim to know how to do every job in the department except their own. They're prone to dishing out free advice to their peers on anything and everything, a trait that will sooner or later make them highly unpopular.

When these characters come looking for a promotion, the difficulty isn't in turning them down; it's in doing it with tact. It's a real headache having to listen to someone tell you how great they are when they botch every job you give them. Fortunately, these types aren't very sensitive, so don't waste any sleep over being too tactful. Simply tell them how their performance has to improve before they can even be considered for promotion.

3. *The minor league whiz.* Many people perform very well at a certain level, but just don't possess what it takes to move up. This is the type of person who does the routine tasks of their job well, but always has trouble in dealing with anything out of the ordinary. It can be difficult to explain to this sort of person why they can't presently be considered for promotion. They may assert—and it's probably true—that they work harder than other people. That notwithstanding, they probably can't handle the more diverse and difficult duties that a promotion would bring. The best way to handle this is to give them a trial period handling more complex work when they ask about getting promoted. When they realize they can't handle the harder jobs, the quest for a promotion will be forgotten.

4. *The credentials buff.* This type looks great on paper, has all of the qualifications to be promoted, but doesn't perform up to expectations. Sometimes people in this category may have held a higher position in some other company. The lack of performance may be general, or it may be limited to one specific trait, such as a poor attendance record, or the inability to get along with other people. The biggest problem with these people is that they tend to overlook their one glaring weakness. All you have to do here is to carefully point out their failing and let them know it's hindering their promotion prospects. It's also prudent to carefully monitor their future performance in the defective area, otherwise they will be back again in six months asserting they have corrected the problem.

5. *The seniority slouch.* Many people are promoted after gaining extensive experience on the job, even though they lack one of the major formal qualifications such as the minimum education requirements. Their performance will compensate for this, and they go on to perform admirably at a higher-level position.

The main problem in this area is that some people think that seniority alone entitles them to be promoted, irrespective of their potential ability and performance on the job. It is these folks that you have to dissuade when they come calling looking for a promotion. They are likely to counter any argument about lack of qualifications with examples of others who were promoted despite this handicap. Therefore, concentrate your arguments on a lack of performance sufficient to justify a promotion as the basis for not promoting those with a lot of seniority.

6. *The whiner.* You may have the misfortune to supervise a whiner who is always complaining about something. They will be the first one at your door when they hear someone else was promoted. These people are just plain annoying, so it's best to quickly dispense with their laments while your sanity is still intact. Just give them the facts about where their performance is lacking. This generally isn't too hard to do, since whiners spend so much time absorbed in self-pity that they rarely shine at their jobs. You might want to gently remind them that more work and less whining might solve some of the problems they complain about.

7. *The buffoon.* If you made a list ranking the promotion possibilities of those you supervise, this type wouldn't even qualify to make the last spot on the list. This is a dyed-in-the-wool dud who is probably on the way to being terminated rather than being promoted. For this reason, you may think it's a practical joke when one of these characters shows up looking for a promotion. If it proves anything, it's that even a dud can have a big ego. Don't even get into talking about promotions with this type of person. Instead, take the opportunity to remind them about getting their act together since their performance is less than satisfactory. At least this approach will discourage them from wasting your time in the future.

8. *The otherwise deserving.* Of all the types of individuals who seek promotions, this is the one case that you can sympathize with. Ordinarily, this person would be promoted; however, organizational constraints such as budget freezes, or the lack of an opening may prevent it. Usually, you can gain some measure of understanding on the part of this employee if you level about the situation. In fact, if you have been supportive in your efforts to promote this person, they will likely appreciate that fact.

The most important thing you can do for this type of individual is to fight for their promotion in the future. A good tactic that will help in this regard is to frequently mention this worker's achievements in your discussions with your own boss and other senior managers. In some instances, you may be able to bargain with your boss to get the person

promoted. For example, offer to cut your department budget somewhere else to compensate for the cost of the promotion.

However, most of the time the best you can do here is to offer future
hope without making any firm commitments. The one thing to avoid is
to hold out false hope to loyal employees through fear of losing them.
It only postpones their leaving for a job elsewhere, and once word gets
out that you were stringing someone along, the impact on morale will
extend beyond the employee in question.

7.3

✹

Handling Promotion Selection
and Its Aftereffects

It can be a no-win situation when you promote someone unless both the promotion selection and reactions from other workers are handled with care.
Otherwise, you may find there are only two people in your department who
think the right person was promoted—you and the person selected for the
position. Serious repercussions can result, ranging from workers seeking jobs
elsewhere, to a decrease in teamwork which can hinder the productivity of
your department. And even when the reaction is nothing more than silent
resentment, the daily atmosphere can be charged with tension. As a result,
even though you rightly feel explanations aren't in order, it makes sense to
carefully manage the promotion procedure to minimize problems and ensure
fairness in the process. Here's how this can be done:

1. Never promote people just because they excel at their current job. This
   is no guarantee that they will be able to handle the duties of a new position. For example, someone may work well under pressure, but show a
   great deal of impatience with peers, and generally have problems in
   dealing with people. If a promotional opportunity comes along that
   involves supervising others, this individual isn't likely to be a good
   selection.

   What you want to look for are employees who demonstrate they have
   the capabilities to perform well in the higher-level position. As a result,
   when you review candidates for promotional opportunities, compare
   them with the requirements of the position they aspire to. This doesn't

mean you should ignore present performance, but it should be balanced against the duties of the job to be filled.

2. Always try to groom your employees for future advancement opportunities by giving them increasingly difficult assignments and greater responsibilities. One good way to do this is to appoint candidates for promotion to act in your behalf when you're on vacation, or otherwise absent for an extended period of time. However, since these occasions are infrequent, look for ways to delegate duties on a regular basis to workers who have promotion potential.

3. When employees are promoted, monitor them closely until they learn the ropes of their new job. This will greatly assist in their transition into the new position.

4. Occasionally, you may have to hire someone from outside your department to fill a skill position for which no one within your group qualifies. Don't worry about this, since if everyone knows they don't have the necessary skills, there will be little or no animosity shown toward the newcomer.

5. Don't become an accomplice in undermining a newly-promoted worker by listening to the petty gripes of those not selected for the position. Of course, be ready to hear legitimate complaints, but if you sense that workers are using you as a means of doing some jealous sniping, quickly call a halt to it.

6. If you had more than one candidate for promotion from within your department, be honest with the losers about their future potential for advancements. If possible, try to find a reasonable way to justify why they weren't promoted. For example, perhaps the person selected had a lot more seniority.

7. Whenever possible, try to give a losing candidate hope for the future without making any specific commitments. If it's practical, try to find opportunities elsewhere within the company for deserving employees.

8. Naturally, you don't want to leave a worker who lost the job feeling unhappy, since they may look for work elsewhere, which means you lose a good employee. But this may happen no matter what you do, so be comfortable with the fact that you made the right decision. If someone chooses to leave because of that, so be it.

9. In the unhappy event that someone you promote doesn't seem to be able to handle the new job, you may want to have a heart-to-heart talk with them. They may realize they aren't compatible with the new position and want to go back to their old job. However, they may be understandably reluctant to approach you with this suggestion. If this is the case, then return the person to their former position.

On the other hand, if the employee insists he can do the job, then it's your responsibility to provide as much assistance and training as necessary to get them to a satisfactory performance level. Of course, if nothing works and the employee is simply beyond his or her ability to do the job, then you will ultimately have to take some action. Needless to say, the best way to avoid this sort of a problem is to be extremely careful about promotion selections in the first place.

7.4

Deflecting Requests for Time Off

As many businesses have adopted flexible working hours, and become more lenient about granting time off to attend to personal business, additional burdens have been placed upon the shoulders of supervisors. The most troublesome problem is often trying to complete the scheduled workload when people seem to be coming and going all day long. As hard as it is to cope with staffing problems when you have advance warning, request for time off on short notice can be even more frustrating.

It certainly behooves you to be accommodating, both for reasons of morale, as well as genuine concern for the needs of your employees. Whether it's child care, the responsibility for an aging parent, or some other personal dilemma, emergencies are bound to arise.

Where the headaches for you come into play is that the same enlightened managers who instituted socially-conscious working schedules, may not be quite so ready to accept that as an excuse if you fall behind in the department's output. All of which can make it that much more difficult for you to cope with requests for time off when you have workload demands that must be met. The end result is that you may not be able to grant all of the leave requests that come your way, even where there is a sound basis for granting the time off. Here are a few tips on how to diplomatically deny requests when it becomes absolutely necessary to do so.

1. Always be sympathetic when you reject an employee's request for time off. This is pretty basic, but the frustrations of a heavy workload can make it easy at times to lose your patience. You have to always keep in mind that the worker you bark at isn't likely to understand the pressure you may be under. Instead, the worker is almost certain to view you as being unreasonable. Therefore, take the time to explain why it's impossible to grant the employee's request. Say something such as, "I really know you need the day off, Charlotte, but it's out of the question because of..."

2. Be fair, but be firm when it's necessary. You may feel bad about refusing a request, but you can't let your emotions overrule the need to say "No" to someone. Sometimes workers may have other alternatives to handling the problem they're requesting time off for. If they view you as someone who always grants any reasonable request, there is little incentive for them to explore other means of coping with their difficulty.

3. Crack down on people who abuse the policy for granting time off. No matter how reasonable you are in giving time off to employees on short notice, there will always be one or two people trying to push the limits a little bit further. Not cracking down on these abuses makes it that much harder when you have to refuse the request of someone who is conscientious.

4. Insist that you be contacted directly when a worker calls in for an unscheduled absence due to illness or emergency. It's common when this practice isn't followed for workers to leave messages for you rather than have to give you a personal explanation of the reason for their absence. It also deprives you of the opportunity to subtly encourage a prompt return to work by a question such as, "Will you be in tomorrow?" More often then not, a worker who is just bagging it will feel compelled to say "Yes," whereas if they don't have to talk to you, there's no psychological pressure against taking an extra day off.

5. Put the monkey on the employee's back when you get a request for time off to handle a personal matter which obviously could have been dealt

with in some other way. Try a response such as, "Francine, you knew about this a week ago. I might have been able to do something about giving you the time off if I had known then."

6. Try to balance the work impact if a leave request is granted against the reason the employee expresses for wanting the time off. Of course, genuine emergencies should be approved, but many lesser reasons for being absent may be important to the employee, but not anything that a disinterested observer would classify as a true emergency. Falling into this category are all sorts of household management problems that working parents must cope with. Although you want to be understanding, employees are ultimately responsible for managing their personal lives so they don't conflict with working hours. So where you may be willing to give someone a couple of hours to run an errand when work is slack, this shouldn't be the case when the employee's job would be affected.

7. Coordinate emergency staffing with your peers in other department if it's feasible to do so. This will allow you to borrow and lend workers to fill in when you're shorthanded. Of course, this isn't practical in some work situations, while in others you may find supervisors who aren't willing to cooperate.

8. Promote teamwork within your department, since among other benefits, it brings peer pressure from the workers themselves when one or more co-workers try to take time off for little or no valid reason. This works especially well where workers are dependent upon other members of a team to get the work done. Furthermore, no matter how good you are at being able to detect who is taking advantage of your flexibility in granting time off, co-workers are even more adept at knowing who is dogging it.

9. One of the best methods of coping with the need to juggle people to compensate for absent employees is to cross-train everyone to do other jobs. That way, you have people who can fill in adequately with a minimum of disruption to your department.

10. Work out a compromise whenever possible. When you will find it difficult to spare the employee for the amount of time off that's requested, look at the possibility for reaching agreement on either a lesser amount of time, or a different time that will meet the needs of both the department and the employee.

7.5

The Do's and Don'ts of Interviewing
Job Candidates

If you don't like the idea of having to say to yourself, "I wish I never hired that dud," than you have to know how to interview job candidates. Otherwise, the odds of hiring someone who doesn't work out will increase dramatically. Naturally, even the best interviewer will be fooled from time to time, but for the most part taking the time to carefully interview job applicants will greatly increase the chances of hiring a good worker. The biggest problem most supervisors face in conducting interviews with job applicants is simply that isn't done often enough to develop good interviewing skills. To overcome this hurdle, try using some of the following techniques the next time you interview people for an opening in your department.

1. Your success ratio in hiring good workers depends as much upon what you do before you start to interview as on the interviews themselves. First, take the job description for the open position and update it if necessary. Then, make a list of factors that are important to you that aren't in the formal description of the position. This is something you should spend some time thinking about. As you know, formal job descriptions are pretty general, and you may well want to place emphasis on hiring someone who meets certain requirements which aren't contained in the formal document. Never lose sight of the fact that the person will be working for you, so be sure to hire someone who meets your specific needs.

2. Take your time in going through the entire hiring exercise. There is sometimes a tendency to rush through the process. This is especially true when you're overworked and are in desperate need of another body. As a result, someone who looks good on paper and doesn't goof in a quick interview is hired on short notice. The new hire turns out to be a disaster and you find yourself in a worse position than if you took the time to do it right.

3. When you furnish your requirements to the human resources department be as precise as possible about the qualifications and experience level you're looking for. This should cut down on the number of applications you have to go through before you select candidates to be inter-

viewed. Of course, how successful you are in getting a good choice of candidates to select from will depend upon the specifics of the hiring process in your company. Sometimes human resources people do the initial screening of applications before sending you those that generally meet the listed requirements. The pool of candidates will also be affected by the means used to advertise for the open position which is something else beyond your control.

4. When you go through the list of resumes/applications you receive, look for both positive aspects that impress you, and potential negatives that you will want to explore with candidates that you interview. The latter will include such things as gaps in employment, a number of jobs over a short period of time, and anything else that you may question. Naturally, if you have a wide enough applicant pool, you may be able to weed out most of the questionable applications without having to interview the individuals involved.

5. Select the best candidates on paper for interviews. Be sure to interview enough people to give yourself a fair selection to choose someone from. This will depend to some extent on both the opening and the candidate pool, but if possible try to interview at least five or six people. As you will discover during the interview process, the people you talk to in person may not be quite as qualified as they appeared to be on paper.

6. In terms of the formalities of interviewing, it's always best if you can have someone else also interview the candidates so you can compare notes. The main benefit of this is that you may discover the person gave different answers to essentially the same questions. If there are significant variances, this may signal a potential problem employee. Although for low-level jobs this may appear to be a lot of effort, it's well worth it if you can weed out problem employees before they get a foot in the door to make your life miserable.

   One easy way to simplify the burden of dual interviews is to coordinate with another supervisor. Offer to conduct interviews for the other supervisor's candidates if he will do the same for you. This is especially useful if you are both familiar with the requirements of the jobs in each other's department.

7. When you interview candidates there are certain fundamentals that should be followed. These include:

- Listen carefully and try to let the candidate do most of the talking. That way you may find out some things you wouldn't otherwise learn.

- Don't ask questions that are prohibited by law, such as on age, marital status, and so forth. Check with your human resources department if you're not certain about what you can and can't ask.

- Observe the applicant's appearance and demeanor during the interview. Someone who walks into your office, slouches down in the chair and proceeds to put their feet up on your desk may be the extreme. But such things as a sloppy appearance and/or a devil-may-care attitude are indicative of someone who really isn't too concerned about anything—which will include the job if you hire them.

- Discuss the candidate's experience as it relates to the job criteria you have established. Ask specific questions that require direct responses, for example, "Can you give me some idea of how you used the software programs mentioned in your application on the job?" Naturally, the nature of your questions will be determined by the job you're filling. What's important is to relate the candidate's experience to the job you have open.

- Only after a candidate has told you about their experience should you tell them about the details of the job opening. Otherwise, if you discuss the open position first, a savvy person will then tie their experience into what you told them.

- Answer any questions the candidate may have about the job in particular and the company in general.

- Don't discuss salary. Let the human resources people handle that aspect when the time comes.

- Thank the candidates for coming in, and tell them they will be hearing from the personnel department within a short period of time. Don't make any commitments during an initial interview.

8. After you have completed the interviews and are ready to choose from one or more applicants, don't overlook your reaction to the candidates in terms of personality. After all, you'll be working with the person selected on a daily basis, and if there's something about a candidate's personality that makes you uneasy now, the chances are it will get worse if you hire them. In general, you're better off with someone who has an easygoing personality, since this type tends to work better with otherpeople.

NOTE: Don't overlook rehiring former employees if the opportunity arises, as long as they were excellent workers and left on good terms. They know the operation and will be able to settle into the job quicker. They may also appreciate the job more the second time around, since they may have left thinking the grass was greener elsewhere, and have now discovered that it isn't.

7.6

The Proper Procedures for Firing Employees

Having to bite the bullet and fire someone isn't an easy thing to do. It's compounded even further if the worker being terminated has worked with you over a long period of time. In fact, because of this natural reluctance, employees who should be let go are often kept on the payroll until the point where the situation has become intolerable for everyone concerned.

To compound the problem, the fear of legal action, as well as the impact upon the morale of other workers, also leads to a hesitancy to take the steps necessary to terminate employees. Nevertheless, not every hiring decision will be successful over the long term, and for one reason or another the decision to fire an employee will have to be made. And even though it isn't an easy thing to do, using the following procedures will at least help you to minimize the difficulties.

1. Be sure to closely follow the company disciplinary policy in terms of documenting warnings that take place along the way. (See Sec 5.1 of Chapter Five on conducting a discipline session.)

2. To protect the company legally, be sure that your reasons for firing someone are valid, and that you have followed company procedure.

3. If you have a situation where an employee just isn't a "good fit" for the type of jobs in your department, but is otherwise a decent worker, if possible try to find another position for the individual within the company. However, don't use this as an excuse to sidestep firing someone, since dumping a dud on another supervisor will come back to haunt you.

4. You may want to informally rehearse what you're going to say when you meet with the employee. If nothing else, it will help put you at ease. It

will also avoid the possibility of fumbling around for the right words when the time comes.

5. The timing of a dismissal can be helpful in lessening the embarrassment to an employee. For example, if it's done late in the day just after everyone else has left, this spares the employee from facing his co-workers as he leaves. It also avoids a public scene if the worker gets angry and launches into a diatribe about anything and everyone.

6. The actual meeting at which the dismissal notice is given to the employee should be one-on-one and in private. Your office isn't a good place for the meeting, since as soon as you have informed the employee, you want to leave and have a personnel representative discuss benefits with the worker.

7. As for what is said, be as brief as possible, don't get involved in a debate, and don't attempt a personal dialogue. This is a traumatic event for the individual, and it's not exactly a day at the beach for you. Simply state the reasons for the termination, and try to say something minimally upbeat and innocuous such as, "Things don't always work out as planned, but I sincerely want to wish you the best of luck in the future." Exit quietly and let the personnel representative take over.

8. Once a decision is made to fire someone, it should be done promptly, since putting it off doesn't solve anything. All too often, supervisors hang on to workers rather than face the unpleasant task of dismissing them. This is rationalized by hoping the worker will land a job somewhere else in the meantime. But what it's really doing is leaving you with a worker you don't want, and the employee treading water waiting for the ax to fall.

9. In situations such as theft, fighting, and other actions which warrant immediate dismissal, don't just fire someone on the spot. Instead, coordinate with personnel and if necessary, suspend the individual until an investigation can be completed as to what took place. Sometimes appearances can be deceiving, and unjustly firing someone can result in an expensive lawsuit.

10. If you are contacted for a reference for an employee who was fired, never make any damaging remarks that could instigate a lawsuit. It's best when the company has reference checks handled by the human resources staff, but if that's not the case state that it's company policy to just verify dates of employment.

7.7

↓

Workable Ways to Deal with Employees' Personal Problems

It's easy enough to rationalize that workers' personal problems shouldn't impact upon their ability to meet the demands of the job, including such requirements as working hours and attendance. However, as you know, that's not quite the way it works. Everyone experiences personal difficulties at one time or another that conflict with and/or affect their job. As a result, supervisors have to exercise tact and flexibility in dealing with these issues when employees are faced with problems in this area.

The most common problems tend to center around the need to temporarily adjust working hours, or take time off to cope with an emergency. Less frequent difficulties include changes in worker job performance resulting from everything from a divorce to the death of a loved one. These aren't easy to handle, particularly if an employee's performance deteriorates and you have no inkling as to the cause. Nevertheless, helping keep employees on course at work is beneficial both for you and the affected workers. A few suggestions that can help you to accomplish this are:

1. Recognize that work–family conflicts exist for many employees. Families with two working parents and single parents face enormous demands in trying to juggle work and family responsibilities. Other workers may have aged parents who need close attention. Even childless dual-career couples who work long hours and/or travel extensively can have trouble trying to bring balance to their lives.

2. Don't take the easy way out when workers come to you with a personal problem that affects their work. See if you can come up with a flexible solution.

3. Always remember that it may be relatively easy to hire other workers, but it's not easy to hire good ones. For this reason alone, it pays to be as adaptable as possible in working to meet the personal needs of those you supervise.

4. To avoid resentment on the part of those without families, take the needs of everyone into consideration. For instance, someone who works

a lot of overtime, or travels a lot, may also need some special consideration in terms of time off.

5. Enlist your group in a cooperative effort to support each other by picking up the slack where necessary. Letting everyone know you're all in the same boat together will help boost morale and increase teamwork.

6. If you get negative feedback from someone who doesn't have personal problems that interfere with their work, play on their sympathy. Say something similar to, "I know you don't have a family, Jimmy, and asking you to pitch in to help someone out may seem unfair to you. But I know if you think about it, you'd want someone to do the same for you. And even if they don't say it, Jimmy, the other people appreciate you helping them out." You might even want to show formal recognition to these people by having a presentation of some minor reward on their birthday or some other suitable occasion. However you do it, the important thing is to show your appreciation for the contributions made by those who don't have work–family conflicts.

7. Don't worry about being singled out by your peers as being too soft on your workers. After you have adopted a practice of being flexible in working to solve workers' personal dilemmas it shouldn't be long before you have statistics to prove that your group has lower absenteeism and higher productivity than other departments. It's also likely that you won't be spending as much time as hard-nosed peers in hiring and training people to replace those who leave because their boss wouldn't work at coming up with solutions to their problems.

8. If you notice that an employee is experiencing a drop in performance and are aware of a pending divorce or some other personal difficulty, talk to the worker about it. Don't bring the problem up directly, but mention the dip in the worker's performance and ask if there's anything you can help with. If you have a reputation for being helpful, chances are the employee will confide in you. At that point, you may want to recommend counseling, ask if the employee needs some time off, or make some other suitable suggestion. Just be careful about unduly imposing your thoughts on the worker if he or she isn't receptive.

7.8
⚜

Several Simple Ways You Can Reward Good Workers

There's nothing better for morale than being able to recognize the efforts of your subordinates. It's not always easy to do this, since you're somewhat limited by the constraints of company policy. This is especially true when it comes to standard methods of recognition such as pay raises and promotions. Pay increases are infrequent, and in many working-level positions the opportunities for promotion are either rare or non-existent. This requires you to seek out alternative methods for showing your gratitude when workers excel at doing their jobs. A few suggestions for recognizing achievement that you can use more or less regularly are:

1. Give them more responsibility. Excellent workers can come the victims of boredom, especially if their jobs are relatively routine and the tasks they perform are repetitive. To compensate for this, look for ways to give your best workers greater responsibilities. One method for doing this is to allow them to act independently in making decisions. It also helps to increase the complexity of their duties whenever it's feasible to do so.

2. Let them do their own thing—within limits. Relax your supervisory oversight and let your best workers have the freedom to use their own judgment in determining when they take breaks, eat lunch, and so forth.

3. Praise them publicly whenever possible. Everyone likes recognition and when workers excel it's important to let them know you appreciate their efforts. However, go beyond just telling people they did a great job. Use every occasion that arises to praise people before their peers, as well as with others outside of your department.

4. If advancement opportunities are limited within your group, seek out promotional possibilities in other departments for your outstanding subordinates. Sure you may lose good workers this way, but this is offset by the goodwill created when workers know that their boss is concerned about their future. People will work harder in dead-end jobs if they can see a light at the end of the tunnel.

5. Whenever possible, try to find special assignments for good workers that will provide some relief from their daily drudgery, for example, serving on some of the typical committees that are formed to organize company social and charitable functions.

6. Reward your best workers with above-average pay raises, so they know there's a payoff for being productive.

7. Don't exaggerate achievements. It's important not to confuse rewarding people for doing above-average work, with doing what they're paid to do. It will take all of the impact away from your efforts to reward achievement if you start praising people for doing their job in a very ordinary way. In short, only reward what's above and beyond the norm.

7.9

The Key Components of New Employee Orientation

Hiring an employee is just part of the equation for adding a fully productive contributor to your group. Equally important is the need to make sure the new hire becomes smoothly absorbed into the unit as quickly as possible. Otherwise, you may find yourself spending a great deal of time in correcting the mistakes common when anyone—no matter how experienced—starts a new job. In addition, the more comfortable new employees are with their surroundings, the quicker they will be able to concentrate on doing their job. Several steps that can be taken to hasten the integration of workers into your group are:

1. Make sure that the new employee's work area is all set up before he or she arrives to start work. Be certain that the necessary tools and/or office supplies are obtained. It's a lot easier for someone to settle into a new job when they have a piece of territory all ready, than to be met with an approach such as, "Well, let's see where we're going to put you." The latter sends a message that getting a new worker off to a good start isn't first and foremost in anyone's thoughts.

2. Avoid making any assumptions about what the new arrival does or doesn't know. Cover all of the bases in your initial discussion, even if it's

done briefly. For example, the personnel department may have covered benefits and other such matters, but chances are the new worker didn't absorb too much of what was said amidst the excitement and anxiety of starting a new job.

3. Spell out the specifics of the job requirements, so the employee knows what his or her duties will be. On the other hand, reassure the worker that you understand everything can't be remembered at once.

4. Go over the basics of time and attendance and leave policies, including such details as when payday is, and where the employee will get his paycheck. Don't overlook minor items such as coffee breaks, when and where people eat lunch, and so forth.

5. Provide a general tour of any areas of the company the employee should be familiar with.

6. Assure the employee that you both expect and welcome questions.

7. Introduce the employee to co-workers, as well as others within the company that the employee should know.

8. Assign a mentor who will in effect be the person's instructor and guide until the person is able to function independently. Take great care in selecting someone who is both knowledgeable about the job, and is generally good at working with others.

9. On the first day, be certain the person has someone to eat lunch with, since this is one of the best times of the day for employees to interact informally with their co-workers.

10. Follow up closely the first few weeks to be sure everything is going smoothly, and that the worker isn't experiencing difficulty in adapting to both the job and the surroundings.

11. Sit down and talk informally with the new worker frequently during the first few weeks. This is important, since new employees are hesitant about contacting a boss with questions. Therefore, it's smart for you to provide a ready, made opportunity.

12. After a few weeks you may notice areas where a new worker needs additional training. If it's of the on-the-job variety assign someone to furnish it, and if it's an external course, schedule it for the earliest date possible.

7.10

How to Make the Best Use of Part-Time and Temporary Help

In today's competitive business environment, part-time and temporary employees are being used more widely, either on a regular basis, or a supplement during periods of peak activity. In some cases, where a part-time worker has held a position for an extended period of time, the problems of supervision are no different than with full-time employees. In other instances, supervising part-timers and temps presents both problems and opportunities that differ somewhat from full-time workers. For example, you don't always get to know part-time employees as well, since they work fewer hours, and don't always stay on one job for a long period of time. They may also be less thoroughly screened when they're hired, especially if it's for a short-term assignment. Some techniques for making the most out of your part-time employees are:

1. Don't wait for an emergency to hire part-time or temporary workers. Try to plan your needs ahead of time so you will have a better opportunity to screen potential hires.

2. Establish good relations with temporary help agencies if you use temps on a regular basis. Ask for details about the training the agency provides for their temps. Most of all, be specific about your needs. If you aren't, then you can't expect to get someone who is a good fit for the available position.

3. Make sure you sit down with temps and part-timers and be certain they fully understand their duties.

4. As much as possible, treat part-time and temporary help as if they were full-time workers.

5. Try to develop a stable of temps and part-timers whom you use regularly. That way, you will have a supply of help that's familiar with your department and can quickly fit into the operation.

6. Brief temps and part-timers on the basics of who they will report to, where to eat lunch, introduce them to co-workers, and so forth.

7. Use part-time help as a means to evaluate candidates for full-time positions. This not only lets you get to know the worker, but it also gives the

worker a chance to get to know the company. This will minimize the odds of hiring someone for a full-time job who won't succeed.

8. If your department is expanding rapidly, it's harder to find top-notch candidates in a hurry. The use of temps or part-timers will give you the chance to fill permanent positions gradually without sacrificing quality in the rush to fill vacant slots.

9. Often, in repetitious jobs, part-timers are more productive than full-time employees, since they work fewer hours, and are less subject to fatigue and boredom.

10. If you get resistance from your boss toward hiring a full-time employee, you may succeed in gaining approval to hire a part-timer, since it's less expensive. Hopefully, after a while, you can get the slot upgraded to a full-time position.

11. A less tangible benefit of part-timers and temps is that it isn't as painful to terminate them when the workload subsides. So if your department has sharp peaks and valleys in its workload, part-timers and/or temps are a better approach than hiring full-time employees.

7.11
♦
Useful Pointers on Explaining Benefits to Employees

Both you and those you supervise have an interest in the amount and type of fringe benefits offered by your employer. The essential difference is that subordinates sometimes expect you to be the expert who can answer their questions about benefits. Probably more often than you would like, someone has come to you and said something similar to, "Can you explain this to me?", as they hand you a copy of some memo issued by the human resources department. Beyond this, you may have to periodically brief your group either on new benefits, or changes to existing ones.

Usually, you can refer employees with complex questions to the appropriate staff person in human resources. Despite this, many times workers see you as the authority figure who can best answer their questions. One reason for this is that you are someone they know and can trust. The end result, for one reason or another is that you may find yourself spending a lot of time answering questions on some aspect of benefits.

From your vantage point as a boss, one of the most useful aspects of fringe benefits is to help rebut worker complaints about low wages by pointing out that fringe benefits also count. To handle these benefits issues most effectively, you may find some of the following suggestions to be helpful:

1. In terms of educating workers as to the cost of fringe benefits to the company you are on the frontline when it comes to management/employee communications. Therefore, you should make every effort to learn the dollars and cents associated with benefits your company provides. In some companies this sort of information will be routinely provided to you. In other cases, you may have to take the initiative in obtaining the facts and figures from the benefits specialist in your personnel office.

2. Get to know the benefit needs of your employees. This isn't insignificant, since workers view benefits from a very personal viewpoint. The best education assistance plan in the world is of little value if most of the workers in your department aren't inclined to pursue continuing education. And even a comprehensive health plan may be of secondary importance to a worker who is covered by a spouse's plan. Knowing the benefits that are most valued by your workers serves a two-fold purpose. It not only gives you information on which to base requests for changes in benefits to upper management, but it also supplies you with the knowledge of which benefits matter most to each individual worker.

   This comes in handy when someone storms into your office complaining about low wages. You can then say something such as, "Don't forget the fringe benefits you get, Carl. Weren't you telling me last week how much the health benefits plan means to you. That along with the other benefits the company offers cost a lot of money which you would otherwise have to pay out of your own pocket. As you know Carl, even if you could make a few bucks more a week somewhere else you wouldn't have the benefits you get here."

3. Health benefits are not only expensive, but also an area where employee dissatisfaction is most likely. This is especially true when new health care providers are selected by the company to furnish coverage. What you have to point out when workers question you is that the alternative

to switching coverage might be either increased employee contributions and/or the elimination of some benefits.

4. It's beneficial to point out to new hires that their compensation package amounts to "X" dollars, which includes so much for wages, and additional amounts for the various benefits the company offers. This information may be furnished to people by the personnel office, but if it's not, you should inform employees of the costs if they can be readily obtained from the staffer responsible for administering the company benefits program. The more information you provide your workers on the benefits initially, will help keep them from pestering you with benefit questions on a day-to-day basis.

5. Whenever you receive a directive on some change in benefits that has been distributed to every employee, questions are bound to come your way from the workers within your unit. Once you're sure you fully understand the changes, hold a meeting with your entire group to go over all of the questions at once. Otherwise, you will waste a great deal of time going over the same ground time-after-time on an individual basis.

6. Whenever you're talking with workers about the positive aspects of the fringe benefits provided by the company, don't neglect the minor fringes, as well as items that may be considered incidental to the benefits program. For instance, the company may offer free parking in a company lot. A worker doesn't see this as costing the company anything. However, the land used for the parking facility, along with maintenance, security, and so forth, all have a cost attached. This particular item is especially important to emphasize if the company is located in a business district, or other densely settled area, where not every employer provides free parking. Other items that tend to be taken for granted by workers include wellness programs, company cafeterias, and anything else that doesn't have a visible dollar cost associated with it.

7. Even though it's time-consuming to learn the details of the fringe benefits the company provides, it's beneficial as a supervisor to do so. Workers will view you as someone who shares their concerns, and as a bonus, keeping workers advised of their value will help reduce grumbling about pay levels. In general it will also reinforce the notion that your company is a good place to work.

Chapter Eight

✦

MANAGING AROUND CRISIS AND PANIC SITUATIONS

You have probably headed to work on more than one occasion with the happy thought that everything was going smoothly, only to be blitzed by your boss before you get your first cup of coffee with some sort of crisis that had to be resolved. If you're one of the lucky ones, this sort of scenario may be a rarity. On the other hand, you may work in an atmosphere where, for one reason or another, a "panic of the day" atmosphere prevails.

Of course, there are legitimate pressure situations which can arise from time to time. However, in other instances the crisis may be more imagined than real. It could be triggered by your boss who may be a perpetual panic provoker, or result from the actions of individuals who perceive anything they're doing to be top priority. It may even result from a more general management structure which tends to operate in a helter-skelter fashion.

Whatever the cause, your ability to read and react to these high-pressure situations will help keep your department functioning smoothly, and allow you to maintain your sanity while all about you people seem to be losing theirs. This chapter focuses on some of the more general causes for crisis, including layoffs, reorganizations, and peak workloads. It also covers how to deflect blame and deal with pressure, as well as what to do in the unhappy event that your own job may be on the line.

8.1

Businesslike Methods for Dealing with Layoffs

Managing your department is never an easy task, even when the economy is booming, and your company is bursting at the seams with new business. That sort of scenario generally brings to the forefront such work-force problems as excessive salary demands, job-hopping, and a seemingly futile search for qualified workers. On the other hand, when business is slow your most pressing problem may be how to maintain productivity and morale in the face of work-force reductions.

Although terminating employees and making other necessary adjustments to cope with a slump in business isn't an easy task, the situation can be made much worse if it's not handled properly. Although the bulk of the responsibility for minimizing the destructive impact of layoffs rests with top management, as the supervisor of workers who are losing their jobs, some approaches you can take include:

1. One of the surest methods for maintaining morale during a period of layoffs is to treat terminated employees with dignity and respect. This lets your remaining workers know that if the ax eventually hits them, they too will be treated with compassion.

2. It's important not to dehumanize terminations by making layoff notices impersonal. Do it privately and be sure that terminated workers are advised about their rights and benefits.

3. When a layoff takes place, it inevitably leaves those people remaining with fears and anxiety about the future. It's valuable to keep your people informed about future business plans. Of course, you won't be privy to a lot of the information on the company's future, since this is in the hands of top management. But to whatever extent you can, let your workers in on what's happening.

4. Hold meetings to keep your people informed as to what's going on. Encourage workers to ask questions, and give answers that are forthright—not bland reassurances that everything will work out alright.

5. Be aggressive in seeking answers to employee concerns about the future. Naturally, you may not be able to get all of the answers you want, but just the fact that workers know you're pursuing the cause will reassure them to some degree.

6. Use the grapevine to gain information about layoffs, but be careful to filter fact from fiction before you give out information to your group.

7. Track down and knock-down rumors that are circulating about future layoffs. Frequently, the rumors tend to be worse than the reality of the situation. Furthermore, the more time your people spend discussing rumors, the less work that gets done. Encourage your people to come to you with questions about layoffs. The quicker you're able to dispel rumors, the less likely it is that workers will pay heed to those who circulate them.

8. Level with your people about what you do and don't know. Don't lull them into a false sense of security if you're not sure of the facts.

9. When layoffs leave your department overburdened, do what you can to redesign jobs to make them simpler, and eliminate any procedures that are outdated. Where necessary, reassign tasks to maintain an equitable workload and absorb the work of the terminated employees.

10. Make every effort to get things back to normal after a layoff occurs. The sooner everyone gets back to the business at hand, the faster the situation will fade into memory.

8.2

Measures to Protect Your Department Against Cutbacks

When top management starts to look for places to save money, labor costs are often placed front and center. Department heads are then typically faced with having to defend their units against cutbacks. The supervisors who win this battle are typically the ones who prepare the best beforehand. A number of strategies you can use to lessen the possibility of your department being singled out for the layoff ax are:

1. Keep accurate figures on your department's output, so you can show favorable comparisons with other groups. Ax-cutting time is when productive groups can survive better than others if they're able to make the case in quantifiable terms.

2. When cutbacks occur, part-time help is usually the first to go. If you've already lost part-timers, don't forget to factor this into your argument that your department has already suffered cuts. For example, say something such as, "Charlie, I've lost two part-time people already, which is the equivalent of one full-time position. That should be counted when figuring cutbacks, since some departments overload with full-timers and don't attempt to save money with part-time help."

3. Cross-training your people has many practical virtues. It can also help when cutbacks are being explored. For instance, you can make the argument that your workers are multi-talented and are of more value to the company because of their ability to perform various jobs. This has some validity when cutbacks are made, since with fewer people, flexibility helps when reassigning people to pick up the slack.

4. Try to justify the need for maintaining your department based upon its value as a revenue or profit center, its importance to customers, or whatever else best justifies keeping your group intact based on the specifics of your situation.

5. Remind your boss of your efforts to keep your department lean while others tried to build empires. If this has always been recognizable, you may be able to survive.

6. Be prepared to do battle, Other supervisors will be looking out for their own interests, so you may have to contend with sniping and back-stabbing. Try to stay above the fray by making your case based upon the facts. However, if it becomes necessary to do so, point out where your department is best retained at full strength compared with others.

7. When cutbacks loom, rally any support for your cause from whatever source you can. This may be external if you deal with customers, or internal, in the form of managers whose groups your unit supports. The higher the status of those you enlist in the cause, the better is the likelihood that top management will spare your group.

8.3

Eleven Ways to Escape the Hot Seat

No matter how good a job you're doing, there will always be occasions when for one reason or another, the finger of blame is pointed toward you. Sometimes it may be a minor problem, while in other instances it could be serious, or even job-threatening. In any event, since it's always nice to be able to wiggle out of the hot seat without getting burned, here are a few tips for accomplishing that. Whether you choose to use one or more of these pointers is left to your discretion. To some extent, it will depend upon the circumstances of the situation, as well as whether you're an innocent victim, or the deliberate target of someone who is using you as a scapegoat.

1. *Blame someone else.* You may on occasion find yourself having to answer for a mistake that didn't originate within your department. There's little difficulty in getting off the hook if you can pinpoint who is really responsible. To be successful at this you must be able to prove both your innocence and the other person's guilt, since unlike the justice system you're not always innocent until proven guilty. To the contrary, when someone points the finger at work, you're likely to be guilty until you can prove you're innocent.

   The real difficulty here is that it's not always possible to do this, which is probably why someone else blamed the mistake on your department in the first place. For this reason, if you're not careful in putting the blame where it belongs, you will not only look like the guilty party, but also give the appearance of trying to frame someone else.

   Consequently, if you know who the real culprit is, but can't prove it, the best course of action might be to just shrug and accept the responsibility without admitting guilt. You may want to say something similar to this. "I don't see how that error could have been caused by us (referring to your department), but I'll certainly take measures so that it doesn't happen again." This means you take the blame, but don't forget who was really responsible, since if they goof again you don't want to be the victim a second time around. Of course, if you feel retribution is necessary, bide your time until you get a chance to make the guilty party look bad.

2. *Share the blame.* In some situations a mistake may be blamed only on your department when actually there is joint responsibility with another individual or group within the company. Here, it's a judgment call on your part as to whether or not to accept total responsibility, or put part of the blame where it rightly belongs. In most instances, the deciding factor will be either your working relationship with the other party, or the position of the person within the organization.

   In the first instance, this usually means accepting full responsibility if you work well with the other individual or unit. Hopefully, your loyalty will be returned somewhere along the line. As for the second factor, it's a no-win situation to try and pin part of the blame on someone at a higher level of management. The best you can hope for here is to make your point known quietly to a higher-level manager you can trust. At least that way, if there are later repercussions, you will have an ally to defend you.

3. *Get a higher-up to agree with you.* One of the best—and fastest—ways to get out from under an accusation of having screwed up is to have someone at a higher level than the accuser agree that what you did was correct. How this is done will be based on the specifics of the situation. One general way is to pitch your position to a higher-up without mentioning that there is an opposing viewpoint. If you make a good case for your approach, the odds are the upper-level manager will agree with you. Then, go back and tell your accuser that the folks upstairs see it your way. That's usually enough to get the matter dropped. But even if the other side pursues the issue with upper management, chances are you will win because you got there first.

4. *Recover quickly.* For every mistake that's made it sometimes seems that there's someone willing to point the finger of guilt. That, of course, isn't true and most mistakes will be accepted in a routine way without any major consequences. However, when you and/or your department are spotlighted for a serious goof, the best way to regain status is to forge ahead and try to diminish the impact of what happened. Naturally, the chance to do something spectacular isn't possible in most cases. Nevertheless, steady performance over a period of time will overwhelm even a serious goof in the mind of your boss and other superiors.

5. *Make it worthwhile for the problem to be kept low-key.* There are times when a good way to keep the lid on a mistake is to plead that making it a major issue will open up a can of worms. For example, if your boss

starts to rake you over the coals about an error, your subtle suggestion that this is commonplace in other groups as well as yours may cool things down. After all, if it's just your department, the boss could blame you as the supervisor. When the problem also exists with the other groups, then the blame more squarely rests with the boss, rather than any single supervisor. Needless to say, use a little tact if you try this ploy, especially if your boss isn't the type to see the wisdom of your kindness in keeping his inadequate leadership under wraps.

6. *Use a valid excuse.* Often there is a justifiable reason why a mistake was made. Whenever your department is criticized, always look to see if there was a contributing cause. Even more crucial, make sure it is pointed out to your boss and others, since the mistake may be noticed while the justification is overlooked.

7. *Plead lack of resources.* Many times deadlines are missed, quotas aren't met, and other misfortunes befall supervisors for no better reason than they don't have the resources necessary to do the job. This is why it's so crucial to make your need for material resources and/or people frequently known to your boss and others. It's preferable to do this in writing so you can refresh failed memories if you're called on the carpet for not meeting production schedules or other performance goals.

8. *Turn defeat into victory.* Nothing can give you greater satisfaction than to be able to turn criticism for a mistake around. For instance, a supervisor criticized for lowered production may offset this with proof of greater quality. The details will vary, but the key is to look for a positive factor that you can use to counter the negative aspect of performance that's being brought to your attention.

9. *Get someone to bail you out.* Occasionally, you may be able to call in a chit for a favor you did in the past which will get you off the hook with a problem. This is simply an alibi defense, where another supervisor or someone else outside your group will support your claim that a mistake wasn't of your doing.

10. *The "No one told me" defense.* This is especially effective where changes were recently made which you weren't told about—or at least no one can prove otherwise. After all, how can you be expected to do something you didn't know you were supposed to do? It's unlikely this tactic will work more than once, so you may want to hold it in reserve for when you really need it.

11. *Admit it, forget it, and keep a low profile.* When your boss, or some other higher authority, admonishes you for making an error, many times the best tactic is to simply admit it, take whatever action is necessary to avoid repetition, and then try to stay out of the limelight for awhile. If you can do this, it won't be long before someone else is on the hot seat, which means your misdeed will be quickly shoved off center stage.

8.4

✹

Handy Ways to Cope with Peak Workloads

Too much work, too little time, more often than not is the fate of many supervisors. It's easy enough to rationalize by thinking something similar to, "I'll just do the best I can." The problem is that your boss may not quite see it the same way, and consequently expects all of the work to be done in a timely manner, no matter how busy you are. If you face this dilemma, here are some suggestions on ways to cope with a seemingly impossible workload.

1. Manage your priorities carefully. When it's impossible to do everything, recognize that some things just won't get done. You have to recognize what's important and what isn't. Otherwise, you will be swamped forever. For more information on meeting priorities, see Sec. 1.9 of Chapter One, and in terms of meeting deadlines on specific projects, you should refer to Sec. 1.10 of Chapter One.

2. Don't be afraid to ask for help. You may think you have to adopt a "grin and bear it" attitude because there's no way you will get additional assistance. However, confronting your boss on the subject can work if you handle it creatively. First of all, be prepared to show the boss detailed facts proving your department is overloaded with work. Comparisons with prior time periods, as well as similar departments, work well. Then, be careful to point out the consequences if additional help isn't forthcoming.

   For example, when you ask for help and the boss says something such as, "How can I give you more help? You know there's a hiring freeze on," then reply with, "All I know is that next month's deliveries won't be met, because I don't have enough people to do the work." This puts the burden of failure on the boss's back, who nevertheless will likely give the old standard response, "Do the best you can." This isn't done to be cruel, but only because the boss doesn't see any satisfactory alternative. At this point, you should be ready to offer a suggestion such as detailing people from other groups, hiring part-time help, or whatever other remedy appears to be viable. With this sort of approach you may just be successful.

3. Delegate everything possible to subordinates if it's your personal workload that's overwhelming. On the other hand, if it's your department that's understaffed, look for ways to delegate tasks to other units. This doesn't have to be complicated, and it doesn't have to be anything of great significance. For instance, if your people make several trips a day to deliver paperwork to another department, let them come to your unit instead. What if they refuse to? Just let it pile up and sooner or later they will complain to your boss. Since the boss already knows you're overburdened, it's likely you will win this battle. There are many procedures such as this which come about from custom as much as anything else. So revising these processes can free up time for your people to concentrate on more important work.

4. Focus your energies on similar tasks. Time can be saved by lumping like items together to be dealt with all at once, instead of piecemeal. The specifics, of course, will vary with the nature of your work, but the principle is the same.

5. Make quicker decisions. Rather than take the time to review matters in detail, make more snap decisions. In most instances, you will find that the rewards in terms of freeing up time will outweigh the risks of a bad decision. Making faster decisions can go a long way toward reducing the pressures of an overload of work. This is actually a necessity rather than a nicety if you're in a situation where your workload has increased significantly due to staffing cuts, layoffs, or corporate reorganization. The increase in your responsibilities may no longer allow the time necessary to evaluate every problem to the extent it was done in the past.

It can be hard initially to recognize this, since experience may have conditioned you to thoroughly analyze every situation before going ahead. This, in fact, was probably what was expected of you by top management. In practice, the unwritten rule may well have been to take the time to make sure every decision was the right one. Of course, with an overload of work, this approach becomes a luxury you can't afford if you want to avoid being overwhelmed by your expanded duties.

6. Skip the trivial tasks that are often ingrained habits. Analyze your duties and see what you may be doing as part of your daily routine that doesn't have to be done at all. Another pitfall to avoid is not to do what you shouldn't be doing in the first place. For example, as a supervisor you're not being paid to do clerical work. However, this can be done in an attempt to speed things along when the person who would normally do the job isn't immediately available. Needless to say, the more work you do that isn't yours, the less time you have to spend on more important endeavors.

7. Eliminate doing anything that will have only minor consequences if it's not done.

8. Make a conscious effort to shorten the length of time you spend on any one matter. This would include cutting long-winded talkers short, either on the phone or in person. Reducing the length of your letters and memos can also be helpful if you spend a significant amount of time on written responses.

9. Accept the fact that you're overloaded with work and have little relief in sight. Simply recognizing the impossibility of your dilemma will help you to carry on without worrying about getting caught up.

8.5

Basic Practices for Handling a Crisis

Everything around here is a crisis" is a common enough complaint in the world of work. Unfortunately, that's often a legitimate gripe, since in many cases the panic button gets pushed for no valid reason. Nevertheless, there are times when by any standards a real crisis can erupt. When that happens, how the problem is attacked will partly determine how much of a hassle you have to handle. Here are some procedures for dealing with the next work-related crisis that comes your way.

1. To a great extent the action to be taken will be dictated by the nature of the crisis. However, there are a number of tactics you can use to help muddle through any mess. First of all, you have to decide what alternatives are available to resolve the crisis. It's important to take the time to do this, even though the urgency of the moment may encourage you to

plunge ahead, since if you pounce upon the problem without any planning, you may make matters worse.

It's not always easy to remain calm in these situations, since the pressure to do something is often exacerbated by a boss who may be standing there screaming, "Do something about this right away." Of course, although you can't, the temptation to ask, "What do you want me to do?" may be great. But if you did, aside from getting your boss even hotter under the collar, it's not likely you would get an answer, since if the boss knew, he would have told you in the first place.

2. Once you have determined the alternatives for dealing with the crisis, try to estimate the results that could be expected from implementing a course of action based upon each possibility. Doing this will help you to weed out approaches that at first glance seem reasonable, but may have unsatisfactory consequences if carried out.

   For example, it may seem proper to appease an angry customer with replacement items that were built for someone else, but haven't yet been shipped. Yet, that can turn into a major headache if production can't be met on the scheduled delivery date for the items that were temporarily borrowed to solve the problem. That actually is a relatively simple problem compared to what can happen by jumping to conclusions when a major crisis occurs. Therefore, never overlook the potential impact down the road when you make a decision to solve a problem, since a hasty decision may come back to haunt you.

3. Naturally, any sort of crisis calls for action to be taken as soon as possible. Not only does this prevent a situation from deteriorating further, but it also hastens getting things back to normal. Therefore, even though decisions should be carefully considered, they shouldn't be left for a "committee of committees" to decide sometime after the next solar eclipse. In short, when it's crisis time, it's time to think on your feet.

4. Once you decide what has to be done, do it. Taking action sends a signal to everyone interested in the matter that someone is in command. This alone does a lot to relieve the anxieties of those affected.

5. It's important to keep interested parties informed as to what is being done. This serves to squelch the rash of rumors which surround any crisis—large or small.

6. If the crisis is of a relatively minor nature, and concerns only internal matters within the company, you can defuse the issue by:

   • Avoiding anger—even if you're provoked.

   • Accepting responsibility for the problem.

   • Stating what will be done to resolve the matter.

   • Moving ahead as quickly as possible to put the problem in the past.

7. To prevent one crisis after another from popping up in the operation of your department, encourage your workers to bring problems to your attention. If workers know that a boss wants to be alerted at the earliest sign of trouble, many minor difficulties can be dealt with before they develop into a major crisis. That sounds simple enough to do, but if employees expect personal criticism when problems are brought to your attention, all of the guidance in the world in the form of, "Let me know about any problems," is wasted effort.

8. To overcome worker hesitancy at being the bearer of bad news, reassurance in the form of ongoing one-on-one communication is important. When employees have regular conversations with their boss—no matter how brief—they gain the self-confidence to discuss potential problems. So encouraging this type of working relationship gives you the information needed to head off problems before they develop into a full-blown crisis. Over the long haul, this is the ultimate crisis management technique, since it encourages difficulties to be resolved before they reach the crisis stage.

8.6

How to Keep Your Cool in Pressure Situations

As a supervisor, it's inevitable that you will face situations that place you under a great deal of pressure. It's great when things run smoothly, but sooner or later there will be some form of disruption which will place you on the hot seat. The circumstances will vary, but every supervisor's job carries with it the potential for encountering a wide variety of pressure situations. These can range from one-shot issues such as trying to meet an impossible deadline, to a more constant and generalized form of pressure such as having to deal with a totally unreasonable boss.

When you have to deal with a high-pressure situation—whatever the cause—it's easy to panic and for emotions to run high. But this sort of emotional reaction will only serve to make your predicament worse. Instead, you have to maintain your composure if you want to turn conflict into success and defeat into victory. That's admittedly not a small order, especially if you have a higher-level manager snarling and pointing the finger of blame at you. Nevertheless, it can be done if you go about it in the right way. Here are a number of approaches for defusing some of the more emotionally-charged dilemmas you may have to deal with.

1. *When your boss yells at you for not meeting your department's goals.* This is a pretty standard situation when production quotas aren't met, deliveries are late, or whatever the case may be in your particular job. The reasons for such failures are many, and even though you're blameless, someone higher up the line isn't about to accept responsibility. This means the fingers are pointed at you. And even though your boss may know the reasons for the failure, he isn't going to be the fall guy. In most instances, he was blasted by his boss and so on down the line all the way to you.

   How should you respond? The most common approach is generally to spell out what the real cause of the problem was. For example, saying something such as, "Last month's production goals weren't met because I don't have enough people to do the job. I've been telling you this for three months, Fred." That's factual, but unfortunately it's really placing the blame on your boss for not allowing you to hire people. Of course, it may well be because of a hiring freeze or some other policy decision made at higher levels of management. But your boss isn't about to go back and pin the responsibility on his boss.

   What we have here is a pretty typical overreaching situation where a management decision was made not to hire additional help in an attempt to increase profits by doing more with less. Unfortunately, the case has now been made that corners were cut just a little too much. However, no one else is going to accept responsibility for poor judgment, so you are now on the spot. But here's where you can turn a situation like this around by coming up with a solution.

   Now is the time to get the help you need, but the way to do it is without saying, "I told you so," to your boss. A good response when the boss wants to know what happened would go something like this: "I'm really disappointed that we didn't meet production last month. I pushed my people to the limit with overtime, but that alone just wasn't enough to do the job. Since these higher production levels are going to continue, why don't we add a full-time slot and a couple of part-time positions? It's less expensive than adding three permanent positions, and it gives us the flexibility of adjusting to the heavier workload in the least costly way possible."

What you've now done is (1) not pin the blame on the boss, (2) recommended more help which everyone at higher levels now knows is needed, and (3) shown a cost-effective way to do it by hiring two part-timers. Summing up, although this is a very specific example, the approach holds true for most instances where someone is looking for an out when something goes wrong. The way to handle it is to avoid debate, and come up with a solution that solves the problem. It's easy to grumble about why it wasn't your fault in the first place, but when someone else outranks you, the choice is often to come up with a solution, or take the rap for someone else's mistake.

2. *When one of your best workers threatens to quit unless she gets a substantial increase in pay.* As you know, good workers are hard to come by, and the possibility of losing one can be a first-class headache. It can practically leave you talking to yourself, especially when you have been extremely fair to someone and they try to take advantage of it. Let's suppose you recently gave Sally, a top-notch employee, a substantial pay hike. Now, she's in your office wanting even more money. She says, "Jack, I work harder than anyone else here and I deserve a 10% raise. If I'm not worth it, then just tell me and I'm quitting. I'm sick of carrying the slack for other people around here."

On the one hand, you don't want to lose Sally since she is your most valuable worker, and you are understaffed to begin with. The flip side of the coin is that you're miffed because she is being unreasonable and taking advantage of the fact that you don't want to lose her expertise. This is just one of any number of situations where subordinates, peers, and others, will try to take advantage of you for their own purposes.

It's tempting to just blow off steam and tell people off. However, that accomplishes nothing and just tends to make an unpleasant situation even worse. The way to handle problems such as these is to calmly deal with the facts and avoid getting drawn into a heated discussion. The reality is that the person isn't going to get what they want, and if they choose to exercise the alternatives available to them, that is their decision. In no event should you let them back you into a corner. With Sally, it would be appropriate to simply say something such as, "Sally, I know you're an excellent worker, which is why you were given an 8% raise a month ago. Your expectations just can't be met. I hate to lose you; however, that's your decision to make. Why don't you think it over? You'll have to excuse me now as I have work to do." The bottom line in these situations is to state the facts and let the chips fall where they may.

3. *You have to deal with an incompetent boss who is always blaming you for his mistakes.* This can be a tricky situation to deal with. You can't just go over your boss's head, since he wouldn't have the job if someone didn't think he was competent. What you have to do is try and establish your credibility with others. This will at least somewhat counteract the boss's constant contentions that you are always making mistakes. In addition, take extra pains to avoid dealing with your boss on subjects that seem to provoke him the most. If the situation gets too unbearable, you really have to confront the problem directly with your boss. If he tends to be hot-tempered, you might want to avoid this sort of confrontation. However, what you have here is basically an insecure bully, and you have to let him know that he'll have to find someone else to push around.

The odds are that you will succeed, since the boss needs your competence, since you're essentially making him look good, but chances are that his behavior toward you will change. Sometimes people are promoted into positions which they really can't handle. To keep their job, they have to cover their mistakes by finding scapegoats. They generally take the path of least resistance and abuse people who can't or won't fight back. Many people leave their jobs rather than deal with someone like this, but unless you're exceptionally thick-skinned, calling the bluff or looking elsewhere for work are really the only two alternatives.

4. *You have taken a new position and find yourself inheriting a mess, even though your predecessor was extremely successful.* This isn't uncommon at any level of management. What happens is that career ladder-climbers take a job and do everything possible to make themselves look good over the short-term. They will cut costs, work people too hard, and use any other measures necessary to make their department excel in terms of output. Then, after six months or a year, they are either promoted internally, or secure a better job elsewhere. The end result is that these people show short-term success and then leave before their tactics catch up with them.

Unfortunately, the person who succeeds them gets the bad end of the bargain. The unit they inherit is generally understaffed, employees are unhappy, the equipment is old, along with all of the other miseries that accompany sacrificing the future for the present. If you ever inherit such a mess, about all you can do is to gradually turn things around. It's highly unlikely your superiors will agree with your assessment of what caused the problems. This is especially true if the culprit has been promoted within the company. In fact, if you're really unlucky, he may now be your boss.

5. *Your boss basically ignores you and deals directly with subordinates.* This is a situation which can make your insides growl, since you're receiving no respect and there's apparently little that you can do about it. All isn't lost however, and it's important to look at why your boss is doing this. If you're relatively new in the position, the boss may just be inadvertently bypassing you. This is most apt to happen when you succeeded your boss in the position you now hold. It may simply be a case of your boss being reluctant to let go of his old ties to the department. Alternatively, your boss could be the type of person who ignores protocol and goes directly to whomever he wants to see. Whatever the reason, if it doesn't subside and is undermining your authority, you might want to mention it to the boss. A good manager will readily understand and take pains to avoid doing this in the future.

NOTE: The examples above represent some typical situations which can put pressure on you to the extent that you might act emotionally rather than analytically. However, the long and the short of dealing with any pressure situation is to keep control of your emotions, identify the alternatives for dealing with the situation, and then select and act upon the best available alternative. This isn't easy to do, and there are any number of events which put unnecessary pressure on supervisors. However, no job is perfect, and it doesn't solve anything to let these problems get the best of you.

8.7

Savvy Ways to Convey Bad News to Subordinates

As distasteful as it is, there are inevitable occasions when you have to be the bearer of bad news. Job transfers forced by reorganizations, a failure to be selected for promotion, or the rejection of a leave of absence request, are just a few of the topics that can place you in the position of a bad news messenger. The subject matter will vary, but the apprehension and uncertainty you have about this most unpleasant of duties will never change. After all, only a heartless clod wants to bring bad news. However, as unpalatable as this chore may be, there are ways to go about it that will minimize the emotional letdown for both you and the affected worker. Here are a few tips that may help:

1. Don't delay in giving bad news. It's natural to have concern about the possible reaction of the worker. However, these fears are generally overblown, and for the most part people are pretty good about adapting to the impact of bad news. Furthermore, the longer you wait, the harder it becomes to get the unpleasant task over with. There's also the possibility that while you're stalling, the worker will get the news indirectly from some other source, which will ultimately make your job even more difficult.

2. Never use some other means such as a memo or letter to avoid having to give bad news directly. This will only serve to create a lack of trust, not only with the employee involved, but with your department as a whole.

3. Always remain sensitive to any personal problems a worker may be experiencing when it's time to deliver bad news. If it's at all possible, delay your discussion until the worker's personal crisis has passed.

4. If it's feasible to do so, try to combine good news with bad news, since the positive will offset the negative to a large degree. However, don't hold out false hope where none exists. For example, if you're telling a worker they weren't selected for promotion, don't make promises about future possibilities if they have no basis in fact.

5. Always avoid humor when you're conveying bad news. It's tempting to try and lighten the atmosphere up a little bit, but the worker is likely to construe your humor as either sarcasm or a non-caring attitude.

6. Expect the employee to feel lousy, and perhaps become emotional. Sympathize with the worker as much as possible in relation to the news you're conveying. For example, you can readily empathize with someone who is losing their position due to a reorganization. On the other hand, if the bad news is essentially self-inflicted, such as notification of a disciplinary action, you shouldn't either display sympathy or get drawn into a debate.

7. Discuss the reasons behind the bad news to the extent possible. Here again, with a disciplinary action, the worker should already be well aware of the reasoning behind it, and little or no discussion should be necessary.

8. If the employee gets angry, don't take it personally, and by no means should you respond with anger on your part.

9. In terms of the logistics of delivering bad news, it should always be done privately. In addition, if there is no urgency attached to the news, try to time it for that part of the day when both you and the worker are at your emotional best. For the most part, near the end of the workday is generally a good time if it's not the sort of news the worker is likely to want to discuss with peers.

8.8

Adapting to Supervision's Changing Role in the Workplace

Historically, business organizations have been basically autocratic, and somewhat similar to the military where orders are given and then carried out with no questions being asked. As competition, both national and worldwide, has intensified, there has been a tendency toward both shrinking the number of layers of management between top and bottom, and to a lesser extent a more participatory involvement of workers in how they do their jobs.

Consultants continually promote new ways to structure companies as well as to empower workers. Some of these are little more than academic theory tuned up to reach a general audience, while others serve little purpose other than to promote the consultant services of someone touting the latest quick fix for the problem of the moment. Many companies even try to adopt some of the more useful ideas with mixed success.

A few theorists have even gone so far as to predict the demise of supervisors, to be replaced by teams of workers who jointly make decisions in the areas formerly reserved for managers. However, before you head off to do something else for a living, keep three things in mind. One, the business world as a whole changes at a glacial pace. Two, what sounds good in theory is one thing, and what works in practice is another. Three, the existing organizational structure of business isn't necessarily bad. Instead, some corporations just became fat and lazy when they didn't have as much competition throughout the world. Many of these have subsequently changed their ways by slimming down to become more competitive.

Whatever changes take place ultimately, there will still be a need for supervision. In fact, the more decision making that's done at lower levels of a company, the greater the need for competent supervisors. All of the jargon about team leaders and facilitators instead of supervisors is essentially an exercise in changing names while the game remains the same. It has about the same impact as changing the personnel department to human resources.

Of course, such concepts as teamwork and worker participation in deciding how they do their jobs are good ideas. But in reality they aren't really new, as many smaller companies have always operated that way. In the same vein, the notion of supervisors encouraging teamwork and worker suggestions isn't new either. Here again, it has always prevailed in some companies, and is still virtually ignored in others. In short, where you work to some degree influences how you perform your duties. Despite all of the debate about the changing role of supervision, a few fundamental practices will stand you in good stead no matter what future changes take place in how you perform your duties. These basics include:

1. *Be flexible.* You may need to become more flexible in determining how you perform your duties. The age-old practice of going by the book will no longer be sufficient. To help meet the needs of your employer in being competitive, there will be less time to mull over operational decisions. Therefore, you will have to react more quickly to get the job done. Beyond this, you will need to be as flexible as possible in managing the people you supervise. This will sometimes require a little creativity in figuring out how to balance the needs of the job against the personal needs of a diverse work force who have responsibilities beyond the walls of the workplace.

2. *Understand the needs of those you supervise.* A quality workforce requires quality people. As you know from experience, good workers are both hard to find and to keep. Therefore, to have the type of workers you will need to meet the demands placed upon you, it will be necessary to recognize the individual needs of employees in terms of working hours, training, and job assignments. Some people will be better positioned to work longer hours than others. On the other hand, some people will get more done in a shorter period of time.

Traditionally, employees work forty or fifty hours a week—some even more—as a matter of standard practice. The more hours someone works, the greater their reputation for being a hard worker. This, despite the fact that people unwilling and/or unable to work overtime often get more done in a shorter period of time. In other words, achievement has generally been recognized by the standard of the quantity of time worked, rather than the quality of work produced. This, in some cases, has led to people just expanding their workload to cover a longer period of time, resulting in unnecessary overtime pay in some instances.

It's likely that the future will bring a greater recognition of the non-working needs of employees, which means a greater flexibility in both the number of hours worked, and the days and hours in which the work is done. To some extent this already happens, but it's likely to become more widespread with the passage of time. This will to some extent dictate job assignments, since some jobs require someone present at all times, while others have more flexibility.

A greater emphasis on employee-training needs will be an ever-increasing necessity. Many prospective employees will need basic skills training in such fundamentals as language and math, as the workforce becomes more diverse, and technology continues to churn out new and complex machinery requiring greater skill levels. This will place increasing responsibility upon you as a supervisor to ensure that these needs are met.

3. *Encourage teamwork.* The greater degree to which everyone in your unit cooperates in getting the job done, the more productive both your individual unit and the company as a whole will be. To the greatest extent possible, every worker should be able to fill in at any job. This not only requires cross-training, but perhaps even more important it means you have to educate your workers on the values and virtues of teamwork. One hand way to do this is to emphasize that the more willing and able workers are to help their peers, the easier it will be to grant requests for time off to meet personal needs. To some degree, you will find workers who are self-centered and not very willing to cooperate with others. To minimize this risk, you should place a high value upon teamwork both in performance evaluations and in your hiring practices.

4. *Promote employee participation in decision making.* No one has a better knowledge of how to do a particular job than the person doing it. Therefore, to maximize productivity it's important to pick the brains of

your employees in terms of more efficient ways to do their jobs. Beyond this, involving workers in the selection of new machinery and equipment can save a lot of wasted time and money. Furthermore, workers are far more likely to be receptive to new equipment and changes in how their work is done if they're involved in the decision-making process from the beginning.

On the other hand, this doesn't mean that workers either should be, or want to be, involved in decisions indirectly related to their jobs, such as hiring and disciplinary matters. In fact, most people if asked would probably prefer to avoid these responsibilities and the headaches that go along with them. So despite the prognosis for the future by a few pundits that most decisions in the business world will be made by teams of workers, this isn't likely—at least on this planet.

5. *Encourage training.* As previously mentioned, the future is likely to see the need for an increased emphasis on company-sponsored training. But beyond this, it's worth your while to encourage your workers to pursue education on their own. For your part, you can help by not letting training play second fiddle to other work requirements. All too often, training is scheduled, and then cancelled because of some work-related emergency. Although there are conceivably situations where this is valid, many times it's done just because it's easier than trying to figure out how to pick up the slack while a worker is away for training. Not only does this mean that the training is perhaps never completed, but it also sends a message to workers that training really isn't a high priority. This can easily serve to discourage those workers who are reluctant to participate in training in the first place.

6. *Exercise leadership.* What will always be needed in a supervisory role is strong leadership. No matter how team-oriented the approach to how work is performed, management and decision-making by committee is both slow and unwieldy. Management will always need strong leadership at all levels, and nowhere more so than in the position of first-line supervision. To succeed in this capacity, you have to be decisive, consistent in decisions that affect people, fair, and set the overall tone for your workers through leading by example.

7. *Correct—don't criticize.* Temperament is important in being the type of supervisor who can function best in a team-oriented environment, and can encourage and inspire workers to adopt a cooperative work ethic on a daily basis. People don't respond well when they're yelled at, or harsh-

ly criticized for mistakes. Even worse, they are less likely to call errors to your attention, which can cause minor problems to go undetected until they become major ones.

For these reasons, it's crucial to correct workers without being critical of them for not doing something right. It's easy to blow your top when careless errors are made, but patience in showing someone the correct way to perform a task yields better results. So if by nature you have a short fuse, try to learn to control it, since it's good for results as well as your health.

8. *Allow room for error.* To enhance the productivity of your unit requires you to allow employees the latitude to make mistakes. Workers won't experiment in doing something in a quicker and/or more cost-effective way if they're going to be condemned for failing. Let your workers know that errors are recognized as part of the process of experimenting with how to do their jobs more efficiently. As workers gradually see you put this into practice on a daily basis, they will accept the risks of trying out new ways of doing old tasks.

9. *Accept and encourage change.* People are creatures of habit and change isn't always a welcome sight, whether it's a major or minor reorganization, or the introduction of a new piece of machinery. As a result, the major areas of concern to any business hoping to become more competitive aren't a mystery. In fact, for the most part, the problems have been around for some period of time. The common hurdles companies seek to overcome include:

- An inadequately trained work force
- Low productivity
- Poor quality
- Widespread competition
- Poor customer service

But there are several factors that tend to be overlooked whenever changes are made geared toward improving operations. First and foremost is the fact that it's a lot easier to identify problems than it is to conceive and implement the correct solution. For example, it may not be particularly trying to recognize that employee training will enhance productivity. However, it's quite another thing to identify who needs what type of training, much less the ultimate benefits that will accrue. In addition, the cost of the training, as well as the impact of time away from the job can't be ignored.

Furthermore, many remedies are looked at in a vacuum without taking into consideration other influences. For instance, is training needed in part because of poor hiring practices, or a compensation policy that pays below industry averages and therefore attracts a less competent pool of job applicants? Is productivity low because of a poorly-trained work force, or are there other elements at work such as poor morale, inadequate working conditions, and aging plant and equipment? And are customer-service complaints the result of employee indifference, poor product quality, or some combination of the two? Suffice it to say that before a solution to a problem can be adopted, any and all related factors must be explored.

In addition, there's often a lack of recognition that while a top executive has the power to initiate change, successful implementation of change rests with lower-level supervisors. In conjunction with this is the frequent failure to clearly define what is expected to be accomplished when changes are made.

Perhaps surmounting all of the other difficulties in implementing change is the need to recognize there are no shortcuts to getting the job done. Solutions may appear to be easy on the surface, but the task of implementing changes to achieve long-term success is fraught with pitfalls that only patience and perseverance will overcome. Therefore, although you can do much to make many changes that involve your particular group, without solid support for change from upper management, there will be many practices you would like to see changed that can't be successfully implemented.

8.9

How to Survive a Reorganization

If you work for any length of time in a mid-size or larger company, you're almost inevitably going to experience a reorganization of one kind or another. Some may affect you directly, while in other instances you may be a disinterested observer if your own department isn't involved. Even here, you may later experience the effects when you discover that people you coordinate your work with have been reassigned elsewhere. There can be little question that reorganizations can be disruptive for both you and those you supervise. A few strategies for making the best of this type of situation are:

1. The groundwork for minimizing the unsettling atmosphere that surrounds a reorganization should be in place long before any changes are initiated. And the foundation of any actions taken to navigate the rapids of any reorganization is good communication. If your workers are promptly informed about any forthcoming changes, this will build their confidence that the disruptive effects of the reorganization will be minimal. All in all, any reorganization is fraught with difficulty, but a failure to communicate with employees—no matter how difficult a task may be—is self-defeating. A lack of information will allow rumors to run rampant, and may even encourage some of your best workers to seek jobs elsewhere.

   Incidentally, if you're reorganizing your own department, how to deal with this sort of change was covered in detail in Section 4.1 of Chapter Four. Here, we're concerned with a corporate and/or division-wide reorganization which is essentially beyond your control. Of course, your ability to explain the changes associated with any large-scale reorganization are limited by the information you receive from your bosses. However, to whatever extent you can, always try to explain why changes will take place, the reasons for them, and the potential impact they will have on the people who work for you.

2. As soon as you hear any scuttlebutt that a reorganization is planned, try to find out all you can through both official channels, as well as those you know who may be in a position to hear about decisions being made at higher echelons.

3. Don't needlessly worry your workers with information about possible reorganizations that haven't been officially given to you by your boss and/or other management and/or staff personnel.

4. If rumors of impending changes start to leak out, and your subordinates seek confirmation or denial from you, try to reassure them that rumors seldom conform to the actual facts. On the other hand, don't convey a false sense of security if there's no basis for it in fact. Simply say something such as, "I've heard rumors too, Alfredo, but whether or not there's any truth to them, I just don't know. Believe me, as soon as I hear anything, I'll let everyone know."

5. Once a reorganization that affects your department becomes official, let your people know the facts, and what, if any, impact it will have upon them.

6. Acknowledge any difficulties that may take place and what will be done to minimize them. All too often, a reorganization looks simple enough on a chart, when it can cause significant inconvenience and/or adjustment for those involved at lower levels.

7. If you will be reporting to someone new, make every effort to get off to a good start. Reassure your new boss that you will do your utmost to make certain the reorganization doesn't hinder the performance of your department.

8. If a group with which your department works closely is reorganized, find out what changes will need to be made in terms of how your group interacts with the other department. This involves the basics of who to see for what, as well as what reassignment of duties has taken place.

9. Sometimes when a group you deal with has been realigned, problems arise when you try to pin down who is now responsible for doing what. This is especially true when people in the department have been either reassigned or terminated. Your people may complain to you that they're no longer able to get any cooperation in getting the job done. Frequently, this results when people in a reorganized unit are reluctant to take on additional responsibilities, and as a result their response when asked who is handling something will be, "I don't know."

   This can happen even when you have been told that a particular individual is assuming the task in question. If you encounter this, immediately bring it to the attention of the supervisor of the other department. If satisfaction isn't forthcoming, get your boss involved so the problem can be ironed out. Otherwise, the performance of your group will suffer, and you will be the victim of a reorganization that didn't directly affect your unit.

10. Any reorganization, whether it involves your group directly or indirectly, will cause some adjustment difficulties. For your part, demonstrate good faith with your workers in ironing things out so everything continues to run as smoothly as possible. By doing this, you will add an important ingredient for a successful implementation of the changes—and that is leadership. And that alone can go a long way toward reducing the pangs of reorganization for everyone who works for you.

8.10

🔱

What to Do When Your Job Is on the Line

For one reason or another, there may come an unpleasant moment when you sense that your job is in jeopardy. Perhaps it's because of a forthcoming reorganization, or maybe you don't see eye-to-eye with your boss. Whatever the cause, it's no time to sit idly by waiting for the ax to fall. The measures you take will be largely dictated by both your personal circumstances, as well as the size and scope of your employer. Nevertheless, there are a number of measures you should always keep in mind. These are:

1. *Watch for warning signs.* Be on the lookout for subtle—or not so subtle—indications that things aren't quite as they should be. For example, perhaps your boss seems more distant in his dealings with you, or maybe you aren't being asked to do any rush jobs or difficult projects anymore. Don't be paranoid about this, since there may be a reasonable explanation for something such as this. However, if it continues over a period of time, or a number of indicators start to appear, it may be time to start getting your resume together. On a less personal level, danger signals such as a reorganization that is in the works while your department's workload has been declining, can also signal that you may be out of a job soon.

2. *Accept reality.* Sometimes people concentrate on their work with little attention given to the organizational politics going on around them. But even if you refrain from involving yourself in office politics, you can't ignore the realities of the situation. For instance, you may be a great supervisor and have a very productive department. Nevertheless, if you're frequently at loggerheads with your boss, or he just doesn't like you for some reason you can't pinpoint, that can spell big trouble. The boss may tolerate having you around for a while because of your competence, but could attempt to get rid of you when it's convenient to do so.

   Many individuals simply assume their future is secure because they're doing a good job. They operate on the basis that hard work and loyalty will be rewarded. They naively believe that everyone else has the same concepts of justice and fair play. Most may have, but there are some that don't. And if you aren't alert to what's going on around you, it's easy to become an unwitting victim.

3. *How dispensable are you?* As you know, everyone can be replaced. But if you're being set up to be let go, the odds are that your boss may already be lining up your replacement. Look around and assess the possibility that someone is being positioned to take your place. Favorites are often played, and if someone has recently been hired who is a potential candidate to replace you, be prepared to look out for yourself.

4. *Don't ignore outside influences.* Even if you are well-positioned for the long haul within the company, external events could be your downfall. For example, are new products threatening to replace those made by your company, or is your company losing business to competitors? Perhaps the entire industry you're in faces hard days ahead. Whatever the reason, if you stay tuned to what's going on in the outside world that may affect your job, you'll be better-positioned to know when it's a good time to start looking for a position elsewhere.

5. *Don't overemphasize the positive.* It's not easy to cut ties to a job—even one you don't like. This is especially true if you have been working for the same company for an extended period of time. Friendships are formed, and familiarity with both your surroundings and daily routine can be reassuring. Nevertheless, you have to force yourself to be realistic. If you're suffering from burnout from overwork, being badgered by an incompetent boss, or just plain bored, it may be time to move on. Actually, stress factors of one kind or another at work can affect your performance without you even realizing the drop-off in your output. One of the hardest parts of looking for a new job is actually just making up your mind to begin your search. So once you reconcile yourself to the fact that for one reason or another you're at a dead end, then it's time to look for a brighter future elsewhere.

6. *Assess your prospects internally.* If things don't look good in your present job, but you generally like the company you work for, then it may pay to look for another position with your present employer. Think about what other positions you are qualified to fill. Do you know the people in charge of those departments, and if so, are they aware of your abilities? Even when you're not even thinking about making a move, it's beneficial to get to know managers who head groups for which you might eventually like to work.

If you're actively looking for another job, when you see a position open up because someone is leaving, or a new slot is being created, discretely inquire about it before it's advertised outside of the company. Everyone would prefer to hire a known quantity, so you have a leg up on any potential competition. If you have reservations about your present job, even though it looks relatively secure, don't wait until it's too late. At that time a position may not be open, so if something interesting comes along, take advantage of it while you have the opportunity.

7. *Don't jump the gun.* Although on the one hand, you have to constantly remain alert for signs that your job may be in danger, you have to take your overall situation into full account before you bail out. For example, even if layoffs loom ahead which might affect you, give some thought to what would happen if that became true. You might be better sitting tight if the possibility exists that the company will offer a generous early retirement package (assuming you're eligible), or if you have sufficient seniority to be entitled to a substantial amount of severance pay. Look at your individual circumstances, both from a personal and financial stand-point. Then make any decisions you feel are necessary.

8. *Be in charge.* You always want to be in the position of being able to act rather than react in terms of leaving your job. Any moves that are made should be at your initiative, and not when someone else forces the issue. Only then can you do what's best for you in terms of your career.

9. *Leave gracefully.* If you accept a position elsewhere, don't vent your wrath before you go. Probably even more important, don't quietly tell a few friends at work that you're really leaving because old Scrungemouth gave you a hard time. Everyone loves juicy gossip, and if the word doesn't spread before you leave, it likely will shortly thereafter. You never know who will surface where, so there's nothing to be gained and much to be lost.

Chapter Nine

CONQUERING THE DAY-TO-DAY DETAILS OF YOUR JOB

It may be the major problems that get your adrenaline flowing, but it's the nitty-gritty details that will consume the bulk of your time. And, in fact, how well you handle the run-of-the-mill chores will dictate to a large degree how many—or how few—larger issues you have to deal with. This chapter focuses on how to successfully manage your supervisory duties in a number of areas which concern your general approach to supervision. Included are pointers on such matters as maintaining a positive attitude, to coping with the pesky problem of office politics. And not to be overlooked are suggestions for coping with both your own expectations, as well as the expectations of the people you supervise.

9.1

How to Be a Boss—but Not an S.O.B.

There was a time when a boss could pretty much tell people what to do, and expect it to be done or suffer the consequences. Questions came down the managerial chain of command, and answers went up. Working-level people were essentially paid to work—not to think. This has changed to some extent in recent years with a greater emphasis being placed on teamwork. Along with this is increasing recognition that the people actually doing the work can help determine the best way to do their jobs. Employees are also being encouraged to make joint decisions in areas such as how they can best work together to become more productive.

As you know, there are a multitude of buzzwords that have been adopted to describe these trends. How enduring any of these terms become is a matter of conjecture. The same can be said for many of the new management techniques filling the pages of business books and magazines. Theories come and theories go, but the work remains to be done. The truth is that in some companies changes will take place faster than in others. The management practices in your own company may not have changed at all, or there may be more rhetoric than reality in terms of what is different. In still other organizations, employee involvement in decision making may have increased a great deal.

How does this affect you as a supervisor? It probably already has to a greater or lesser degree, depending upon how much—or how little—management practices have been altered within your own company. Above and beyond anything else, it has probably led you to do a great deal of thinking about your own role in all of this. As a minimum, you may have wondered how you can go about being a better supervisor in an era of employee empowerment.

Despite all of the hoopla surrounding this subject, the fact remains there will always be a need for supervisors. In fact, with more responsibility being delegated down to the working level within companies, the role of those whose major responsibility is supervision will only increase. The bottom line for both the present and the future should be to treat every employee with respect and dignity. The tactics for doing this include the following essentials:

1. *Earn respect—don't demand it.* Employees aren't about to do much beyond the minimum required to keep their jobs for a boss they don't respect. You can't dictate or demand the sort of credibility that earns the respect of those who work for you. It has to be built up over time as your subordinates observe your actions as their boss. If they gradually come to see you as someone who shows respect for them, is willing to listen to their concerns, looks out for their work-related interests, and is fair in your dealings, they will give you the respect you rightly deserve.

   On the other hand, the fact that you are their boss will do nothing to command respect. It might create resentment, or perhaps even fear, but unless you treat people with dignity, the power of your position is meaningless in terms of gaining respect.

2. *Fight for your workers—not with them.* Some people are short-tempered by nature, while a hectic work pace can arouse anger in even the most mild-mannered supervisor. Combine this with a touchy subject and/or a tired or stressed-out worker and you have the ingredients for an argument. Admittedly, there are situations which can push anyone to the brink of anger, but no one ends up a winner in a heated disagreement. Therefore, always contain your anger, even if provoked by a surly subordinate. It's much easier to handle a situation when you can deal with it calmly. If you do happen to lose your cool on occasion, try channeling it into defending your workers when they're criticized by others. That way, you not only relieve your tensions, but you also earn the gratitude of those who work for you.

3. *Tell—don't yell.* There are more than a few supervisors who firmly believe that the only way to manage is to intimidate people. They yell, rant and rave, make accusations, and are even known to throw things around. Any boss who has to act in this manner obviously hasn't earned the respect that would gain attention without this childish behavior. In the long run, rather than tolerate this abuse, many workers seek employment elsewhere, while those that remain look for opportunities to sabotage the boss's career. Intimidation may work in the short term, but over a period of time, upper-level managers will realize that good workers are leaving because of poor supervision. When that happens, the supervisor will likely be the next person out the exit.

4. *Promote your people—not yourself.* When you receive credit for work done in your department share it with your workers. By saying something such as, "Thanks, but Herb and Joan did all the work on that and deserve the credit," you accomplish a couple of things. First of all, you gain the respect and gratitude of the workers who were mentioned. Second, you are recognized as a loyal and unselfish boss by the person who gave the praise. Third, you demonstrate self-confidence by showing your willingness to give other people the credit they deserve. And finally, you encourage your employees to do their best with the knowledge that they will receive credit for what they do.

5. *Be a leader—not a follower.* There can be a tendency on the part of some supervisors to take their cues from their peers or bosses in terms of how they interact with those they supervise. For instance, if a manager oper-

ates through fear or intimidation in dealing with subordinates, some lower-level supervisors will do likewise. If you subscribe to this practice, then the net result will be that your workers view you as an S.O.B., along with all the rest of the managers who do likewise.

This sort of situation is most common where someone lacking in management skills is placed in a top -evel management slot. They don't have a clue as to how to motivate people other than through fear. This generally happens in technical or professional areas where someone with extensive specialized skills or knowledge is suddenly thrust into a position where they now have to manage a large number of people. What happens is that lower-level managers—who perhaps know better—will mimic the boss's style rather than stick with the courage of their convictions.

The irony is that this often takes place even though top management doesn't consider this to be a proper approach to managing people. In other instances, it is simply condoned as long as the bottom line results are satisfactory. However, inevitably operating through fear and intimidation catches up with people who operate this way, since ultimately high labor turnover and declining productivity alert top management to the cause of the problem. When that happens, a dictatorial boss will be on the way out, and those who mimicked his practices will quickly change their ways if they don't want to follow suit.

Conversely, if you adopt a more humane management style that realistically recognizes the proper way to treat people, you will reap the benefits of comparison with your hard-nosed counterparts. This may in the short term result in some needling by hard-liners about you being soft on your workers. However, over a period of time the benefits to you will far outweigh any disadvantages. You will find yourself with more loyal workers who are willing to go that extra mile to get the job done during crunch time. Furthermore, you will have to spend a lot less time hiring replacements than your counterparts. Last, but by no means least, you will ultimately have the satisfaction of seeing other supervisors adopting your style of management when their higher-level role model goes down in flames.

6. *Recognize that a worker's failure is your failure.* Just as you rightly reap the benefits by managing your unit effectively, you should also accept the responsibility when things go wrong. There are supervisors who are more than willing to accept the credit when things go right, who quick-

ly look to a subordinate to blame when there's a mistake made. Of course, when workers make errors they should be given constructive criticism in how to correct the problem. However, that should be kept within the confines of your department. If a manager or staff person confronts you with a mistake made by one of your workers, accept the responsibility and then go about correcting what went wrong. After all, you're the one charged with seeing that your department runs smoothly, so a worker error is to some extent your responsibility.

7. *Practice fairness—not favoritism.* If there's anything that can alienate workers in a hurry it's a supervisor who practices favoritism. Nothing gnaws upon a hard-working employee's mind more than seeing a co-worker who is the boss's pet do little or nothing day after day. And even when a supervisor tries to be fair with everyone, this is an area where perception sometimes overwhelms reality.

For example, if you give a desirable assignment to a worker as a reward for doing an excellent job on a continuing basis, there will likely be a couple of people who see this as playing favorites. Naturally, this isn't the case, and quite frankly, you can't spend time worrying about the jealousies of everyone who works for you. However, since it's such a sensitive area, it's prudent to avoid the appearance of playing favorites to the maximum extent possible.

Nevertheless, this shouldn't deter you from rewarding top performers for their achievements. Just make sure you let it be known that it's performance—not popularity—that's being recognized. There may still be a couple of people who mumble to themselves about favoritism, but over a period of time most of your workers will realize that you're fair to everyone.

8. *Use disciplinary measures as a last resort.* There are supervisors who are known for dispensing disciplinary warnings at about the same pace as samples are handed out at your local supermarket. When this occurs, it often signals that someone is in a supervisory role who doesn't belong there. It can also be a sign that an incompetent boss is using workers as the scapegoats for his or her own lack of performance.

When workers make mistakes, the proper course of action is to show the worker what must be done to prevent and/or minimize repetition of the type of error that was made. As long as a worker is making a diligent effort to do the best job possible, failures shouldn't be treated as crimes.

On occasion, workers just may not be cut out for the type of work they're doing. In these instances, whenever possible every attempt should be made to either realign the job to meet their capabilities, or else find them a job better suited to their talents.

If disciplinary action is taken haphazardly by a supervisor, workers won't take any chances in doing their jobs. The supervisor will be consulted on how to do even the most routine functions. The end result will be an overwhelmed supervisor, and a department where productivity is low because workers are operating in a climate of fear where risks are avoided and caution takes precedence over performance.

9. *Set reasonable expectations.* Both on an overall basis, and in terms of individual performance, workers shouldn't be expected to perform beyond their capabilities. If the workload is overwhelming a department, it's the responsibility of the supervisor to either obtain more help, or gain relief in the form of a reduction in the amount of work. There's little that can be achieved by driving workers beyond their limits. To the contrary, it will only result in needless mistakes, accidents, and poor morale.

The same applies on an individual basis. Workers have varying talents and energy levels, and everyone shouldn't be held to the standard of the department's star worker. The particular talents of each individual should be developed to the maximum extent possible. Some people will work faster than others, yet their slower peers may produce higher quality work. Others may be better at handling tasks that immerse them in details, which their co-workers wouldn't have the patience to handle. With a little bit of effort it's possible to maximize the overall productivity of your group by developing the strengths of each employee.

9.2

Responding to Questions You're Not Prepared to Answer

There are occasions when people will ask questions that you're either not prepared to answer, or for one reason or another don't want to answer at that time. It may be your boss, other managers, one of your workers, or anyone else within the company. For that matter, if your job requires you to interact with people outside of the organization, it might even be a customer or supplier. Who it is doesn't really matter. What does count is that you know how to avoid giving an immediate response without appearing to be evasive.

The circumstances under which this sort of a situation develops will naturally vary. Some general ways to deal with this problem, as well as a few responses you can use in some of the more common areas where this is likely to occur include:

1. The most basic reply is, of course, "Let me look into that and get back to you." This routine response fits most any situation where an immediate answer isn't expected. Sometimes people want to know when a reply will be forthcoming, while in other instances it's left to your discretion. What you have to be careful of here is that you don't promise someone a reply by a date or time that can't be met. That not only damages your credibility, but it may also cast doubt on the reliability of your answer when you do respond. So if you discover you can't respond as promised, let the other party know about it, offer a reasonable explanation, and give them a revised date or time when they can expect a reply.

2. One of the most difficult moments can occur when someone expects an immediate answer and you don't have the information to give an honest reply. Often, people will try winging it and end up talking in circles. This not only frustrates the other party, but it makes the person who is fumbling around appear to be incompetent. Even though it's difficult to do so, sometimes you just have to say, "I don't know," when a question is posed that you can't answer. Then, go on and offer to get the answer. When you're expected to know something and you don't, it's preferable to admit to the fact, rather than spend five minutes waltzing around the question just to prove you don't have an answer.

3. Occasionally, when an immediate answer is expected, you may be able to satisfy the individual by giving a partial reply and offering to pursue the matter further if additional information is needed. Say something such as, "Those were shipped last week. If you need an exact date, I'll get it for you."

4. If you're asked a loaded question for which you want to carefully phrase your response, stall for a minute or two while you mentally prepare your reply. In fact, it's always good to pause briefly before you answer someone, since this implies you're reflecting on what was said. People often

get trapped into saying something they don't want to by blurting out an immediate response.

5. You may have someone ask you a misleading question, which if it is answered directly will convey the wrong impression, for instance, "Why did you send that shipment to the wrong address?" The speaker is looking for an explanation which will confirm the contention that you made an error. Assuming you're not responsible for the shipping error, you will reply, "I didn't," with some explanation of why it wasn't you, and/or who was responsible for the error. You're actually answering the question, "Did you send that shipment to the wrong address?" Simply leaving off the word "Why" changes the entire context of the question. The way questions are framed can lead to giving the wrong reply if you're not careful in responding. Whenever you're asked a question which is misleading, simply answer the question you want to answer, not the question which was asked.

6. Another technique you can use to fend off unwanted questions is to answer a question with a question. For example, "Why won't you lend me two people for a couple of weeks?" can be responded to with "Why does your department need two people?" You have shifted the focus from being on the defensive yourself, in explaining why another department can't borrow help, to putting the other supervisor on the defensive in terms of explaining why help is needed. This approach doesn't always avoid answering the original query, but as a minimum it gives you a lot of time to think of a good response.

7. You can divert the focus away from the question that was asked in some situations. This is especially true when the question is asking for your opinion, or some form of advice. For instance, if your boss asks your opinion on transferring one of your workers to another department, you can use this platform as the jumping-off point in a plea for more help. An example would be something similar to this: "Bob, what do you think about moving Jones over to the model shop?" with a response such as this: "Are you kidding, Jack? Let me show you why I need a minimum of two more people as it is..."

8. Once in a while you can fend off an unwelcome question by simply dismissing it as irrelevant. Just be careful whom you choose to do this with, since your boss, or any other top manager, won't take kindly to being brushed off with a wave of the hand and a comment such as, "That's not even worth discussing." This tactic is best reserved for pests who con-

sistently badger you about something you have already discussed with them.

9. There are times when you can challenge the validity of the question itself with something similar to an "Are you sure?" response. This at least gives you time to think about the topic, and if you're lucky, the person may decide that they aren't yet ready to pursue the subject.

10. If it's practical, an easy way to dodge giving an immediate answer to a question is to act surprised at what is being said. Plead ignorance and vow to dig into the matter right away. Sometimes you can combine this with an alibi as to why you are uninformed, such as being on vacation, attending a meeting, or whatever else might fit the circumstances.

9.3

Using High-Tech Communications Tools to Make Your Job Easier

Whenever you're concentrating on completing a task, or have a deadline to meet, you may have cause to regret the technology which has placed instant means of communication at everyone's disposal. After all, it's getting harder to even temporarily avoid people since car phones provide contact on the road, people can fax or send an electronic mail message to you at work, and beepers can get you just about everywhere else. Of course, technology has also provided some message avoidance courtesy of answering machines and their voice mail counterpart. But, on balance, even though you can still stall, it's virtually impossible to ignore any message for long.

Despite the occasional frustrations you may experience if you're on the receiving end of a deluge of faxes, phone calls, and computer messages, the continual upgrading of communications technology is a positive development in helping to increase your effectiveness as a supervisor. A more difficult problem you may face is how to sift through the sales pitches and literature, as well as the pleas of your workers, to decide what new equipment you need for your department. Some of the factors you have to consider in determining what you need, as well as how to use it effectively are:

1. As with most equipment expenditures, the process first requires an analysis of the purpose to be served. Will the equipment help to

increase the efficiency of your department, or meet some other justifiable need?

2. If you need something, don't continually wait for the latest technology update. Although you don't have to be on the cutting edge of every new development, don't hold out forever, since most types of communications equipment are being regularly updated.

3. If you decide to order new equipment, take the time to adequately test it beforehand. Vendors aren't going to point out the pitfalls of their particular product. Furthermore, they aren't likely to be familiar with your special needs. What works well somewhere else may not be suitable for your department.

4. Don't let salespeople downplay the amount of training that may be required. Always try to pin down the learning curve for the new equipment. If you don't do this carefully, it can result in escalating training costs, employee discontent, and equipment that isn't being fully utilized. Not to be overlooked in this regard are the equipment manuals. If they're not easy to understand, it will take employees considerably longer to use the new equipment productively.

5. Although it's not cost-effective to spend a great deal of time on relatively inexpensive purchases such as a fax, even here a little bit of thought can increase the productive value of your purchase. For example, when purchasing a fax, features such as an automatic feeder and paper cutter save time. The flip side of the coin, no matter what you're buying, is to get features you need, while skipping the "bells and whistles" which only increase the price.

6. What often gets overlooked when new equipment is being considered is the human element. Getting your workers involved in the process early-on helps ensure the ultimate effectiveness of the equipment. This was covered in detail in Section 3.5 of Chapter Three.

7. Of course, how much or how little say you have in determining the purchase and use of communications technology for your department will depend upon the policies of your employer. Naturally, major items such as a voice mail system will be determined at the corporate or division level. In fact, even low-cost items such as a fax machine or copier may be bought without asking for your input. However, whatever it is, if it will be in your department, always try to make your needs known. Otherwise, you may be stuck with equipment you don't want, can't use,

and even find it charged to your budget. Incidentally, if you're the one initiating a request to buy equipment which needs higher-level approval, how to justify your request is covered in Section 4.11 of Chapter Four.

9.4

Reading Likes and Dislikes—and Using Them to Advantage

One of the best ways to get people to see and do things your way is to learn their likes and dislikes and use this knowledge to get your job done. This isn't as difficult as it may seem. You may already do this to a limited degree. For instance, your boss may be unbearable to deal with early in the morning, and less so as the day wears on. As a result, you likely avoid approaching him with anything of consequence until late morning or afternoon when his mood has improved. This is just one of the many ways you can take advantage of individual traits to do your job better and make your life a little easier. Some others are:

1. Many people have pet peeves. Avoid discussing them if at all possible. Even if they have nothing to do with work, if a certain subject aggravates someone, this attitude may carry over into other matters, including a work-related topic that you're discussing. Of course, if you share the particular annoyance with the other person, this can help establish a good working rapport. It may not be as enjoyable as a round of golf together, but if a common dislike can contribute to a good working relationship, then better that than nothing.

2. Individuals' likes and dislikes may include other people within the company. If a dislike for another person is both deepseated and obvious, it pays to tread carefully in this area when you have to work closely with someone who harbors these feelings. For example, whenever possible, avoid trying to get them involved in any project which would require them to work closely with their nemesis. If it's unavoidable, downplay the involvement of the two individuals in any discussions you have with either of the two adversaries.

   Above all else, work around any situation which would involve the two people in face-to-face meetings. This is particularly true if you're working on something that requires the agreement of both parties. Otherwise, their personal animosity may carry over into the work at hand, and you may experience difficulty in getting either one to agree to anything, because of their bickering.

The flip side of the coin when someone dislikes another person with a passion is that you may be able to use this to your advantage. For instance, if you're trying to get something approved by someone, the slightest hint that their nemesis opposes the project will likely get an approval with no questions asked. Needless to say, if you're inspired to work both sides of the fence with this ploy, you better hope that neither party finds out what you're doing.

Incidentally, if you have the misfortune to supervise two people who have an intense dislike for one another, you may eventually have to transfer one of them out of your unit. Even when their conflict doesn't affect their work on the surface, it can create enough tension so that their co-workers are uncomfortable.

3. In terms of likes and dislikes, some folks are almost fanatic in their enthusiasm for certain personal interests such as a particular sports team, or perhaps an activity they pursue with avid dedication such as golf, running, sailing, and so forth. Whatever it may be, if you're aware of it, it's easier to soften someone up to see things your way if you express an interest in it. By the way, you don't have to go overboard about it. If you hate golf, don't go slogging around doing eighteen holes every Saturday just to curry favor with someone, unless establishing the particular working relationship is awfully important to you. A more sensible approach is to just inquire about the person's favorite activity, and then let them ramble on about it. Just don't look bored, or give them fifteen reasons why their favorite activity stinks.

4. Some people have peculiar quirks about certain aspects of their work. Recognizing these likes and dislikes can go a long way toward making the job easier to do. For example, there are people who hate anything to be put in writing, while others want everything that way. A few people appear to call a meeting every other minute, while others avoid them like the plague. There are managers who go by the book and follow every procedure to the letter, while others play it strictly by ear. Learning the little nuances of how people approach their work will help get the cooperation you need in a timely manner.

5. Everyone has a time cycle where their energies tend to run high or low. If this is apparent with someone, don't bother them when their batteries are running low. Of course, there are certain times when it's generally unwise to bother people. These include before they have settled into their routine each morning, just prior to lunch, or near the end of the workday. Confronting someone with a weighty business matter at these times is likely to irritate them, or else have them give you a quick brush-off.

Naturally, a general rule such as this can have exceptions. For instance, you may know from experience that your boss will quickly sign-off on anything if you present it just before lunch. Therefore, if you're looking for a quick approval without too many questions being asked, that would be a good time to get it. On the other hand, if you want to spend some time discussing something, or you're looking for a little guidance, another time of day would be more appropriate. The important point is to look for patterns in how people react at different times of the day. Once you notice any, use them to your advantage whenever possible.

9.5

How to Be Pleasant with Unpleasant People

The pressures that go along with being a supervisor are difficult enough to deal with. If you also have the misfortune of having to deal with someone unpleasant at work your days may seem even longer than they actually are. Most people try to cope with this sort of hassle by limiting their dealings with anyone who is habitually disagreeable. Of course, this may be less frequent than you would like if a close working relationship is required. So simply avoiding nasty people doesn't always work. What's more, this approach may limit your ability to work effectively, or even affect your career prospects if the person is in a position of influence. Therefore, rather than just ducking people, it can be to your advantage to disarm them with a touch of charm. Here are a few tactics you may want to try:

1. Be doubly pleasant when you're dealing with someone who is habitually nasty. It's hard even for a grouch to be nasty with someone who is always smiling. Be careful not to appear phony when you do this, since

you don't want to have a smile interpreted as a smirk. That may only serve to make the person more unpleasant even though that may seem to be impossible to do.

2. Emphasize courtesy. Go out of your way to be courteous with disagreeable people. Sometimes good manners will disarm ill-mannered people, especially if they are used to dealing with individuals who tend to be brusque. And a lot of folks are when they have to deal with someone who is miserable.

3. If you have the patience, see if you can pinpoint the reason for the person's bad attitude. Sometimes people will be gruff in an attempt to mask a personal problem which they don't want to discuss. Perhaps they are lonely, or have recently lost a loved one. Whatever the reason, if you are willing to endure their hostility, they may eventually become less hostile, at least in their dealings with you.

4. Sometimes people will use humor in an attempt to overcome unpleasantness. Be careful here though, since unpleasant people aren't always appreciative of humor. They may instead view it as an attempt to make fun of them and become even more hostile. Therefore, using humor is a high-risk venture with grouchy people.

5. One of the easiest ways to defuse people who are looking for an argument is to agree with them. After all, it's not easy having a disagreement when there's no one to disagree with. This isn't always possible in work situations, since you can't very well agree with someone when the subject of the discussion is a work-related matter which you don't agree with. Nevertheless, even here you may be able to finesse the disagreement by saying something similar to, "I see what you're saying." All this is really doing is acknowledging that you understood what the person said. However, it may be preferable to engaging in a war of words, especially if there are alternatives available other than having to settle the issue with the grouch.

6. One of the most practical approaches to dealing with someone who is nasty is to grit your teeth and concentrate on the task that has to be done. Simply ignore the unfriendly demeanor of the other party. If you need to, you can always rationalize that you may have to deal with this person once in a while at work, but at least you don't have to live with them. Someone probably does, so just be grateful that it's not you.

7. If you're the type of person who has a philosophy of "Don't get mad, get even," an unpleasant person can be a good soldier in disguise. If the situation presents itself, sic 'em on someone you want to get even with. If you're really in luck, and both parties are equally unpleasant, you may be eligible for a matchmaker of the century award.

8. If you have unpleasant people who work directly for you, and their personality affects their job performance, then you have to talk to them about it. This is especially true if they deal with people outside of the company, such as customers or suppliers. Speak to them in private and let them know that they will have to change their attitude in dealing with people. If they don't, and complaints continue to come your way, then you have little recourse other than to follow the disciplinary procedure. You may have to go all the way to eventual dismissal if an attitude correction doesn't take place in the meantime.

9. Infrequently, a bad attitude may stem from something as simple as boredom. If you think a worker may have this problem, give out more difficult assignments and see if it cures the problem.

10. Naturally enough, as with so many other facets of your role as a supervisor, you have to set the example in terms of dealing with people in a courteous and pleasant manner. There will be people who will test your mettle at times, but if your employees see you act angrily, then they may well view it as an acceptable course of action.

9.6

How to Keep a Positive Attitude Through Thick and Thin

There will inevitably be times when you wonder whether being a supervisor is worth all of the aggravation that goes with your job. Admittedly, it's not easy being responsible for managing others in the performance of their duties. You may reminisce about that time in the past when you had no one to worry about except yourself. It may seem that you didn't have a care in the world when all you had to be concerned with was your own performance. In reality, that may or may not be true, since when nothing seems to be going right, it's easy to visualize how good things used to be—even though they weren't quite as wonderful as they now seem.

Even though it's hard to see when everything is at it's worst, if you stay on course things will make a turn for the better in short order. We all tend to overemphasize both the good and bad aspects of our lives. Generally, everything is neither as wonderful, nor as terrible, as it seems when we're experiencing it. Knowing that alone will help you to keep on an even keel, even though the ship appears to be sinking. Accept the fact that there will be days when everything at work seems to go wrong. Allow yourself to feel a little lousy about it. But remember that there are good days as well as bad ones. So if you're presently in a slump, the advantage is that you have a string of good days to look forward to.

Above all else, work at conquering the headache of the moment, and you will soon find out that there's a light at the end of the tunnel. Most of all, don't ignore the fact that there are actions you can take to turn things around. A few suggestions that may help you to maintain or regain a positive outlook are:

1. Confront—don't avoid—what's specifically bothering you. If you need more help, sit down and discuss the possibilities with your boss, rather than just stewing about being overworked. If you have someone who isn't performing and should be terminated, then find the courage to do it. Carrying a deadbeat may be helping them, but it isn't doing anything for you other than giving you grief.

2. Concentrate on the major problem that's giving you the most difficulty, rather than trying to tackle everything at once. Once you wrap one task up, then go on to the next one, until you whittle your problems away one-by-one.

3. Don't overwork yourself. If you continually work long hours, fatigue will set in. The end result is that you'll be tired all of the time. Conversely, you may accomplish more if you cut your hours back and get some much-needed rest.

4. Always remember that it's only a job. Put your priorities in order. If you are bothered by the fact that you're working late nights and perhaps missing your son's baseball game, take a night off and enjoy the game. The work isn't going anywhere, but your son will soon grow up.

5. Get away for the weekend, or do something special that you enjoy. The relaxation will help to recharge your batteries.

6. Don't neglect to take your vacations when they're scheduled. All too often, there's a tendency to postpone vacation time indefinitely because

of the work crisis of the moment. Take the time off. If you feel bad about it, cheer up. There will be another crisis soon after you return.

9.7
✧
Twelve Ways to Take a Break When You're Busy

The never-ending flow of work coming your way may have you tied down to the point that you seldom or ever get away from it. You may be working away from the moment you arrive in the morning until the minute you exit for home. If this is done on a regular basis, it can cause problems for you. Beyond anything else, going straight out from dawn till dusk can burn you out both physically and mentally. From another angle, a few minutes away from the work area will give your mind a chance to reflect on some of the issues you have to deal with. So no matter how busy it may be, you should always squeeze in a little downtime in the form of a break. Here are a few ways to do this, some of which are obvious, and others less so. Obvious or not, if you're not taking any breaks, it's worthwhile to consider some possibilities. These include:

- It's common practice when someone is busy to stay at their desk, or within the work area, when they take a break. However, this doesn't give you a chance to relax, since people will interrupt you either by phone, or in person. Therefore, no matter how busy you are, have your coffee in the cafeteria where you can escape from the pressures of the job, even if it's only for ten or fifteen minutes.

- Take a walk outdoors for a few minutes and get some fresh air. This is a sure way to get a little solitude. It's also a good way to get some time to quietly reflect on how to handle some problem that's awaiting your return to the office.

- Go out to lunch by yourself. Pick a nice, quiet place you know where you can let your thoughts wander away from the worries of work.

- Combine going out to lunch with rewarding one of your workers who has been an excellent performer by taking them along as your guest. Of course, if you do this with one person, then in the future you'll have to do the same thing for other stellar performers. Then again, if you have enough hard workers, it will give you an excuse to go out to lunch on a fairly regular basis.

- The third option for lunch is to make it a business lunch by taking your boss or someone else to discuss business matters. This won't get your mind away from work, but it's better than nothing, especially if it's difficult to lunch out without having a business-related reason.

- Another option to get away from the building for a while is to run a personal errand. This is certainly justified, especially if you have been working long hours which has made it difficult for you to do your personal business after work. A variation of this theme is to take your boss somewhere on personal business. For example, if your boss is looking for a new car, suggest a dealer you know and offer to take the boss there. You can do this with any number of shopping-related ventures. Not only does it get you out of work for awhile, but you score some points with the boss for being so helpful.

- If you just need a few minutes away from your desk, go chat for a few minutes with someone you share interests with who works in another part of the building.

- Take a business-related break by going to personnel to see how much vacation time you have accrued. When you discover how much time you have on the books, this alone may make your day brighter as you mentally plan your next fishing excursion or golf trip.

- Be your own courier and deliver something that has to go to another department. At least it will get you away from your desk for a few minutes.

- Find an out-of-the-way spot and take a few minutes to read your newspaper. Be careful how you go about this though, since you don't want to give the impression you're goofing off. One way around this is to combine your reading break with a business visit to another department. Then, if you're challenged, you can say you're waiting to see so-and-so on business.

- If a temporary absence from the area is impractical, then at least take a break in place. Put your feet up on your desk for a few minutes and just let your mind wander.

- Another alternative is to make a personal phone call to someone you haven't talked to in some time. Catching up with what has been happening in the life of your friend will at least force you to think about something other than the work at hand.

9.8

Painless Ways to Deal with Office Politics

Office politics are a reality of any work environment, even though not everyone plays the game. Sometimes they can cause problems for you as a supervisor, either in terms of your own career, or else with a subordinate who may spend more time politicking than working. Whatever the case, office politics shouldn't be taken lightly, since they can either harm or help your career depending upon how you approach the topic. They also can create resentment among your employees, since everyone has their own perception of what is and what isn't apple polishing. Several factors that should be considered if you want to survive the political game at work are:

1. Discourage workers who go out of their work to cozy up to you. If they succeed, it will cause animosity within your group as other employees will resent the fact that you play favorites. However, in resisting the apple-polishing efforts of a subordinate, try to do it in such a way that you don't alienate the person. For example, politely turn down suggestions to go to lunch by giving a reasonable excuse.

2. Don't confuse people who are just being friendly with office politicians. This isn't always easy to do, which is one reason why it's important to be sociable with workers without socializing with them.

3. As a supervisor it's wise to avoid establishing personal friendships with those you supervise. Even if it's not true, other workers will think you give special treatment to any employee you socialize with. This not only makes it difficult for you in terms of supervising your group, but it also presents difficulty for the employee, since other workers will be leery of saying things that might get back to you.

4. If you have people who work for you who spend too much time playing office politics, keep them busy. Otherwise, they'll spend their time on self-promotion wherever and whenever you can.

5. Some people who play office politics to the hilt have a two-fold strategy. First, they try to edge their way into favor with people who are in a position to do them favors and/or give their career a boost. But if they're unsuccessful in their attempts, they never miss an opportunity for revenge on anyone who resists their politicking. So if you know an overt office politician or two keep one thing in mind. They'll be happy to leave their footprints on your back if you let them walk all over you.

6. Don't ignore the reality of relationships where you work. For example. if another supervisor is a close friend of your boss, be careful not to be critical of the boss in front of this individual. In fact, the cardinal rule is not to criticize anyone behind their back. The grapevine usually sees to it that negative comments get back to the person who was criticized. When that happens, whether it's another manager or the mail clerk, you've made an enemy. And if you don't think a mail clerk can get even with you, you may find out otherwise the hard way.

7. Even though you aren't particularly skilled at and/or receptive to playing office politics, you should always strive to adhere to the unwritten rules of the corporate culture where you work. For example, if it's expected that everyone attend company social events, such as the annual summer outing or holiday season party, you stand out by being absent. Even if you have valid reasons for not attending, such as a distaste for mingling with co-workers who have had too much to drink, it still behooves you to attend. At least make an appearance and go through the motions of enjoying yourself. The odds are you can slip away early, since once the alcohol starts flowing, most folks won't remember who stayed and who left. If you avoid these events, you will be cast as a loner, or even worse, someone who is anti-social. No matter how competent you may be at your job, this sort of image can be damaging to your career.

These unwritten rules of the game may also apply to such factors as how you dress, and even with whom you eat lunch. For instance, if all of your peers tend to eat lunch together, you will miss out on a lot of the scuttlebutt if you don't do likewise. As far as what you wear, don't deviate too much from the norm. Of course, the extent and variation of these aspects of corporate culture will vary from company to company. The important point is to recognize them and make at least a minimal effort to comply.

8. Know where the power lies within your organization. This isn't quite as simple as analyzing an organization chart. As you may have observed in your own company, two people holding equivalent positions may not exert the same influence with other people in the company. One of them may be constantly sought for counsel from higher-level bosses, while the other person may be virtually ignored.

   Knowing who has power and who doesn't serves a couple of purposes. First of all, if you want to cultivate those in a position to help your career, you have to know who is who. Otherwise, you can spin your wheels getting yourself liked by someone who is on their way out the door. From another angle, if you just want to know whom it's most important not to alienate, knowing who has influence and who doesn't is essential. Then, if you get in the position of being forced to choose between satisfying the work demands of two people, you will know whom it's best to satisfy first.

9. You may think you're in a position where it's unnecessary for you to have to cultivate contacts beyond your immediate boss. Perhaps you're well-liked by your boss, and do a good job, so you feel reasonably secure that your present job is safe, and your career is on the right track for the future. However, things can change rapidly in the business world. Reorganizations, your boss getting shifted to another job, and any number of other factors can all change things virtually overnight. So even though you may not see the immediate need to cultivate good relationships with others within the company, don't overlook the future, since it will one day become the present.

10. No matter at what level you choose to play the office politics game, always be courteous and friendly with everyone. That way, even if you don't necessarily make any friends, at least you avoid making enemies.

11. Don't neglect the self-defense aspect of office politics. If you totally refuse to play politics at work, you leave yourself at the mercy of those who will use you as a scapegoat. What happens behind your back can be vital to your future. And if a peer decides to knock you unfairly at every opportunity, it's easy to do if you don't have supporters to defend you. So even if you don't want to play the political game to get ahead, it might be wise to do a little politicking just to protect your current turf.

9.9

✸

Tactics to Protect Your Subordinates from Unfair Criticism

There will always be people offering some form of criticism of your employees. Some of it may be justified, much of it may not be. And on occasion it may just be substituting for criticizing you directly. Whatever the cause, and whatever the reason, you should do your utmost to defend your people, since they generally aren't in a position to defend themselves against these behind-the-back assaults. Furthermore, the criticism is equally aimed at you if it's work-related, since it's your department, and therefore your responsibility to see that everything runs smoothly. Although how you handle the situation when one of your workers is criticized will largely evolve from the specifics of each individual instance, a number of helpful ways to deal with common problems in this area are:

1. Try to avoid putting workers in situations where criticism is virtually guaranteed. For example, don't assign someone to a task that will require them to work with people outside the department who have complained about them in the past.

2. Don't assign people to projects working with people where there is a known personality conflict.

3. Don't delegate tasks to workers which they don't have the ability to do. You certainly want to develop the skills of those who work for you, and as part of this process it's important to assign them work that expands their capabilities.

   On the other hand, don't overdo it by assigning work that is beyond a worker's ability to perform. For example, someone who has difficulty stringing two sentences together shouldn't be assigned a task that requires extensive writing of memos and reports. The key is to channel employee development by assigning work that will develop their skill without pushing them beyond their limits. Otherwise, workers who totally fail when given an assignment will lose confidence, and perhaps lose all interest in developing their ability to accept greater responsibility. Preventing this from happening requires a keen awareness of the strengths and weaknesses of each worker.

Although this principle applies across-the-board in terms of employee development, it's of even greater importance on projects that will require working with staff people or other departments. First of all, the primary interest of outsiders will be to get their work done, and they aren't likely to be understanding about the fact that you're trying to stretch the abilities of one of your workers. Beyond that, the worker is more likely to be criticized by outsiders, which will only serve to discourage the employee.

For these reasons, try to assign employee development tasks that will require a minimum of interaction with other departments, at least until you're confident of the worker's abilities. If the nature of your work is such that working with other departments is required for most tasks, then take the precaution of closely monitoring developmental assignments to prevent unfair criticism of workers.

4. Insist that anyone who has complaints about one of your workers see you when they have future dealings with your group. That way, you'll be able to closely monitor what is taking place.

5. If another department head consistently tries to pin blame on your department, investigate the complaints and be prepared to counter these assertions with facts when it happens again.

6. If another supervisor appears to be using your group as the scapegoat for his own department's failures, sit down privately with your peer and see if you can resolve the matter. If the problem continues, go on the offensive by letting your boss know what the real problem is, and proving it with any available evidence.

7. Make people who unfairly complain go by the book in terms of following operating procedures in future dealings with your department. Frequently, cumbersome procedures are generally ignored, since they can slow things down considerably if they're strictly adhered to. But if you have someone who is giving your people a hard time, forcing them to follow the correct procedure will slow their work flow down. Once this happens, the guilty party will want to sit down and discuss things. Let them diplomatically know that if they lighten up on their criticism of your workers, then you'll lighten up in terms of being a stickler who insists on going by the book.

8. Enlist the support of other supervisors who are having difficulties with a finger-pointer. Invariably, an incompetent department manager who is

trying to pin mistakes elsewhere will generally have problems with a number of other groups.

9. If it's feasible to do so, look for a way to change operating procedures to eliminate the problem that is being complained about.

10. Let your workers know that extra care should be taken when working on anything for someone who is consistently complaining.

9.10

What Subordinates Should Expect from You

Your workers have certain expectations of what you as a boss should do for them. They also have expectations of what you shouldn't do. These will to some degree vary from worker to worker. For example, some employees practically want their hands to be held, while others would essentially like to be left alone. Although every worker won't have the same notions, there are a number of common practices that can be considered to be reasonable in this regard. These include:

1. *Respect for their opinions.* Workers want recognition that they know their jobs and have valuable ideas on how their jobs should be performed. This requires a willingness to listen carefully to employee suggestions on job-related matters. But if this hasn't been standard practice in the past, you have to take the initiative to actively solicit employee opinions. Otherwise, most workers won't voluntarily make suggestions until they see that their ideas are both welcome and taken seriously. Furthermore, if after careful consideration an employee suggestion can't be adopted, the reasons why should be discussed with the worker.

2. *A willingness to listen to their job concerns.* If a worker has concerns about some aspect of his or her job, the only one they have to go to who has the power to deal with what bothers the worker is their supervisor. In a busy work environment, it's easy to brush employees off when they approach you with what seems to be—and often is—an insignificant complaint about some aspect of their job. However, what is insignificant to you can be extremely important to the employee. Therefore, it's crucial to find the time to listen when workers want to express their feelings about work-related matters. The advantage this gives you is that work-

ers will feel you genuinely care about them, and this pays big dividends in terms of how people perform their jobs.

3. *A recognition of their personal concerns.* Workers have problems to deal with in their personal lives which can affect their jobs. These can range from child care to illness, or various other difficulties. When employees raise personal problems with supervisors with the intent of trying to work out some form of accommodation, they expect a reasonable consideration of their request. Workers will be less upset with being turned down than they will if they feel their boss didn't even make an effort to help. An understanding of the worker's situation, and a willingness to help if it's possible to do so, is equally as important as whether or not time off or a flexible working schedule can be granted. A worker can accept rejection if they know it's impossible to comply with their request.

4. *Fair treatment.* Workers expect fair treatment from their supervisors, not only in terms of how they're treated individually, but also in respect to the group as a whole. This means that even the appearance of favoritism will cause employee resentment. Even beyond this, workers expect an even distribution of the workload. Good workers can become bitter if they see they're continually asked to do more than co-workers who are being paid as much for doing a lot less. And if a worker continually goofs off, co-workers are more likely to hold the supervisor responsible than the offending worker. The feeling is that the worker wouldn't be loafing if the boss took some action. So when it comes to the concept of fair treatment it extends to the need not only to avoid overloading certain employees with work, but to make sure those who aren't doing their jobs shape up or get shipped out.

5. *Answers to their questions.* Workers look to their supervisor for answers to their questions on a variety of topics, ranging from rumors about lay-offs, to how to perform a particular task. When their questions are given short shrift, or shrugged off with a, "See me later; I'm busy now," response, they quickly assume their supervisor doesn't know anything about anything.

Once that happens, a supervisor may have to deal with a group of alienated workers who have no respect for their boss. Therefore, when employees do ask questions they should be carefully considered and answered. If an answer can't be given immediately, the worker should be told when to expect a reply. Since in a busy workday it's entirely possible you may not have a chance to get back to the worker, or, being human, could just forget, it's a good idea to tell workers to check back if they haven't heard from you by a certain time.

6. *Credibility*. Workers not only want answers to their questions, but they also want to be able to believe what you say. For this reason, avoid speculation and conjecture when answering workers' questions. If you don't have—or can't get—a definitive answer, say so and give the reason why. In addition, it's important not to make promises which are beyond your control to keep.

   Above all else, don't try to deliberately deceive workers even though you're in possession of information that isn't meant to be relayed to workers. If you're in the awkward position of knowing something a worker asks you about, but can't give out the information, simply say something such as, "That's not a subject I'm at liberty to discuss just yet." Doing this both preserves your commitment to confidentiality, and avoids telling a falsity which will be revealed when the news comes out. This type of situation sometimes happens when layoffs or a reorganization are pending and you are privy to news that hasn't been released yet. Workers have excellent networks for gleaning information, and an employee may ask you for confirmation of what is circulating in the rumor mill.

7. *Workers want to know your expectations.* There's nothing quite as discouraging to workers as being criticized for not doing their jobs when they honestly believe they were performing their work satisfactorily. This unfortunate event happens more than it should simply because workers don't know what is expected of them in terms of quality, quantity, or anything else. To prevent this, every worker should be told exactly what is expected of them, not only in terms of doing their job, but in such areas as observing time and attendance policies, keeping their work area clean, and any other matter relative to their job. This should be reinforced periodically by letting employees know that they're meeting and/or exceeding your expectations. On the other hand, they should be counseled when they don't perform up to par. And this should be done long before performance deteriorates to the point where disciplinary action becomes a consideration.

8. *Employees expect you to be decisive.* Workers lose respect for a boss if they seek a decision on something and are met with waffling, stalling, or even worse, a comment such as, "What are you coming to me with this for?

You should know what to do about that." People differ in their ability to make decisions, and some workers will see a boss's approval on subjects that they could rightfully decide on their own. With these people, it's necessary to build their confidence to the extent that they will be willing to take more risks. This can be done over time if they learn they won't be criticized for making the wrong decision.

On a more general level, when employees seek you out for a decision on what to do about a particular problem, tell them what to do, as well as why that's the best approach to take. If a worker approaches you with a matter that you have to get higher approval on, explain the need to do this so workers don't misconstrue it as stalling on your part.

9. *The tools to do the job.* Whether you supervise an office or factory floor operation, employees get disenchanted when they don't have the equipment and supplies they need to perform their work. This extends beyond the equipment itself to the maintenance necessary to keep everything in working order. There's nothing more aggravating to a worker rushing to complete a task than to hit a bottleneck when the copier breaks down. As a supervisor, it's necessary to establish simple procedures to see that supplies don't run out and equipment maintenance schedules are adhered to. Not having the proper tools to do the job just gives people another excuse for why they are behind in their work.

10. *Proper training.* Unless employees receive the proper training to perform their jobs, frustration will set in, and morale will suffer. These feelings of inadequacy can be compounded if workers are criticized for making mistakes in performing functions for which they were never properly trained. This is especially prone to happen when a worker's job is upgraded or the duties changed without any prior training. Workers also expect that when they're scheduled for training, it won't be cancelled due to work requirements, budget constraints, or some other reason. If this happens, the message sent to workers is that doing their jobs properly is secondary to other considerations. And workers who interpret the cancellation of training in that manner aren't going to worry too much about the quality of their work.

11. *Rewards based on performance.* When workers excel at doing their job, they expect to be rewarded for their exceptional performance. All too often, the worker who excels receives nothing more than co-workers who barely meet minimum standards, or at the most a pat on the back. There's nothing wrong with the latter, since praise is always appreciated,

but workers who excel want to see the fruits of their labor in their paychecks, or in some other form of monetary reward. A good supervisor should use a merit pay system to reward those who deserve it. It's also crucial to see that your top performers are put in for company awards when appropriate. Nothing bugs good workers more than seeing people in other departments consistently receive awards when their own boss never even submits people for consideration.

12. *Appreciation.* Every worker isn't a stellar performer, but most people strive to do their job to the best of their ability. These day-to-day stalwarts often go unnoticed, especially if they aren't the type to toot their own horn. These people may not have a big ego, but they do have feelings. They would like to hear an occasional, "Nice job," "Keep up the good work," or similar sounds of praise from their supervisor.

There are some people who will work for years at a job, occasionally hearing criticism, but never a word of praise. Then, when they are leaving for employment elsewhere, they're shocked to hear how much they were appreciated and how badly they will be missed. The supervisor who makes a conscious effort to praise people regularly won't have to tell many people they will be missed, since people who are appreciated aren't as likely to leave.

13. *Workers expect their boss to defend them against unfair criticism.* When other managers make accusations against workers, a supervisor who expects loyalty from subordinates better jump to their defense. It may be hard to believe, but there are supervisors who accept as fact every accusation that's made about one of their workers. They then either criticize the worker, or in extreme cases give them a disciplinary warning. Of course, some derogatory statements may be true, but others are clad in no finer cloth then a personal dislike for the worker who is being castigated. On other occasions, other managers are just using the employee as an excuse to knock their boss, or to cover up a mistake within their own department.

Whenever someone from outside the department criticizes a worker, it's imperative to get the facts before taking any action. As far as what to say when a charge is made, a noncontroversial comment such as, "That's surprising to hear, since Jones is a really hard worker," will work nicely. If it ultimately turns out that the other manager was wrong, the supervisor of the accused worker should make a concerted effort to let everyone involved know where the blame really rests.

14. *Consistency.* Employees are more at ease with a boss who handles the same matters in a consistent fashion time and time again. For example, if people are allowed to do one thing one day, only to be reprimanded for doing the same thing the next day, they just won't know where they stand in terms of what's expected. Therefore, always try to be consistent in the approach you take to handling common situations.

15. *Flexibility.* Although consistency is an employee expectation in terms of your day-to-day actions, workers also expect supervisors to be flexible enough to make exceptions to the general rule when it's called for. This is particularly true in areas such as dealing with personal problems which may be causing a worker temporary difficulties in adhering to the standard policy on time and attendance. In these cases, workers appreciate a boss who will strive to find a solution to the problem, even if it means expending a great deal of time and effort in an attempt to help the worker out.

16. *A positive attitude.* Employees can't be expected to look at the bright side of the ledger if their boss always sees the dark clouds on the horizon. It may not be easy to do, especially if you're not the bubbly personality type, but it's crucial to morale for a supervisor to maintain a positive outlook through thick or thin. Always try to show enthusiasm on the job, since this will tend to keep employee spirits up even under the pressures of a heavy workload.

9.11

What You Should Expect from Subordinates

Just as those who work for you have expectations regarding your working relationship with them, you have your own ideas on what you expect from your workers. Of course, to some degree these expectations will vary from supervisor to supervisor. But in terms of what should reasonably be expected, the following list is representative of the common interests of supervisors in general. After reading the list, you may have a couple of pet peeves of your own to add.

1. *Do their jobs to the best of their ability.* This is the prime expectation of any supervisor. The only caution needed is that it's necessary to recog-

nize that each employee will have differing abilities. As a result, even though everyone should be expected to meet a minimum standard, some workers will outperform others.

2. *Bring problems to your attention.* Minor glitches can develop into major hassles when workers don't let you know about problems they're experiencing. As long as you let employees know you want to hear about problems, and don't criticize them for bothering you, most workers should meet this expectation. Be careful here though, since a few timid types may still not feel secure about approaching you, so you have to try and build their confidence to do so.

3. *Accept and follow directions.* If there's anything that can make a supervisor regret being a boss, it's workers who refuse to follow directions, or even worse, want to debate the issue over and over. There are two aspects to this dilemma. One is to exercise a lot of patience and repeat directions as often as needed to be sure they are understood. If feasible, show the worker how to do what you want done. The other bar to compliance is the fact that some people are just plain stubborn.

Within this category are a few people who insist on resisting any sort of authority. With this latter group, these individuals are better off working at a job where they can exercise their independence. If your problems with this type of individual become severe, your best course of action may be to help them achieve their goal of not having a boss by bidding them farewell when you process their walking papers.

4. *Comply with time and attendance policies.* You should reasonably expect that workers comply with working hours and leave policies. Even when unscheduled absences take place due to illness or an emergency, workers should be expected to notify you directly. Frequently, the same people who are likely to give you trouble in this area are the ones who would be most upset if checks were handed out an hour later on payday.

5. *Cooperation with co-workers and others.* You certainly can't expect your workers to all be the best of friends. But it's a reasonable expectation that they treat everyone with courtesy and cooperate with others in getting the job done.

6. *Don't sow discontent among co-workers.* Every supervisor has enough to deal with without having to cope with the problems created by troublemakers. Of course, gossip is to be expected, but what isn't necessary are individuals who go out of their way to stir up trouble.

7. *Loyalty.* If you consistently look out for the interests of those you supervise, it's reasonable to expect that they will show a little loyalty toward you. This can take many forms, but it includes avoiding criticism of you outside of the department, and pitching in to do a little extra when peak workloads hit, or you're short of help due to vacations or illness.

8. *A positive attitude.* Just as workers expect you to demonstrate enthusiasm, you too should reasonably expect workers to take a positive approach to their job. However, personality plays a big role here, so to some extent this is more a wish list item than an expectation. Some workers will always be positive, while for other people it would be entirely out of character. Probably the best you can expect in this regard is that people aren't openly negative, since that can directly affect the morale of your department.

9. *A little bit of understanding of your position.* Every time a worker complains about something that you have done your utmost to resolve, you have probably wished they would see things from your point of view. That, of course, will never happen, but just as workers expect you to understand how they feel about issues at work, they also should have some regard for the problems you face. Needless to say, some workers will recognize at least some of the difficulties you have to deal with, while others will always have the attitude that you're the boss, and that's what you're being paid for. That unfortunately is a reality you have to live with.

9.12

Eleven Minor Irritants
That Can Cause Problems

Most major areas that can cause problems from a supervisory perspective have been covered in individual topics throughout this book. However, there are any number of minor irritants that can cause grief if they're not nipped in the bud. It's impossible to pinpoint them all, since individual situations differ widely. Nevertheless, among the most common irritants that you may have to confront are the following:

1. *Office romances.* They say love is grand, but you may have a different opinion, especially if an office romance is blossoming within your

department. There are a couple of sensible rules in this area that you ignore at your peril. The first and foremost is that meddling on your part will only make matters worse. So if there's no impact on the job performance of the individuals involved, let love take its course.

Conversely, if a budding romance is affecting job performance, it is and should be your concern. However, your approach should be based on the poor performance of the worker or workers involved, not on their romantic interests. If there's too much idle time resulting from one of your employee's romantic involvement, deal with it just as you would any other situation where a worker is goofing off.

Don't even raise the relationship issue in your discussion. However, the employee may foolhardily attempt to justify the goofing off by saying something such as, "Alice and I are dating, which is why I'm talking to her more than usual." If this happens, counter with a noncommittal remark such as, "Your personal business isn't my concern, Vince. What's important is that you're wasting a lot of time chitchatting, which is preventing you from getting your work done. No matter whom it is with, you will have to limit your discussions during working hours."

2. *Personality clashes.* People can't generally choose whom they work with. As a consequence, differing personalities will result in individuals sniping, griping, and bickering. Here again, this isn't something you should dwell upon. It does help when possible to avoid putting people with a dislike for one another in situations where they have to interact. Of course, if individuals who work directly for you carry their disdain for one another far enough to interfere with their work, then intervene and tell them directly that it won't be tolerated.

3. *Special projects.* On occasion, your boss may saddle you with a special project which will take away from work on your regular duties. Do your share of these tasks, but be careful about getting stuck with a "can't win" assignment. If you can spot one of these before it's assigned to you, beg off with an excuse of being overburdened at the moment. But do so with an attitude that implies you would ordinarily be glad to accept the assignment. For example, say something such as, "Usually, I'd be glad to take that project on, Fred, but I'm way behind because of the number of orders we received this month."

If you regularly accept special jobs without complaint, you'll probably be able to duck one that looks like trouble now and then. This is especially true if you tend to be more cooperative than other supervisors in accepting these chores without complaint. Incidentally, if you're really desperate to avoid a project, you can suggest someone to your boss, and give a more or less logical reason why they would be an appropriate choice. Don't do this to a friend, though, if you value the friendship.

4. *Routine paperwork.* There's a certain amount of routine paperwork that has to be done, yet it can eat up a considerable chunk of your time. Rather than grumble about it, delegate this work to a subordinate whenever possible.

5. *Procedural changes.* Just when it seems like everything is flowing smoothly, along comes another change in operating procedures that requires an adjustment in the way things are being done. Whenever feasible, take your time about implementing these changes so that you can minimize your adjustment hassles by learning from the experience of other supervisors who are further along in the process. Be careful though, that you don't try this on something that is of significance to superiors.

6. *Infighting.* You may have the misfortune of having to deal with peers and higher-level managers who are constantly jockeying with one another for career advancement at the expense of cooperation and teamwork. There's nothing you can directly do about this, but it pays to be aware of these situations, so that you can minimize any impact on your own career. Whatever you do, avoid getting drawn into choosing sides when a couple of managers are trying to undermine each other's credibility.

7. *Critics.* In your dealings, you may run into one or two people who constantly criticize everything and everyone they come into contact with. When necessary, defend yourself against these nitpickers, but for the most part you can ignore them, since they probably have a well established reputation for being negative. Above all else, avoid anger when dealing with these people, since they consider it an accomplishment if they can get under your skin.

8. *Deadwood.* One of the minor irritants for anyone who works hard is having to observe someone who, day after day, does nothing—and gets away with it. There are varying reasons for this, including nepotism, favoritism, and friendships. Whatever the reason, accept these situations for what they are without letting them get under your collar. What you do want to avoid if it's at all possible is to get someone's deadwood

assigned to you, since they will occupying a slot which could be filled with a productive employee.

However, stay tuned to the internal politics of these situations, since on balance you can profit by having a top executives' favorite nephew sitting around in your department twiddling his thumbs. Just be sure to grit your teeth and say, "He's doing great," when the loving uncle inquires about his performance.

9. *Sneaks.* When you encounter a sneak, the odds are that they're trying to cover the tracks of their errors. It makes little sense to invest the time and energy to catch a sneak in one of their lies or other forms of deception. What you do have to avoid is placing any credence in what they tell you, since deciphering fact from fiction can be difficult. If you have such an individual working for you, and you do catch them lying, let them know you won't tolerate it. It's also a good idea to put them in a job where they can't do too much damage. This usually means a position where they have few dealings with other people.

As for confirmed sneaks who work elsewhere, try to avoid dealing with them, since they can leave you high and dry by giving you false or misleading information.

10. *Indecisive people.* If you work with someone who can't make a decision, learn how to work around this trait. The simplest way is to offer your own solution to every situation where they have to make a decision. In effect, deal with indecisive people by becoming their decision-maker.

11. *Intimidators.* There are individuals who deliberately attempt to intimidate people as a means of getting what they want. As a general rule, with this type of individual, the trick is to remain calm while sticking to your position, no matter how badly they berate and belittle your ideas. However, over a period of time they may sense that your refusal to get emotional is a sign of weakness. So if you have to deal with this sort of bully on a regular basis, don't let too many occasions pass before you let them know you have no intention of being their patsy.

Chapter Ten

SUPERVISORY
SELF-IMPROVEMENT
PRACTICES

The bulk of this book has contained advice to help you perform your supervisory duties more effectively in terms of dealing with workers, bosses, and peers. This chapter focuses on the issues that matter most to you from a personal standpoint, which are furthering your own career along with coping with the headaches and hassles of work. Issues as general as handling stress and as specific as making the most of your commute are covered at length. You will also learn how to do a little bit of self-promotion, and cope with back-stabbers and others who aren't anxious to see you succeed. Some tips on assessing your own performance are included, and last of all, some general rules you can refer to on the overall aspects of being a successful supervisor.

10.1

Getting Yourself Accepted and Respected
in a New Job

Whenever you change jobs, no matter how much supervisory experience you have, it's still necessary to gain the acceptance and respect of the people you will supervise in your new position. You're a new quantity as far as they're concerned, which means essentially proving yourself all over again. The more experience you have, the easier this will be to do. But, nevertheless, you will still have to learn the best way to deal with each individual, as well as the group as a whole. The following tips will help in getting off to a fast start in doing that.

1. Proceed slowly in making any changes until you learn the capabilities of your subordinates.

2. Keep an open mind about comments you hear concerning people, whether they're positive or negative. Someone with an ax to grind may view a new boss as the ideal vehicle for revenge on a co-worker, or alternatively to falsely tout the skills of a friend.

3. Be friendly, but be cautious in participating in social activities until you have sorted out the who's who of the company.

4. Get involved in the nitty-gritty of everyone's job so you quickly learn who does what, as well as how good or bad they are at doing their work.

5. Get off to a fast start in terms of demonstrating how you intend to supervise your unit. For instance, if you tend to be a "hands-off" manager, show that you leave the details to your workers. On the other hand, if you like being closely involved, encourage people to operate this way. The one caution here is that if your management style differs significantly from the prior supervisor, your workers will take some time to adjust to the change. If that is true, then be understanding about the difficulty some people will have in adjusting.

6. Show respect for the job knowledge of your new subordinates. If you ask lots of questions, this will not only educate you about the new operation, but it will give your workers the chance to show you what they know.

7. If difficult decisions come up which you're unsure of how to handle, consult with your boss. When you're in a new position, it's expected that you will need guidance initially.

8. Don't try to wing it, since workers will quickly sense this, and may decide you're a phony without giving you the benefit of the doubt.

9. If after several months in your new position you realize that you made a bad move by taking the job, don't try to hang in there too long. Once

you have been in a job long enough for the newness to wear off, you can be fairly certain that things won't get better, Rather than trying to make a bad situation work, put your resume in play and try again somewhere else.

10.2

Valuable Pointers on Assessing Your Own Performance

Many people quibble, either openly, or more likely to themselves, whenever they receive a performance evaluation from a boss. There's nothing wrong with that other than most people make little or no effort to evaluate their own performance beforehand, instead leaving it to second-guessing after a boss has done it. This leads to comparison, especially if any aspect of performance didn't get a top-notch rating.

On the other hand, one of the best ways to assess your performance is to conduct your own self-appraisal periodically. Not only will this better prepare you in achieving your career objectives, but it might also help you to pinpoint areas where you want to improve your performance. Some questions to ask yourself when you do this are:

1. You really can't evaluate your performance without first deciding what's most important to you in terms of a job, since that tends to influence your actions. Three areas of concern for most people are career advancement, job security, and a good balance between work and outside interests. These can conflict with each other in several ways.

   For example, if you're career-driven and focused on getting promoted, then your performance should be geared toward doing what's necessary to achieve that goal. On the other hand, if you value your personal life and prefer to spend time with your family, you may not be willing to work long hours that a career "fast track" would require. If job security is paramount in your mind, it may well be that you're willing to work for less money, or in a thankless position, as long as it offers long-term security. These alternative choices mean the first question to ask when assessing your own job performance is what are your primary goals? This should be the criteria against which you assess your performance.

2. What are your strengths? Are you good at motivating your subordinates, promoting teamwork, or meeting deadlines? There are a whole range of factors that you should consider and then decide which ones you are best at.

3. What are your weaknesses? This is a hard issue to confront, but it's critical to giving yourself a fair assessment of your performance. By pinpointing areas where you would like to do better, you can then decide what has to be done for improvement.

4. Do you learn from your mistakes? Have you received repeated criticism from your boss on some aspect of your performance? Incidentally, this includes subtle comments, as well as outright criticism. If so, then the chances are you're ignoring an area that needs improvement.

5. How good are you in the eyes of your boss? When thinking about this, consider how you have fared in your performance evaluations, as well as the size of the pay raises you get.

6. How do your workers view you? Consider direct comments which show appreciation, such as, "Thanks for helping me out with that." Longer-term factors that show you're viewed with high regard as a boss include a low turnover rate where few workers leave for other jobs, and requests from other employees to work in your department.

    By the way, if you appear to be rated highly by your boss, and not so by your workers, give some thought to this. Does this indicate you're too hard on your workers at the expense of pleasing your boss? Perhaps not, but it does deserve some thought. Of course, the reverse can also apply, where your workers value you highly, and your boss doesn't. If this is the situation, then maybe you're not meeting management's expectations in terms of your supervisory responsibilities.

7. How do your peers view you? If other supervisors seek you out for advice, the odds are that you're a good supervisory role model.

8. Are your talents recognized by higher-level managers other than your boss? If not, it may mean you have to work on improving your visibility in terms of receiving wider recognition for your efforts. It may also indicate that your boss isn't the type who shares the credit with those who work for him.

9. Do you try to take on tasks that will get noticed by upper management? This can be either in the form of work-related projects that are of par-

ticular importance to top management, or volunteer activities that will get you known to people throughout the company.

10.3

Effective Approaches to Handling Stress

If you work for an employer who has reduced the work force recently, you may find yourself trying to cope with an increase in an already hefty workload. Even if your company hasn't been cutting the payroll, there may be competitive pressures to work harder. An unfortunate side-effect of a demanding workload is the possibility that it will create job stress and burnout. Actually, even the desire to succeed can create self-imposed pressures which make job stress a distinct possibility. So if you're in a busy environment (Who isn't?) it pays to take the time to evaluate what steps you can take to make your life a little easier. And since you're supervising others, it's worthwhile thinking about what you can do to reduce stress on your workers. The following suggestions should help on both counts.

1. If you're a "do-everything" person, learn how to more effectively delegate tasks to subordinates, and say "No" to another assignment when you're already overburdened.

2. Use your vacation time. A well-planned vacation can recharge your batteries and give you a new outlook on life. Be careful here though, since some people turn vacations into survival exercises by seeing how many activities they can cram into their schedule. Take a vacation that lets you relax, instead of a whirlwind tour that doesn't allow you to wind down.

3. Try to stay physically fit. If you feel good about yourself, then that alone can put a better perspective on the strains of the job.

4. Know your limits. Don't try to do everything to please people. You're not invincible, so don't be a dumping ground for work that your slower-paced peers plead they can't handle. Let your boss know how overwhelmed you are with work, and if necessary make comparisons with others who hold comparable positions. Your boss may come to you with work for no better reason than you readily accept it and dig in to get it done. In effect, it's the path of least resistance for your boss. It's certainly admirable that a boss would have this sort of confidence in you,

but there's a limit to everything, and when it's reached, it's time to speak up.

5. Leave work at work. Put some balance in your life by making time for leisure activities, whether it's golfing, or just relaxing with your family and friends. Constantly bringing work home with you either leaves you no time for anything else, or if you take it home and don't do it, you may feel guilty about it. So leave it where it is and pick up where you left off tomorrow.

6. Don't procrastinate when you have a big project to finish. The closer you get to the deadline, the greater the pressures will be. Tackle the project a chunk at a time and it won't seem so daunting.

7. Organize your work so that you won't suffer the anxiety of wondering where something is when you're looking for it in a hurry. Be careful though not to become obsessed with organizing everything down to the last detail, since you can end up spending more time on organizing what to do rather than getting it done.

8. Don't be a perfectionist. When workloads are excessive, something has to give. You can either do less work with everything done just so, or do more work with less of an emphasis on perfection. There are a lot of tasks that don't have to be perfect, so place less emphasis on those to give you more time to spend on important matters.

9. In terms of lessening the stress on those you supervise, try the following approaches:

   • Avoid being vague when you make assignments. Let workers know what they're responsible for when you assign tasks.

   • Consult with employees before implementing changes, and follow up to be certain everything is going smoothly.

   • Don't make your best workers carry more than their share of workload. When rush jobs need to be done, it's natural to seek out your top performers. But if you do assign them additional tasks, take some of their other work away to compensate.

   • Try not to impose unreasonable deadlines for the completion of tasks. In the event you must—for example, top management pressures— assure the assigned people that you know it is in fact an unrealistic goal. Let them know that you only expect them to try their best.

- Avoid assessing blame when things go wrong. Look for cures instead of culprits.

- Make sure your subordinates are trained properly. Often, people are expected to perform functions that they weren't trained to do.

10.4

Little-Known Ways to Improve Your Promotion Prospects

It's easy to moan about losing out on a promotion. However, blaming the boss—or anyone else for that matter—is an exercise in futility. If you want to escape being on the losing side of the promotion ledger, you better learn how to improve your chances for success. It's necessary to outline your goals, and decide what you have to do to accomplish them. If you're optimistic enough to believe that hard work alone will do the trick, you will have plenty of time to groan as your peers pass you by.

1. Know your boss's priorities. Everyone has their pet peeves and their pet projects. Learn what your boss's are, then work to avoid doing anything that your boss dislikes, and jump to the fore when you're working on the boss's favorite projects.

2. Assess your relative ranking against supervisors you're competing against for promotion. How are you viewed by your boss and other upper-level managers in comparison with the competition? This requires a little speculation on your part, but with a little effort you can pretty much figure out where you stand on a comparative basis.

3. Evaluate the chances for promotion within the company. If everyone above you is likely to stay put for the indefinite future, you may want to look elsewhere. As a general rule, a long-term career with one company is often the best route for career advancement, since every move you make involves proving yourself all over again. However, factors such as company prospects and promotional opportunities also have to be considered.

4. Avoid criticizing your peers so you won't be pegged as a back-stabber.

5. Don't be shy. If you think you deserve a promotion, ask for it. Even if the immediate response is negative, letting your boss know your expectations may help your cause at a later date.

6. Don't undercut people in the chain of command by going over their head. When it's absolutely necessary, make certain you fill the boss in on why you left him out of the loop. Otherwise, you won't need an explanation as to why you were the loser when the next promotion is made.

7. The people who hold power in a company aren't always the ones with the important job titles. So get to know who's who in terms of the power structure at work.

8. Get yourself noticed by working on fund-raising committees and other charitable endeavors at work. This will give you an opportunity to interact with executives you might not normally meet.

9. You may want to consider a lateral career move to gain experience that can help you earn a future promotion.

10.5

Strategies to Protect Yourself Against Back-Stabbers

It's unfortunate but the business world has its share of back-stabbers and buck-passers who may slyly attempt to belittle you, or otherwise use you as the scapegoat for their own failures. You may be lucky enough not to be exposed to one of these unsavory characters where you work. On the other hand, you may not be so fortunate, either now or in the future. Therefore, it pays to be aware of how to protect yourself from becoming an unwitting victim. Here are some ideas on how to deal with these problems.

1. The key to avoiding back-stabbing is seductively simple—it's awareness. The problem is that vigilance against back-stabbing is often overlooked until it's too late. And that's probably the main reason it's so prevalent. After all, it's natural to assume that everyone else has your sense of fair play. But while you're shooting straight in conducting business, someone else may be setting you up as a target for their dirty tricks.

2. Back-stabbers tend to take on greater duties than they can handle, and when something goes wrong, seek to pin the blame elsewhere. So unless you want to hold the ladder of success for someone else, don't set yourself up as a victim. That means knowing your job responsibilities, and asking lots of questions, particularly when meetings are held.

   A favorite tactic of back-stabbers is to get you involved in a meeting, so they can later claim you agreed to something, even though you didn't. This leads to situations where your presence serves as support for an idea that you don't agree with. So make your thoughts known at meetings, or you may be silently setting yourself up as someone's scapegoat.

3. One favorite ploy used to unwittingly involve you in a project that's in trouble is to seek your concurrence on a memo about the subject. It's easy during a busy day to quickly sign off on something handed to you for concurrence based on verbal assurances. However, be careful here, since a back-stabber's favorite line is, "This is just...The boss wants it right away."

4. Don't breach confidences, since a subordinate can get you in trouble by repeating something you were told to keep confidential. It may even be inadvertent, as some people love to broadcast anything they hear that is prefaced by, "Don't tell anyone." But whether it was accidental or not, the net result is that you're in hot water with someone.

5. If an employee is constantly questioning your authority, and otherwise criticizing you behind your back, put a halt to it immediately. Confront the employee directly and calmly state that you expect the behavior to stop. Incidentally, it's a good idea to let your boss and others know about this behavior, since back-stabbers are best controlled by letting people know about their tactics. That way, their credibility is destroyed.

6. If you're dealing with people outside of your department who are back-stabbers, one way to stay off their list of targets is to put them in the position of owing you a favor. Do something for them which will make them feel obligated to you. This is one situation where you shouldn't be in any hurry to have someone return your favor, since the longer a back-stabber is obligated to you, the better off you are.

7. To discourage back-stabbing by your subordinates, avoid assessing blame when something goes wrong. Instead, put the focus on what can be learned from the situation, as well as what can be done to avoid future repetition.

10.6

✙

Talking Others Into Seeing Things Your Way

Whether you're talking to your subordinates as a group, trying to get a point across with your boss, or making comments at a meeting, it's necessary to be convincing. This isn't as hard as it may seem to be, but to be successful requires more than just showing up and having your say. After all, you may be convinced about the wisdom of something, but the person or persons you're talking to may have a different viewpoint. Here are several pointers that can assist you in getting people to see things your way. Obviously, you won't win all of the time, but at least you can be confident that you gave it your best.

1. Don't use jargon or technical language when you're talking to someone who won't understand it.

2. If you're trying to convince someone of something, think about what you're going to say beforehand. Also give some thought to possible objections, and what you can say to counter them.

3. Whenever possible, put any suggestions you make in terms of how it will benefit the person you're talking to.

4. Be truthful. If you try to shade the facts, you'll never be believed.

5. Know when to stop talking. Make your point and then quit. The more you say the harder it will be for the person to recall the beginning of the discussion.

6. Be sincere and enthusiastic, otherwise people won't think you really care about the subject of the discussion.

7. Keep eye contact without staring at people.

8. Speak slowly enough for people to understand what you're saying.

9. Pause occasionally to give people a chance to absorb the points you're trying to make.

10. Relax when you talk to others. It's common to worry, especially if you expect to be questioned about some aspect of your work. But always keep in mind, when you have been the one working on something, you know far more about it than anyone else.

10.7

Several Sure-Fire Ways to Show Leadership Qualities

Much has been written about leadership in business. The leadership role models touted in articles and books range all the way from swashbuckling generals to ancient philosophers. While all of this may make for interesting reading, it doesn't do much to explain the basic day-to-day practices needed for effective supervision in the business world.

One of the problems often pointed out is that managers are fundamentally concerned with achieving planned objectives in an orderly fashion, while leadership involves change, risk-taking, and vision. However, for practical purposes, good managers do handle both roles to varying degrees. In fact, perhaps too much emphasis is placed on trying to define the difference between the two roles rather then pinpointing how they can work in harmony. So let's look at some methods you can use as a supervisor to be a better leader.

1. Encourage teamwork and worker participation before making tough decisions. Any significant issue will find varying opinions about the course of action to be taken. Nevertheless, don't go overboard in seeking consensus. Even workers who don't agree with the ultimate decision will respect your leadership if they have been given an opportunity to voice their concerns beforehand.

2. Be enthusiastic about the future even when things aren't going well at the moment. Enthusiasm is just as contagious as gloom and doom, so your attitude will be reflected by your workers.

3. Remain calm under pressure. Maintaining control under stressful conditions is important in a couple of ways. First, it helps you to make better decisions. Second, it demonstrates to employees that they have a leader who can be relied upon in critical situations. This sort of reassurance also encourages employees to keep their cool when work pressures intensify.

4. Be willing to admit your own mistakes. Employees know when mistakes are made, and a supervisor who can admit to them shows the self-confidence of a leader.

5. Accept the blame when things go wrong. Supervisors who assume responsibility for errors made by people working for them encourage

their workers to do the same, rather then pass the buck or point fingers elsewhere. Of even greater importance, employees are more willing to take risks when they know they won't be singled out for criticism.

6. Encourage debate and dissent. A supervisor who is a good leader will encourage workers to express their concerns. You might think this is essentially a "no win" headache for yourself, when in fact, it can be a valuable asset. If workers know they won't suffer by being open and honest they will bring problems to your attention that might go unnoticed until they erupt into a crisis.

7. Be open and honest. If you are willing to level with employees, they will be willing to level with you. Being forthright with workers on a consistent and continual basis will pay dividends when you have to relay unpleasant news. It also builds a foundation for the trust that's needed to be an effective leader.

8. Give credit where credit is due. Praise employees for a job well done, but don't overdo it. When someone performs exceptionally well, take the time to let them know. On the other hand, don't arbitrarily scatter compliments about, since this detracts from praise that is truly deserved, and can create resentment by deserving employees when they see marginal workers receiving equal credit.

9. Try looking at things with a critical viewpoint in terms of seeking a better way to perform existing tasks. Many routine functions continue to be done the way they are simply because no one has really given any thought as to how they can be done better.

10. Question things that don't make sense. More than a few administrative routines are continued longer after they have outlived their usefulness. These include certain types of periodic meetings and/or reports which were started for a reason which no longer applies. They continue simply because no one questions their present-day purpose.

11. Try to recognize changes taking place within your department, division, company, or industry, and look for ways to benefit from them. This is the sort of forward-looking vision that distinguishes leaders from followers. Naturally, the extent to which you can react to change will relate to your particular position. As a supervisor, your sphere of influence will be significantly less than senior managers. Nevertheless, it's not so much the potential impact as the thought process that's important in fostering leadership abilities.

12. One of the best leadership traits you can practice from a personal standpoint is to know when to let go. This applies not only to the need for delegating work to subordinates, but also in recognizing that there is life beyond work for yourself. An effective supervisor and leader knows when to call it a day and head for home, which is a leadership tactic anyone can relate to.

10.8

✟

Quick and Easy Ways to Practice Personal Public Relations

Working with other people always requires a certain amount of tact and a dash or two of diplomacy. But to gain the cooperation of other people on a regular basis, you have to consistently strive to present your best image. After all, people are more receptive to those they like and trust. So the better you are at practicing a little bit of personal public relations, the more often you'll meet with success in dealing with others. This isn't difficult to do, but it does require a constant awareness of the importance of presenting yourself in the best possible way. Some practical ways to do this include:

1. Ignore the petty things that annoy you. Some of the personal traits of people you deal with may not meet with your approval. But rather than show your displeasure, simply ignore them. If someone is boring or obnoxious, that's their problem, not yours. You're not going to change anyone's personality, so why try when it will only serve to make them dislike you. On a personal level, you probably couldn't care less whether these individuals like you or not. But you have to work with them to accomplish your job, so it's preferable to overlook some of the minor annoyances in your life.

2. Agree on inconsequential matters, even when you disagree. On subjects not related to work, there's nothing to be lost by avoiding disagreement with people on their personal viewpoints. Whether it's politics or sports, let people have their say. Some people carry over their personal likes and dislikes to their work life. As a result, they may be less willing to cooperate with you at work simply because you don't see things from their viewpoint on social issues. Even though you don't openly agree with

them, at least avoid arguing about something that has no relevance to work. In fact, you can apply this same principle to minor work-related issues that don't affect you.

3. Find something nice to say—even when it seems impossible. It's not easy to be polite when you're dealing with people who are downright nasty. But complimenting them will give you the satisfaction of not letting them get under your skin. It may also make it easier to work with someone who is unpleasant, but even if it doesn't, it certainly won't make things worse.

4. Be friendly—it's free. Your personality may be such that you're inherently friendly. However, if you find it difficult to start a casual conversation with people you don't know well, make the effort anyway. You will find that most people like to talk, so just being a good listener will do the trick. It's a lot easier to get things done when people are comfortable about talking with you.

5. Don't be a non-conformist in your appearance or your actions. Some companies are more flexible than others in terms of how people dress, as well as the relative formality or informality of conducting business. The simple approach to success here is to pretty much follow the unwritten rules as to what is acceptable and what isn't.

6. Be thoughtful, if you want to be thought of favorably. People appreciate the little touches. So go out of your way to congratulate people on important milestones in their personal lives, such as birthdays. And to the extent possible, show an interest in what interests them in their life beyond work.

10.9

Sensible Ways to Tackle a Tough Commute

If you have the misfortune of having a burdensome commute to work, it can guarantee a hassle-filled start to every working day. Even if your commute is usually pretty routine, on occasion it may become a headache due to bad weather, construction delays, or the inevitable traffic-snarling accident. But whether your daily journey is a constant headache, or simply falls into the category of just plain boring, there are a number of things you can do to make the most of any commute.

Of course, as any police officer patrolling the highways can testify, many drivers already use their commuting time for everything from combing their hair to talking on the car phone, to eating breakfast. And when you encounter one of these busy-bee commuters paying less than proper attention to the flow of traffic, you might be the first to suggest they would be better off simply enjoying their favorite music on the car stereo.

However, making the most of a commute can go far beyond either munching or musing while you're behind the wheel. In fact, a little bit of planning can help turn the hassle of commuting into a more bearable part of your overall day. Unfortunately, commuting to work is such a habitual routine that most people simply accept it as a necessary burden without looking for ways to make the best of this daily journey. With this in mind, here are a few possibilities you may want to try to lessen your daily commuting headaches.

1. Get ready for the morning rush the night before by putting out the clothes you want to wear, and placing everything you are taking to work where you can quickly find it. If you have to start searching for your car keys, or anything else, the first thing in the morning, you will be off to a bad start before you even get out the door.

2. If you're constantly rushed in the morning, try getting up fifteen or twenty minutes earlier. It will allow you to get ready for work at a more leisurely pace so you won't feel stressed out right at the start of the day.

3. Conquering a difficult commute should start before you even sit down behind the steering wheel. First of all, get your initial traffic reports before—not after—you leave home. There's nothing quite as frustrating in the morning as hearing the urgent voice of a traffic reporter on your car radio warning you about a traffic bottleneck you're already tied up in.

4. Consider the timing of your commute. A little bit of thought can help cut both your commuting time and the hassle of stop-and-go traffic. For example, due to traffic flows, leaving ten minutes earlier may save you twenty or thirty minutes on the road.

5. Additional commuting time is one of the overlooked hazards when people agree to either picking someone else up, and/or sharing the driving. Only after you have entered into such an arrangement will you discover the additional time involved may be more than you bargained for. Therefore, despite the possibility of cutting commuting costs, and hav-

ing a companion for conversation, don't quickly commit to sharing a commute. It can cause real headaches if you work late on a regular basis, or on that rare occasion when you want to leave early.

6. If you do decide it's worthwhile to have a rider, either to reduce expenses, or just the pure altruism of being neighborly, make sure your commuting partner is compatible. Otherwise, a lengthy drive every morning may be doomed to start your day off on the wrong foot. Incidentally, on balance it's not a good idea to commute with someone you supervise. Not only does it give other workers the notion that your commuting partner will receive favored treatment, but it can present a sticky situation if you have to consider taking disciplinary action against your driving companion.

7. If your main commuting problem is nothing more than boredom, then simply try varying the route you take to change the scenery. This also has the advantage of giving you familiarity with alternative routes for times when road repairs or other factors make your routine route troublesome.

8. A little experimentation with different routes may lead you to vary the route you take home from the one you use going to work. Sometimes, this can be a real time saver. For instance, if your commute covers and area where there are strip shopping centers and/or a mall, you may encounter few traffic problems in the morning before the stores open for business. On the other hand, traffic may be heavy in these locations on your evening drive home when the shopping traffic is heavy.

9. Don't neglect preventive maintenance on your car. There's nothing worse than your car breaking down on the way to work in the morning. And as fate would have it, it always seems that this happens when an early morning meeting with your boss, or some other important matter is awaiting your arrival.

10. Don't neglect to consider the commute when you're considering a new job. Of course, salary, fringe benefits, and career opportunities should take precedence. Nevertheless, a back-breaking commute can in the long run become burdensome enough to overwhelm the other advantages of a new job.

    Therefore, don't let the career appeal of a position lull you into thinking an eighty-mile round trip to and from work won't be a burden. Conversely, don't be fooled by commuting mileage alone when choosing between job opportunities. Instead, check out the commute for yourself. You may discover that a fifty-mile ride on a highway may be quicker and easier to endure than a hard-to-get-to or congested destination that's much closer to your home.

11. The same considerations that apply to a new job also shouldn't be ignored if you're buying a new home. The allure of finding your "dream house" may lead you to initially treat a long commute to work as a sense of adventure, only to have it give way to discontent after a month or so. And with either a new job or a new home, commuting expenses shouldn't be ignored. Gas, maintenance, and buying a new car more frequently can quickly eat away a salary increase, or the lower price of real estate in an area which requires a longer commute.

12. Above all else, whatever your present or future commuting trip may be, don't let minor irritations get to you. It makes little sense to stew about commuting problems, and doing so doesn't get you to and from work any quicker. Although commuting may not be your favorite pastime, with a little thought at least you can make it manageable.

10.10

Ten Tips for Successful Business Travel

If your position requires you to travel occasionally on business, you not only have to be concerned about the trip itself, but also about keeping your unit running smoothly while you're away. Of course, as any seasoned traveler knows, business trips aren't extended vacations. And more than one road-weary employee would like nothing better than not to have to face another whirlwind tour of congested airports and the frustrations of jet lag. Flight delays, lost luggage, and missed connections, are just a few of the many hazards that can confront you on a business trip. It's certainly frustrating, but no matter how carefully you schedule your travel plans, things can still go awry. In the final analysis, since many of these difficulties are beyond your influence, there is little you can do about them other than grumble and growl a bit.

On the other hand, a productive trip depends upon many other factors which are well within your ability to control. And it's how you manage these matters that can significantly affect your on-the-road productivity, as well as the amount of work that awaits you upon your return. So a little preventive management can avoid the burden of having to play catch-up with your workload after every business trip.

1. The starting point in increasing your travel-related productivity is to see that your department continues to function smoothly in your absence. Otherwise, as is often the case, you will return from a trip to discover that anything of importance has been put on hold awaiting your return. This is a real problem if a business trip takes you away from the office for several days. Therefore, it's important to delegate the authority to a trusted subordinate to make decisions in your absence.

2. Delegating the authority to supervise the department in your absence goes beyond just saying something such as, "Joe, take care of things while I'm away." Such a blanket statement isn't likely to yield the expected results for several reasons. First of all, the designated subordinate probably won't react to anything that isn't directly brought to his or her attention. After all, even dedicated employees aren't about to go looking for additional chores to add to their own workload. Furthermore, even the most conscientious individual may be hesitant about making decisions in your absence that could backfire on them. To counter these difficulties, it's necessary to be quite thorough about briefing the person who will be filling in for you. Let him or her know specifically what decisions can and can't be made in your absence.

3. For a number of reasons, other people in your department may be unwilling to bring problems to your fill-in for resolution. This can result from simple inter-office rivalry, or perhaps a lack of confidence in the person left in charge. Therefore, it's imperative that everyone in your department be told by you that this individual is acting in your behalf while you're on the road. Subordinates should also be instructed to refer all routine matters to that person. This puts everyone on notice, and prevents people from complaining that work wasn't completed on schedule because they were delayed by your absence.

4. What often gets overlooked is the appointment of someone to act in your behalf when you will only be gone for a day or two. However, if you travel a lot, one-day trips can add up to a lot of lost employee productivity during the course of a year. For this reason, it's valuable to have a subordinate who is appointed on a permanent basis to act in your absence.

5. Even when you have satisfied yourself that steps have been taken to ensure the continuity of work while you're away, don't stop there. Leave a copy of your itinerary with both the person left in charge and your boss. Of course, do the same thing with anyone else who may have to contact you in an emergency. Don't overdo it though, since you don't want to be constantly interrupted while you're trying to conduct trip-related business.

6. As an additional safeguard, you may want to set a certain time of day at which you will call work. This will allow people to be prepared with questions when you call. However, be careful about doing this, since it encourages an indecisive fill-in to leave even minor decisions for discussion with you on the phone.

7. On the trip itself, travel as light as you can, and carry any papers you need with you. That way you won't be hampered if any checked baggage gets lost.

8. Incidentally, you may want to make car reservations before you leave on your trip. Last-minute car rentals and/or scrambling for taxis can throw all of your plans out of kilter.

9. Making the most of any business trip requires careful attention to time constraints. So don't forget that minor irritants can ruin everything. For instance, it's easy to assume that you can buy any minor items you need at a local store. However, finding what you want quickly isn't always so simple when you're in an unknown environment. Therefore, bring along the headache remedy and an extra shirt or blouse, since shopping can be a bigger time-eater on the road than it already is at home.

10. Although many suggestions are offered as to how you can use flight time and layovers for work purposes, that isn't necessarily wise. After all, if you're going to be conducting important business at your destination, it's necessary to be alert and well-rested. Jet lag and other travel-related pressures in themselves can be a drain on your physical and mental well-being. Therefore, rather than spending flight time in pounding out work on a lap-top computer, use your time to relax and think. Doing that will have you ready to go when you arrive at your destination. That, combined with knowing you won't be returning to a department that's been on downtime, can help make your business trip more productive.

10.11

↯

Forty Nifty Nuggets for Successful Supervision

What makes a successful supervisor? If you ask someone that question, they probably will talk about the ability to deal with people effectively. There's little doubt that is a necessary trait for the job. However, the requirements go far beyond that. A supervisor's job is compounded by the fact that the people he or she interacts with often have competing interests. Subordinates view matters from a different perspective than upper-level managers. Even with supervisory peers, there is competition for limited resources. So beyond being good at people skills, you also need the ability to work with people who may have conflicting interests. And that is about as tough a job as anyone could ask for.

But it doesn't stop there as you well know. There are the operational specifics of your job that have to be mastered. Then there are the pressures of often being asked to do your job with too few people for the workload you're responsible for. To make matters even worse, sometimes the cooperation you require from others may not always be forthcoming when you need it. All in all, it can be one problem after another. For these reasons, there are many things you have to master to be an effective supervisor.

Although they all aren't of equal importance, at one time or another many different topics have to be dealt with. The list which follows contains many of the elements which will contribute to your success. You don't have to be an expert at all of them, but if you generally follow most of these principles, your job should be easier to cope with.

1. Treat everyone with respect.
2. Exercise leadership.
3. Try to maintain a positive attitude.
4. Questions things that don't make sense.
5. Learn to listen carefully to what people are saying.
6. Don't jump to conclusions.
7. Work hard to promote teamwork.
8. Learn how to say "No" when necessary.
9. Offer praise when it's deserved.
10. Reward top achievers.

11. Don't work employees beyond their limits.
12. Know your own strengths and weaknesses.
13. Control your emotions.
14. Avoid favoritism.
15. Correct mistakes without being critical.
16. Defend your subordinates against unfair criticism.
17. Provide meaningful feedback to subordinates.
18. Make sure workers understand their assignments.
19. Use follow-up effectively to monitor performance.
20. Encourage your employees to make decisions on their own.
21. Concentrate on priorities.
22. Avoid procrastination.
23. Delegate tasks whenever possible.
24. Solicit employee suggestions.
25. Keep a lid on internal conflict.
26. Resolve complaints quickly and fairly.
27. Don't do anything that doesn't have to be done.
28. Stay on top of routine tasks so they don't pile up.
29. Be organized to avoid wasting time looking for things.
30. Keep workers informed about matters that affect them.
31. Eliminate distractions.
32. Minimize interruptions.
33. Don't hold or attend unnecessary meetings.
34. Practice rumor control.
35. Be flexible when employees have personal problems.
36. Ensure employees receive the proper training.
37. Fight for the resources you need to do the job.
38. Discipline when necessary as a last resort.
39. Don't be outflanked by office politicians.
40. Don't let job pressures get to you.

Index